READY-TO-USE

Motor Skills & Movement Station Lesson Plans
for
Young Children

Joanne M. Landy
& Keith R. Burridge

THE CENTER FOR APPLIED RESEARCH IN EDUCATION
West Nyack, NY 10994

COMPLETE MOTOR SKILLS ACTIVITIES PROGRAM

Library of Congress Cataloging-in-Publication Data

Landy, Joanne M.
    Ready-to-use motor skills & movement station lesson plans for young children / Joanne M. Landy and Keith R. Burridge
        p.   cm. — (Complete Motor Skills Activities Program; bk. 3)
        Includes bibliographical references.
        ISBN 0–13–013943–2
        1. Movement education.   2. Motor learning.   3. Education, Elementary—Activity programs.   I. Title: Motor skills & movement station lesson plans for young children. II. Burridge, Keith R.   III. Title.

GV452.L357   2000
    372.86—dc21   00–020250

Acquisitions Editor: *Susan Kolwicz*
Production Editor: *Mariann Hutlak*
Interior Design/Formatter: *Dee Coroneos*

Printed in the United States of America

10 9 8 7 6 5 4 3 2 1

ISBN 0-13-013943-2

**THE CENTER FOR APPLIED RESEARCH
IN EDUCATION**
West Nyack, NY 10994

www.phdirect.com

DEDICATION

To all the children of the world who will hopefully benefit from
being involved in quality movement experiences that will foster and enhance
enjoyable lifelong activity . . .

&

To our parents who have provided us with constant love and
encouragement through the years to pursue our dreams . . .
Our sincerest thank you.

Joanne M. Landy earned a B.Ed. degree, graduating with Great Distinction from the University of Regina, Saskatchewan, Canada in 1974. She also completed a post graduate international P.E. study course through Concordia University in Montreal, Quebec, and a Personal Trainer course through Renouf Fitness Academy in Perth.

Joanne's professional background includes 10 years of secondary teaching in physical education/health and mathematics; 10 years of specialist teaching in primary physical education, as well as several years of University demonstration teaching in P.E. methodology and pedagogy programs, in the Canadian school system. In 1988 Joanne and her late husband, Professor Maxwell Landy, were part of the leadership team at the National Youth Foundation Fitness Camp in Los Angeles. She is also co-author with Maxwell of the four-book series *Complete Physical Education Activities Program* (Parker Publishing, 1993).

Joanne now resides with her children in Perth and operates a Lifestyle Education consulting business which provides in–depth workshops and inservicing in physical education at all levels, including University P.E. teacher training programs. She is also a member of the Board of Consultants for Sportsmart/Sportime Australia (Melbourne-based), which markets a wide range of innovative and educational manipulative equipment in physical education. In the recreational areas, Joanne has been instrumental in developing and coordinating youth activity-based programs which include a Junior Basketball Skills Development Program, a "Tune-Up-Kids" program for young children from 5–12 years of age which focuses on development of fundamental movement skills, and a personal development program for teenage girls (13–18 years of age) called "On the Move." She has also set up "Tune Up" programs for adults and runs team-building and motivational sessions for school staffs, corporate business groups, and other community groups.

Joanne has presented at major HPERD (Health, Physical Education, Recreation and Dance) conferences in North America, Australia, and New Zealand. She also has facilitated many workshops in primary/secondary P.E. teaching at the University of Western Australia, Notre Dame College of Education, Western Washington University, Washington State, University of Regina, Saskatchewan, and major university centers throughout New Zealand. This year, Joanne lectured at Murdoch University, Education Faculty, in the Primary Physical Education teacher training program. She maintains an active lifestyle and is still involved in many sports on a regular basis.

Keith R. Burridge earned a Dip. Ed. from Nedlands Secondary Teachers College, followed by a B.P.E. degree (1978) and M.Ed. from the University of Western Australia, Perth. Keith's professional background includes 15 years as a secondary physical education and science teacher, 5 years as a primary physical education specialist, and 4 years of special education working with children with movement difficulties. From 1995-97 he was employed by the Department of Education of Western Australia (Perth)

as a school Development Officer in Physical Education and was responsible for professional development in P.E. for over 80 schools. He has represented Australia at the elite level in canoeing.

Keith was one of the key writers for the Western Australia Department of Education's 1998 Fundamental Movement Skills Package. He has lectured at Notre Dame College of Education and Murdoch University, and facilitated programs for early childhood education. Keith has presented F.M.S. and best practices in teaching workshops throughout Western Australia. He is the co-author with Joanne Landy of the newly released book *50 Simple Things You Can Do to Raise a Child Who is Physically Fit* (Macmillan, 1997). As a F.M.S. specialist, Keith has contributed in the writing of a book called *Why Bright Children Fail* (Hammond, 1996). He is also the designer for a K–3 computer assessment package for identifying children at an early age who have coordination problems. This program is in operation in over 400 schools in Western Australia.

Presently, Keith is teaching at Willeton Senior High School in Perth and piloting a special program to work with children at educational risk.

ACKNOWLEDGMENTS

We take this opportunity to once again thank our publisher and editor, Win Huppuch and Susan Kolwicz, the production staff of Diane Turso, Dee Coroneos, and Mariann Hutlak at Prentice Hall Direct for their editorial and production expertise, and constant support in the making of this book.

Also our thanks go out to the thousands of teachers in the field and in training institutes and to the children who have contributed to the direction and development of this comprehensive series by their enthusiastic participation in a variety of workshops over the years. We hope that they will enjoy the benefits of using this resource in their day-to-day involvement in quality activity!

INTRODUCTION TO COMPLETE MOTOR SKILLS ACTIVITIES PROGRAM

The *Complete Motor Skills Activities Program* consists of three books:

▶ Ready-to-Use Fundamental Motor Skills & Movement Activities for Young Children

▶ Ready-to-Use Fine Motor Skills & Handwriting Activities for Young Children

▶ Ready-to-Use Motor Skills & Movement Station Lesson Plans for Young Children

This program has been designed as a motor skills program for teachers, professionals, and parents in related fields (remedial, rehabilitation, and medical areas), working in the school environment, the home environment, or the community environment to assist children who have coordination difficulties in the performance and mastering of fundamental movement skills.

The focus of this program is to provide enjoyable developmentally-appropriate movement experiences in the teaching of these fundamental movement skills so that the children gain both competence and confidence in successfully performing these skills. We emphasize that if the strategies are to be successful, teachers and parents need to be aware that although children may be able to perform the tasks adequately in terms of task completion, focus must be directed to *how* the task is completed; that is, focus must be directed toward quality of the movement—not just the outcome of the movement.

FUNDAMENTAL MOVEMENT SKILLS

Fundamental Movement Skills (FMS) are gross motor movements that involve different body parts such as feet, legs, trunk, head, arms, and hands. FMS are the foundation movements for more complex and specialized skills required to play low-organized games, sports, gymnastics, dance, and recreational activities. These skills can be categorized into three main skill areas:

1. **Body management skills** involve controlling body balance whether on the move (dynamic balance) such as rolling, stopping, landing, turning, twisting, bending, swinging, stretching, and dodging; or being stationary (static balance) such as balancing on one foot. Body management skills also include awareness of body parts, and how the body moves in personal and general space.

2. *Locomotion skills* are movements that take the body in any direction, from one point to another. Locomotion skills should be learned from an early age onwards, and include walking, running, dodging, jumping and landing, hopping, leaping, skipping, and sliding.

3. *Object-control skills* involve hand-eye or foot-eye coordination in manipulation of such objects as balls, hoops, jump ropes, racquets, bats, and hockey sticks. They involve underhand throwing, overhand throwing, catching, bouncing, dribbling, rolling, striking skills with one or both hands, and kicking and trapping skills.

Motor memory is also an important component to this learning process and relates to the child's ability to visually and auditorially copy single movements, movement patterns, and rhythm patterns.

Current research suggests that if children do not reach a degree of competence and confidence in fundamental movement skills by the sixth grade, they will not engage in regular physical activity or sports for the rest of their lives.

SEVEN ESSENTIAL KEYS

Successful skills teaching in fundamental movement skills can result if you incorporate the following seven essential keys:

1. *Show enthusiasm, care, and interest.* These are qualities that cannot be written into any program. They come from you, and without them the program is not going to be so effective as it could be.

2. *Use visual demonstration with instruction* whenever possible. You may even need to physically move the child through some of the actions.

3. *Give praise, encouragement, and feedback.* These are an essential part of the learning process. Simply to say "do your best" does not bring about a constructive change. What is needed is good information about techniques and feedback (information about what the child has done). For example, "I watched the way you held the ball correctly in your fingers" or "That was a great effort; this time let's put your other foot forward."

4. *Create a positive, fun learning environment.* Sometimes we get preoccupied with telling the child what he or she is doing wrong or what he or she has not done instead of focusing on what he or she should be doing. A positive comment indicates to a child approval; the child can then develop trust and a willingness to keep trying.

5. *Keep the information simple and easy to follow.* Teaching by small-step progression is ideal. Progress may be a lot slower than you think and so patience definitely becomes a virtue.

6. *Keep the home play sessions shorter, more frequent, yet allowing for ample practice.* Some parents may be too enthusiastic and make the session simply too long. By keeping the sessions shorter, you can ensure that physical and mental fatigue do not become a factor and that the child's interest level is sustained.

7. *Avoid showing frustration; be patient.* If *you* feel frustrated, imagine how the child must feel. Frustration on your part is easily picked up by the child and compounds difficulties. Try saying "I think this is a good place to stop for today. Let's continue tomorrow."

BALANCED PHYSICAL EDUCATION PROGRAM

This book provides teachers with an important resource for the fitness component of a balanced P.E. program. Below is our suggestion for what we feel should be the total key components of a balanced P.E. program.

COMPONENT	GRADE/AGE GROUP
Motor Skills	K–7 / 5–12 years
Fitness	K–12 / 5–17 years
Fine Motor	K–10 / 5–15 years
Games	K–12 / 5–17 years
Movement Awareness	K–3 / 5–8 years
Rhythm and Dance	K–12 / 5–17 years
Gymnastics	K–10 / 5–15 years
Sport	4–12 / 9–17 years
Outdoor Education	8–12 / 12–17 years
Aquatics	K–12 / 5–17 years

ABOUT THIS BOOK

Here is a comprehensive collection of lesson plans focusing on progressive skill development and developmentally appropriate activities, along with movement stations to further reinforce skills. The book has been divided into two major sections:

► **Section 1** deals with the "teaching tools" that will provide effective and efficient classroom management and organizational strategies; the key teaching methods that can be used in teaching quality P.E.; the formations that provide variety in teaching the skill components; and the basic starting positions; break signals; and fitness signals.

► **Section 2** consists of 10 hands-on **Foundation Movement Lessons** for developing good listening skills; reaction and alertness; spatial and body awareness; collection and dispersal of equipment; organization and class control; and health-related and performance related fitness. These 10 introductory lesson plans are progressively developed over three levels, are segmental in design, and based on a 30-minute time allotment. In Level 1, the foundation movement lessons are designed to occur over two teaching sessions, in order for quality learning, practicing, and consolidating to occur. In Levels 2 and 3, the foundation movement lessons are revised and extended.

A set of 50 lesson plans follow, one set for each of the three levels, and each lesson focuses on one of the fundamental motor skills. Each lesson is comprised of two sessions: a Teaching Session and Movement Stations. Fitness activities are built-in throughout these lessons so that fitness becomes an inherent part of every lesson. In total, this material should provide for 30 weeks of movement skills teaching.

FORMAT

The format for Level 1 provides for the first 10 lessons to be focused on the foundation movement lesson plans, followed by the 50 lesson plans on movement and motor skills. Levels 2 and 3 have a slightly different format in that a foundation movement lesson is taught first, then a movement revision teaching session, followed by another foundation movement lesson, and a movement session. This cycle is repeated until the foundation movement lessons have all been revised; then lessons follow the same format as for Level 1.

Fundamental motor skills are categorized into three areas: *body management skills*; *locomotion skills*; and *object control skills*. Research indicates that about 450 minutes are required to adequately teach a FMS–object control skill; therefore it is advisable to teach only 5–6 of these fundamental motor skills in a 40-week school year to ensure that quality learning and sufficient practice in mastering the skill occurs.

TEACHING SESSIONS

Within each teaching session is included the Movement Area and Specific Movement skill (for example, Body Control/Dynamic Balance); Teachable Points for that movement; Equipment Required; Teaching Goals; Teaching Progressions; and Activities, which provide for small and large group play to reinforce movement skills taught in that lesson.

We emphasize at this point that the program is *not* content driven; it is not a "cook-book" approach per se. The main goal is to teach through *progressive skills development*, not try to teach through every lesson. In fact each lesson may contain more content than you may be able to get through in a 30–40-minute time allotment. Factors such as the ability levels of the children, the general "mood" of the class, the teaching area, the weather, special events, and so on may have a direct bearing on how much of each lesson is taught. Moreover, you should be prepared to repeat some of the lessons or part(s) of the lesson as a good principle of teaching.

> **To ensure a balanced lesson, each teaching session should include a Warming-Up Segment (4-5 minutes) and a Closing Segment (4-5 minutes). Refer to Section 1's Fitness Signals for a selection of warm-up activities and games, strengthening activities, and cooling-down activities which include closing activities and games and stretching ideas.**

MOVEMENT STATIONS

The movement stations consist of six activity stations that allow for further practice, mastering, and reinforcement of the skill(s) learned in the teaching session. Generally two stations are designed to revise previous learned skills; two stations provide practice of the new skills, one station will allow for free structured play or cooperative play, and one station for skill assessment. You will divide the class into six groups and assign each group to a starting station. The order of rotation will then be established; for example, on signal each group will rotate clockwise to the next station. Rotation will occur about every 5 minutes.

The instructions/demonstrations should be concise and kept simple for each station in order to maximize participation time. In fact most of the explanation and set-up organization can be accomplished in the classroom, with each team assigned a station or stations to set up and take down. The diagram or layout of each station can be photocopied from the actual movement station lesson plan and given to that particular team. The task and/or activities presented at each station are designed to accommodate the different ability levels of children and will include, for example, varying throwing distances, targets, equipment. They are also designed to promote maximum participation.

Option 1: First teach the activity tasks at each station, observe performance of children at each station, and offer individual feedback as you move around.

Option 2: Position yourself at the assessment station, while parents and/or teacher helpers assist at the other stations. Each group will rotate through to the "teacher" station. Focus on the skill being assessed, observe the performance of a

new skill, make comments, and then later follow-up with strategies to help the individual child who may have coordination difficulties. It is preferable to give the assistants key points to observe while the children are moving.

Option 3: Have groups rotate through the five skill stations. Select 4–5 students at a time, one from each group, to go to the assessment station. The order could be predetermined in the classroom for efficient use of time.

(Ideally we recommend that parent helpers and/or senior students be available when a movement station lesson occurs. Senior students involved in this program could be given special recognition at assemblies as well as a certificate for their efforts.)

NOTE: The assessment procedures and recording sheets for each FMS can be found in Book 1, Ready-to-Use Fundamental Motor Skills & Movement Activities for Young Children. Each recording form contains a checklist of observable teaching points, assessing procedures, and scoring system.

Included in Book 1 are reproducible Teaching Points Cue Cards for easy reference when teaching the different motor skills, and identifying common faults and corrections for each of those common faults (remediation).

☛ **Blank Teaching Session and Movement Station formats are provided at the end of this book to allow for creation of additional lesson plans.**

MOTOR SKILLS LEVEL GUIDELINES

The following are guidelines for teaching these motor skills over a 3-year period:

LEVEL 1	LEVEL 2	LEVEL 3
Locomotion Skills		
Running	Running (Revision)	Running (Extension)
Dodging	Dodging (Revision)	Dodging (Extension)
Hopping	Hopping (Revision)	Hopping (Extension)
Leaping	Leaping (Revision)	Leaping (Extension)
	Skipping	Skipping (Extension)
	Slide-stepping	Slide-stepping (Extension)
Body-management Skills		
Static Balance	Static Balance	Static Balance
Dynamic Balance	Dynamic Balance	Dynamic Balance
Jumping/Landings (Horizontal/Vertical)	Jumping/Landings (Horizontal/Vertical)	Jumping/Landings (Horizontal/Vertical)
Object Control Skills		
Receiving a Rolled Large Ball	Receiving a Rolled Small Ball (Revision)	Receiving a Rolled Small Ball (Extension)
Catching a Large Ball (Hands/Body) and (Just Hands)	Catching Large Ball (Two Hands)	Catching Different Ball Shapes and Sizes (Two Hands/One Hand)
Catching a Small Object	Catching a Small Ball (Two Hands)	Catching on the Move
Bouncing and Catching with Two Hands (Using a Large Ball)		
	One-Handed Bouncing (While Moving)	One-Handed Bouncing (Changing Directions)

LEVEL 1	LEVEL 2	LEVEL 3

Object Control Skills   *(Cont'd)*

LEVEL 1	LEVEL 2	LEVEL 3
Underhand Throwing	Underhand Throwing (Revision)	Underhand Throwing and Catching (Small Objects)
		Two-Handed Passing
Overhand Throwing	Overhand Throwing (Revise)	Overhand Throwing (Extension)
Single-Handed Striking (Using Hand/Tee)	Single-Handed Striking (Forehand/Racquet)	Single-Handed Striking (Backhand/Racquet)
Two-Handed Striking (Bat and Tee)	Two-Handed Striking (Bat and Tee)	Two-Handed Striking (Moving Ball)
		Dribbling, Trapping, Passing, Shooting with (Floor Hockey) Stick
Dribbling/Trapping	Dribbling/Trapping (with feet)	Dribbling/Trapping (with feet)
Kicking for Distance	Kicking for Distance	Kicking for Distance (Extension)
Kicking for Accuracy	Kicking for Accuracy	Kicking for Accuracy (Extension)
	Punt Kick	Punt Kick

CONTENTS

SECTION 1
USING EFFECTIVE TEACHING STRATEGIES IN PHYSICAL EDUCATION

SECTION 2
THE MOVEMENT LESSON PLANS

LEVEL 1 *(Cont'd)*

LEVEL 2

LEVEL 2   *(Cont'd)*

LEVEL 2 *(Cont'd)*

LEVEL 3

LEVEL 3 *(Cont'd)*

LEVEL 3 *(Cont'd)*

MOTOR SKILLS ACQUISITION MODEL

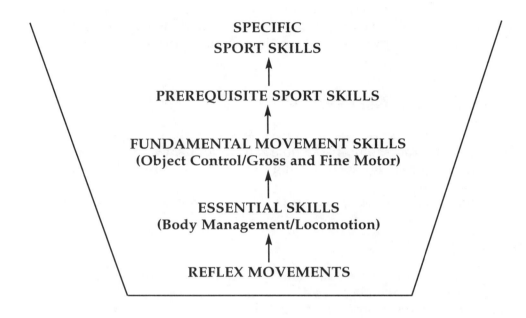

SPECIFIC
SPORT SKILLS

↑

PREREQUISITE SPORT SKILLS

↑

FUNDAMENTAL MOVEMENT SKILLS
(Object Control/Gross and Fine Motor)

↑

ESSENTIAL SKILLS
(Body Management/Locomotion)

↑

REFLEX MOVEMENTS

➤ Fundamental motor skills are part of a movement continuum that begins before birth and continues for the rest of our lives. Soon after birth, an infant displays reflexes that gradually give way to essential voluntary movements that will allow the infant to socialize, explore the environment, and to literally stand on his/her own two feet. With exposure to movement experiences, the young child begins to learn rudimentary fundamental movement skills that, ideally, will be refined through good modeling, quality instruction, and opportunity to practice. Although children will reach different levels of competence, they move through similar phases.

➤ If children are not taught, or do not practice and master the "small step" progressions from fundamental motor skills to sport specific skills, they could experience frustration and even failure which could have detrimental effects on their pursuing activity on a regular basis as a teenager, and later on as an adult. For example, a young girl learning to play T-Ball for the first time, who has not developed good catching, throwing, and striking skills, could become very discouraged by her lack of ability, and simply quit. This becomes a negative experience for her.

➤ Thus the importance of children acquiring competence and confidence in mastering fundamental motor skills at an early age cannot be emphasized enough!

Children who consolidate these fundamental motor skills in early life will be more likely to pursue and experience success at a multitude of recreational activities and sport specific avenues. This will open the door to a lifetime of active lifestyle that will be both habitual and enjoyable!

ASSESSING STUDENTS

When looking at assessment in movement—whether it be gross motor or fine motor—a number of stages need to be considered dependent upon what level of understanding you require of student performance. Below is a guideline to some aspects of assessment that need to be considered.

STAGE 1: GLOBAL ASSESSMENT

During this first stage, you should observe and monitor the children in formal and informal situations. You should make qualitative judgments on the children's level of coordination. For those children appearing to have difficulties, you should make some anecdotal comments.

This monitoring is ongoing and provides the foundation for reporting.

STAGE 2: SCREENING

This optional stage involves assessing children on the standardized tests that are available and recognized as reliable and valid.

The results provide important information on the levels of coordination of the children in these areas. This information is extremely useful for class and individual student programming.

STAGE 3: ONGOING QUALITATIVE ASSESSMENT

This stage involves your monitoring and making qualitative observations in the different skill areas. Using checklists, information can be gained that provides the foundations for teaching, individual correction, and feedback in the class. Again, the need is for you to be familiar with the key movement points given for individual skills.

STAGE 4: INDIVIDUAL ASSESSMENT FOR THE PURPOSE OF REMEDIATION

If, from your global observations and from standardized testing, a child is recorded as experiencing difficulties, then you should use checklists to try and find the most probable cause of the difficulty Do not eliminate the possibility that the cause of the difficulty is sensory in nature and that referral to a medical professional might be required.

FITNESS AWARENESS

➤ Parents should have reasonable expectations for their child's abilities and for potential skill changes.

➤ Children with movement difficulties often do not learn as well or as quickly using conventional methods of instruction, as do coordinated children.

➤ Parents need to be aware that children experiencing movement difficulties require more time to learn a skill. They need constant feedback and quite often need to be physically taken through movements (kinesthetic assistance).

➤ Parents should be aware that some difficulties will disappear with maturity; some will not. The longer we allow inefficient physical movement to continue, such as incorrect handwriting grip, the harder it becomes to correct because the child practices poor movements which become habits, and then these have to be undone. Also, if these difficulties are left too long, some children begin to display avoidance behavior because they are not experiencing success.

➤ Identifying the physical problems early can result in a favorable prognosis for improvement. However, this requires consistent, cooperative, and effective intervention by the school and by parents.

➤ Try to make your child as independent as possible. To do this you must resist the temptation to complete the tasks for him or her, including such daily requirements as tying shoelaces, cutting food, and dressing. Instead, be there to assist your child to complete the task.

➤ If your child does have a specific weakness in one or two areas, we recommend that you try to spend three 15-minute sessions per week, focusing on these areas of weakness in addition to the normal home play.

➤ It is very important to promote the strengths of the children as well as assisting with their difficulties. You can achieve this by choosing some of the activities that you know your child is good at; for example, the child may have difficulties tying his shoelaces, but is great at cutting out shapes; therefore, do some cutting sessions or include cutting as an enrichment session.

Be patient with your child because it does take longer for children to learn skills than we think. Praise the child's efforts as well—we all need encouragement. Try to be consistent in following this program.

SECTION 1

USING EFFECTIVE
TEACHING STRATEGIES
IN PHYSICAL EDUCATION

BLANK VERSO

The most effective teachers are those who not only know *what to teach*, but *how to teach* it. They are not "just do it" teachers; rather they use the "teachable moment" and are willing to explore different ways of providing quality teaching and creating positive learning experiences.

A number of teaching methods are presented here. The stimulation and motivation provided by use of a variety of teaching methods cannot be overlooked. All decisions in a lesson are made by either you or the child, but the amount of decision-making transferred from you to the child is the determining factor in which method is used.

Teaching methods should also be selected to fit the circumstances that exist: the content to be taught, the number of children in the class, the equipment and facilities, the time allotted, the space provided, and the ability levels of the children. Good teachers will use many different methods, often within the same physical education lesson, mixing and matching as the situation dictates The result could be a refreshing sparkle and stimulating challenge for the children and the teacher alike!

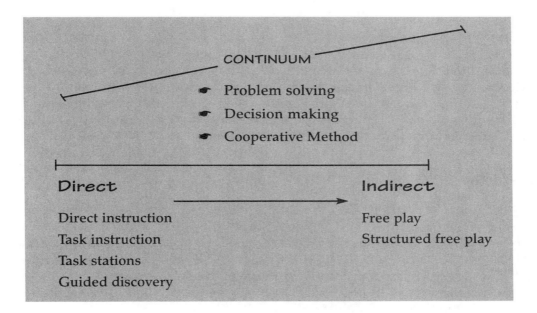

TEACHING METHODS

DIRECT INSTRUCTION

This is the best method for initially teaching fundamental movement skills. You provide step-by-step instruction (small-step progression) and all decisions are made by you. This method provides a good starting point for beginning teachers and acts as a spring-board to the use of other methods. Although this method of teaching is economical in the utilization of time available to learn new activities or skills, it should be used sparingly in total-class instruction as it tends to discourage creativity and initiative, leads to stereotyped movements, does not allow for individual differences, and restricts the development of decision-making and leadership abilities.

TASK INSTRUCTION

Task teaching involves the shifting of decision-making from teacher to children, while they work toward the perfection of predetermined skills. Let the children decide at what pace they may work. How the skill is completed remains set, as well as where the skill is completed.

TASK STATIONS

This method is very useful when teaching large groups of children; when there is insufficient or minimum equipment and apparatus for the entire class, but enough for a small group; when you wish to be free to give individual attention to children, by rotating to each group; when you wish to provide children with opportunities for responsibility and leadership; and when skills learned can then be further practiced, reinforced, and extended through station work.

GUIDED DISCOVERY

The basic difference between this method and the previous styles mentioned is that in guided discovery you never tell the children the answer. You solicit certain responses from the children through questions (cues) that are designed to gradually lead the child to the discovery of a predetermined target—hence, success! You present the tasks and then ask the children to think about how they can best solve these tasks.

PROBLEM SOLVING/DECISION MAKING

In the guided discovery method the child's movement response is prompted by your cues, but in the problem-solving method, the child is *expected to determine the answer all on his/her own.* This method is open-ended; that is, there is no predetermined final skill. In fact, there are no right or wrong responses at all. Each child is made to feel that his/her response is acceptable and worthwhile. The assumption is that the children have the prerequisite skills and knowledge to solve the problem. This method is therefore not suitable for younger children.

   Usually you use the problem-solving technique to introduce the skill by posing a question as to what has to be accomplished by the skill and the children experiment to find the best alternative. This method thus encourages initiative, self-inquiry, and self-actualization in the child. The child is involved in the thinking, sensing, comprehending, analyzing, and reasoning processes, with the freedom to think, to work alone or in groups, and freedom to work with available apparatus and equipment. Note that Decision Making is a process, not a method of teaching.

COOPERATIVE METHOD

This method has been called "cooperative" because the teaching–learning–evaluating role is shared between you and all the children in the class in a cooperative effort to assist each other to learn. This method retains the formal style of instruction of the direct and task methods, the informality of the practice session and utilization of task cards as used in the task method, and the self-actualization associated with the guided discovery and problem-solving methods. There is a further shift in decision-making and responsibility in this method that involves the children in the teaching–learning–evaluating processes. The responsibility also extends to handling of equipment and class organization.

FREE PLAY

This can be considered as a method and is valuable in that time is allowed in the lesson for children to "freely" and safely explore their new equipment without specific instruction, thus enhancing creative play opportunity.

STRUCTURED FREE PLAY

This method can be used for all years where limitations are put on the responses that can be made and is a prerequisite to problem-solving, but is more individual than guided discovery. Limitations may be in the form of spatial demands, time, force, use of body parts, and equipment.

MANAGEMENT TOOLS

Signals are **"management tools"** used to create effective and efficient classroom organization, arrangement, and mobilization of children, thus maximizing participation time and reducing behavioral problems. Through learning and reacting to these signals, the children develop better listening skills, alertness and reaction; improve in overall spatial and body awareness; develop good body management and control while moving or stationary; and develop and improve locomotion skills. Through using signals, cooperation is enhanced, efficient mobilization of children to equipment or equipment to children (collection and dispersal of equipment) is established, and an effective positive learning environment in the P.E. classroom is created.

Signals involve both a verbal and a visual signal and are classified into **Organization** signals, **Formation** signals, **Starting Positions,** and **Break** signals. These need to be taught early at the beginning of the year and consistently reinforced throughout the school year. You must be both patient and insistent that these signals are responded to immediately by all children and that quality of movement is evident. Once children have learned to react to the basic signals, then these become the "management tools" for teaching movement skills and all other components of the lesson. Furthermore, this concept can be extended to include the development of other signals, thus creating a movement or signals vocabulary—a movement language—that can be constantly expanded. When the signals are well learned, the verbal signals can be taken away so that only the visual signal is responded to. It may be necessary under certain conditions—for example, if you are teaching outside or using a lot of music inside the gymnasium—to use a whistle, which becomes the immediate attention-grabber. Then the signal can be given, which becomes the indicator to do something. Once you become more confident and competent in using these tools, you will find yourself spontaneously creating more signals and usage. Enjoy the challenge!

The Organization and Formation signals, Starting Positions, and Break signals are now described. The "Teamness Concept" is also introduced along with the Team signal. These tools are incorporated in a variety of ways in the first 10 lessons, illustrating how they can be effectively taught and used.

ORGANIZATION SIGNALS

The following signals provide ways of effectively mobilizing children and of developing their listening skills and spatial awareness. Identify the boundaries of the play area in which children will move around. Use a minimum of 6–8 cone markers or witch's hats spaced evenly apart around the area. Establish the following signals that children can quickly learn and respond to. Single-out good listeners and praise them!

1. ***Homes!*** (*Hand Signal:* Make a roof overhead with hands. Mats, hoops, carpet squares, or deck rings could also be used as "Homes.") Find a free space in the play area. Check that you cannot touch anyone or anything. This is your "Home!" Remember it. Now leave your home and touch 5 different markers, with 5 different body parts. Return to "stand tall" in your home space. Go!

2. ***Scrambled Eggs!*** (*Hand Signal:* Roll hand over hand.) Listen carefully to how I will ask you to move. Then move in this way, in and out of each other, without "touching" anyone. Example: "Scrambled Eggs—Walking!"

3. ***Iceberg!*** (*Hand Signal:* Raise one hand in the air with thumb up.) This is your stopping signal. When you hear or see this word, stop immediately by "jump-stopping" or landing on your feet at the same time, knees bent, hands out for balance.

4. ***Quiet Signal.*** (*Hand Signal:* Raise one hand overhead.) This is your "stop–look–listen" signal. Stop what you are doing and raise your hand overhead, giving me your full attention!

5. ***Dead Bug!*** (*Hand Signal:* Thumbs down.) Quickly and safely lie on your back, raising your arms and legs in the air. Wiggle them gently.

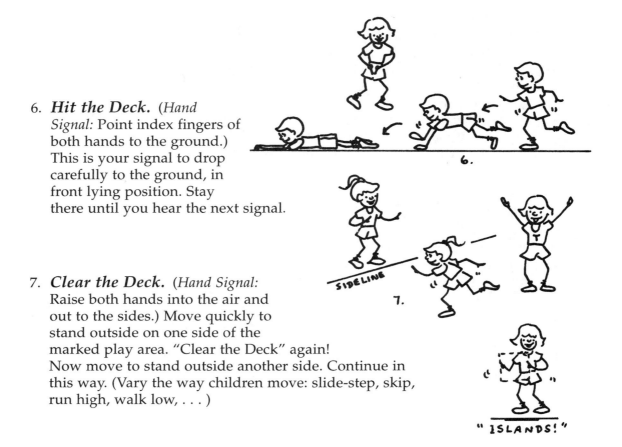

6. **Hit the Deck.** (*Hand Signal:* Point index fingers of both hands to the ground.) This is your signal to drop carefully to the ground, in front lying position. Stay there until you hear the next signal.

7. **Clear the Deck.** (*Hand Signal:* Raise both hands into the air and out to the sides.) Move quickly to stand outside on one side of the marked play area. "Clear the Deck" again! Now move to stand outside another side. Continue in this way. (Vary the way children move: slide-step, skip, run high, walk low, . . .)

8. **Islands.** (*Hand Signal:* Use both hands to draw a "square" shape in the air.) Each team or group moves to its designated island taking the necessary equipment along and sets up as instructed. This is a group/team learning square that can vary in formation, size, and number. Cone markers, ropes, 4´ × 6´ light carry mats, Station Cards, etc., can be used to indicate each island location and space. Each islander can still find a "Home" (individualized learning space) within his/her island. You designate one square to be the "Main Island" (the teaching square). Some examples for different teaching skills are illustrated.

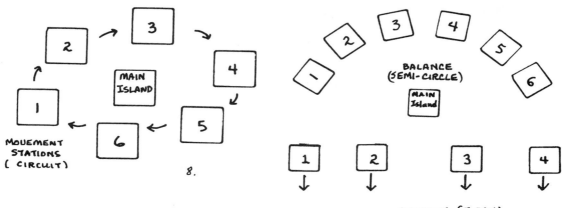

FORMATION SIGNALS

Formation signals effectively and efficiently organize the children into location and position. If teaching the P.E. lesson outside, ensure that children are not looking directly into the sun. Use markers to clearly indicate the boundaries of the play area.

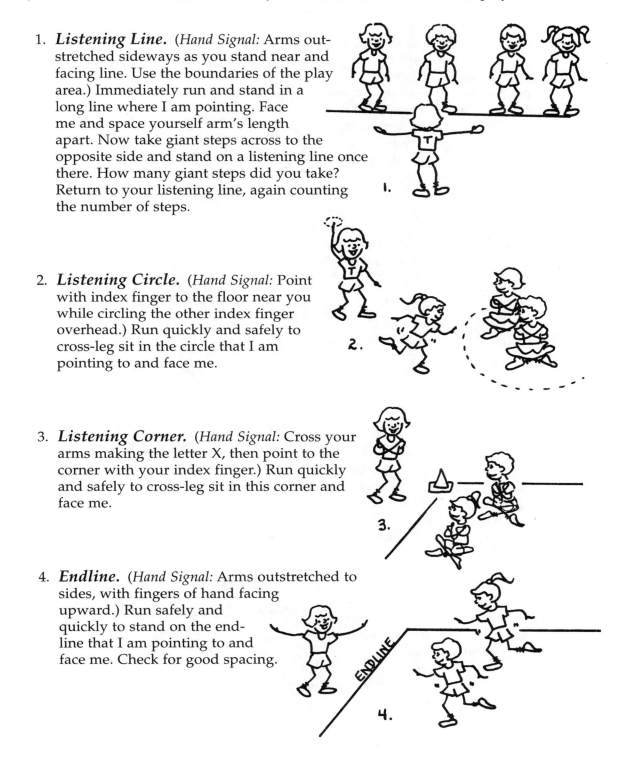

1. *Listening Line.* (*Hand Signal:* Arms outstretched sideways as you stand near and facing line. Use the boundaries of the play area.) Immediately run and stand in a long line where I am pointing. Face me and space yourself arm's length apart. Now take giant steps across to the opposite side and stand on a listening line once there. How many giant steps did you take? Return to your listening line, again counting the number of steps.

2. *Listening Circle.* (*Hand Signal:* Point with index finger to the floor near you while circling the other index finger overhead.) Run quickly and safely to cross-leg sit in the circle that I am pointing to and face me.

3. *Listening Corner.* (*Hand Signal:* Cross your arms making the letter X, then point to the corner with your index finger.) Run quickly and safely to cross-leg sit in this corner and face me.

4. *Endline.* (*Hand Signal:* Arms outstretched to sides, with fingers of hand facing upward.) Run safely and quickly to stand on the endline that I am pointing to and face me. Check for good spacing.

5. *Groups—"2!", "3!" . . .* (*Hand Signal:* Indicate group size by showing that number of fingers, followed by the Home hand signal.) Children quickly sit in a group indicated by the number of fingers shown.

"2's"

5.

6. *Teams!* (*Hand Signal:* Both hands held out in front parallel to ground as you stand near a designated line.) Children quickly fall into their teams, with the captain at the front and the co-captain at the end of each team. Everyone cross-leg sits in file formation (one behind the other).

Team
1 ◎ • • • • ▣
2 ◎ • • • • ▣
3 ◎ • • • • ▣
4 ◎ • • • • ▣
5 ◎ • • • ◂ ▣
CAPTAIN   CO-CAPTAIN
"TEAMS!"
6.

7. *Waves!* (*You move from facing the file to position on either side as shown in diagram.*) Children, in stand tall position, space themselves arm's length apart, with each wave on a designated floor line or 3 giant steps away from the wave in front.

"WAVES"
7.

8. *Circle Up!* (*Hand Signal:* Hand raised overhand, circling in a clockwise or counterclockwise direction. Children run in the given direction, single file, around the play area.

CW   CCW
8.

9. *Snake!* (*Hand Signal:* Use listening line hand signal, then point to line of direction, such as a wall.) Children quickly run to stand on the listening line, then turn to file formation (one behind the other), facing the direction you indicate. Children stay in this file order as they move.

XXXXXXXXX→   "SNAKE"
9.

10. *Shuttle!* (*Hand Signal:* Use team hand signal and then split the team into two groups.) Each team splits into two groups that stand in file formation, each half facing opposite the other and spaced a designated distance apart.

X X X   X X X
5 3 1 →   2 4 6
10.

STARTING POSITIONS

Starting positions signals provide an efficient way of getting children in the appropriate body position for demands of the skill, activity, or game. Teach the following, emphasizing good posture.

1. *Stand Tall.* Stand with feet comfortably spread apart and toes turned out slightly. Arms are at the sides, hands relaxed, eyes looking forward.

2. *Cross-Leg Sit.* Sit with legs crossed and arms resting on the knees.

3. *Long Sit.* Sit with legs outstretched and together. Lean back on your hands for support.

4. *Hook Sit.* Sit with legs together, bending at knees, and feet flat on the floor. Lean back to take weight on the hands.

5. *Half Hook Sit.* Sit with one leg outstretched and the other leg bent. Lean back to support weight on hands.

6. *Wide Sit.* Sit with legs outstretched and comfortably apart. Lean back on hands for support.

7. *All Fours.* Support your weight on hands and knees, facing downward.

8. ***Knee Sit.*** Sit upright on your knees, hands resting on your knees.

    Kneeling Sit. Sit back on your knees.

9. ***One Knee Up, One Knee Down.*** Sit with one knee up and the other knee down as shown. Keep your back straight.

10. ***Front Lying Position.*** Lie face down with your legs extended backward and together, arms by your sides at chest level.

11. ***Front Support Position.*** Support weight on hands and toes, facing downward. Hold body straight.

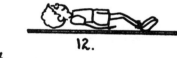

12. ***Back Lying Position.*** Lie facing upward, legs straight and arms at sides.

13. ***Back Support Position.*** From hook sit position, take weight on hands and feet, raising body off the floor. Keep legs straight and extended, arms slightly bent at elbow.

14. ***Hook Lying.*** Lie on back with knees bent so that weight is on feet and arms are relaxed at the sides.

15. ***Squat.*** From standing position, bend knees to raise heels off the floor. Place hands between your legs and rest them on the floor.

BREAK SIGNALS

A "Break" is a short informal activity that, when introduced spontaneously throughout the lesson, can provide a further benefit and extension of signals in the following ways:

➤ Provide a change of pace from the current activity being performed—from passive to active involvement, or from active to passive activity to provide a rest.

➤ Provide a variety of ways for children to interact and respond to different signals and enhance their alertness training.

➤ Provide extra fitness, challenge, and fun—even the element of "surprise."

➤ Mobilize children to equipment or equipment to children and assist in dispersing and collecting equipment.

➤ Create transitional flow between lesson segments.

In the following movement lessons and teaching sessions, several examples of breaks are presented so that you can get the idea of how to effectively implement them in your daily lesson plan.

1. *Equipment Break.* On signal "Bounce!," bounce the ball clockwise around the play area. Then place the ball in the container and fall into teams.

2. *Organizational Break.* Touch a mat, a bench, a rope, and a hoop with a different body part each time, then find a partner and cross-leg sit side by side.

3. *Tempo Change Break.* On signal "Cocoon!," sink to the ground, then slowly—ever so s-l-o-w-l-y—uncurl to stand in tall position, stretching high into the air.

4. *Partner Break.* When you hear the signal "Leapfrog!" find a partner and leapfrog from sideline to sideline. (Leapfrog by placing hands on partner's back and straddle-jumping over partner.)

5. *Stunt Break.* "Thread the Needle." From stand tall position and with fingers interlocked in front, lean over and try to put one leg through, then the other leg. Now reverse to the start position. Remember to keep hand-hold throughout this activity!

"COCOON!"

"LEAPFROG!"

"THREAD THE NEEDLE"

"TEAMNESS CONCEPT"

T.E.A.M. (TOGETHER EVERYONE ACHIEVES MORE!)

"Teamness" is an important aspect of organizing your classes within the physical education classroom setting. By placing children into teams, you are creating a sense of belonging for that child, so that social exclusion problems will not occur, and cooperation can be fostered and enhanced in a positive learning environment. Moreover, operating your P.E. classroom through teams will allow for efficient setting up; dispersing and collecting equipment; and mobilizing children for station work, low-organized games, lead-up and minor game play, and other interactive play experiences.

Place children into teams early in the school year, from kindergarten onward. Ideally the team size should be confined to 5–6 members and the number of teams determined by the class size. For example, in a class of 30 children, try to create 5 teams of 6 and balance these teams as best as possible. You may need to readjust the teams from time to time to "balance them" and, after a certain time, may decide to change teams around.

Within each team, appoint two leaders: a captain who sits at the front of the file and a co-captain who positions at the end of the file, thus "containing" the team. Strive to have a girl captain and a boy co-captain or vice-versa. After a period of two weeks, let the captain and co-captain change roles. After a month has passed, appoint a new captain and co-captain for each team. Continue this pattern until each member has had a turn at being a leader. List the teams for each class on a large paper flipchart using a colored "starring" (*) system, for example, to record captains and co-captains. These charts also become your "cues" to help you learn the children's names for each class, quickly!

CO-CAPTAIN   CAPTAIN

The duties of the captain and co-captain include such responsibilities as:

➤ dispersing and collecting equipment
➤ reporting on team absenteeism
➤ relaying instructions to team
➤ providing leadership in different activities and games
➤ providing "pastoral care" to ensure that everyone on the team is looked after, and receives fair and equal treatment (gender-equity)
➤ promoting cooperation, communication, and collective decision-making

Each team creates a name and a team cheer for itself. Have each team in turn demonstrate this cheer to the other teams. Team names could be selected on the basis of rainbow colors; the alphabet; special groups such as animals, birds, dinosaurs, planets, and so on. Several ideas are provided in the first 10 lesson plans to foster leadership skills, respect within the team, responsibilities, equality, team spirit, communication, contribution, and cooperation through team-building activities—all important skills for functioning positively in society and the community at large.

FITNESS STRATEGIES

"FIT" GUIDELINES

➤ **Observe the children at play.** Take a "mental snapshot"—Is the child active? Energetic? Enthusiastic? Receptive? Responding positively to challenges? Enjoying? Interacting with you and with others?

➤ **Make fitness fun!** Children are not mini-adults! They simply obtain their fitness by doing activities that they enjoy. Imposing "training" on them will only create an uphill battle of resistance.

➤ **Children do activity intermittently.** Remember that they tire easily, but recover quickly.

➤ **Play is the fundamental "key"** to life and contributes to the overall development of the child. Children can explore, create, express, discover, interact, and learn about the environment around them and about themselves through "playful" experiences. Play is about "promoting lifestyle activity for youth." Play is also for adults participating in the lives of children!

➤ From an early age, **educate children about what it means to be "FIT":**

"**F**"—How often should we do activity? (*frequency*)

"**I**" —How much effort should be put into it? (*intensity*)

"**T**"—How long should we do the activity? (*time*)

　　—What types of activity can we do? (*type*)

➤ **Moderate activity is valued and beneficial.** Active children become active adults. Any activity is better than no activity. Experts recommend that primary school-aged children accumulate at least 30–60 minutes of age- and developmentally-appropriate physical activity *daily*! Encourage more than 30–60 minutes; discourage extended periods of inactivity for children.

➤ **Fitness should be inherent** throughout the physical education lesson rather than taught as a training regime. Exposure to a variety of interesting, enjoyable, and beneficial activity at the developmentally-appropriate age level is highly recommended!

TWENTY EXERCISE RECOMMENDATIONS

1. Establish boundaries and mark them clearly for each activity session. Use such markers as witch's hats, domes, or throwing rings.

2. Establish a set of signals for starting, stopping, and movement. These signals will enhance children's listening skills, alertness and reaction, and spatial awareness. Practice these until the children can respond immediately.

3. Give instructions clearly and concisely. Demonstrate whenever possible.

4. Warm up gently and rhythmically, using as many of the major muscle groups involved in the main activity. Begin in a slow, controlled manner, gradually increasing intensity.

5. Keep the warm-up simple. Use easy, "catchy" names that children will remember.

6. Identify the activities with names that children can easily remember and associate the movement with the name; for example, "Dead Ants"—children quickly and carefully drop to the floor on their backsides with limbs waving in the air.

7. Include specific stretching and movements that are used in the activities to follow.

8. Avoid tag-type games in the early part of the warm-up.

9. Modify and adapt according to age level, space available, and weather conditions.

10. Use music with a moderate, steady beat to enhance the enjoyment and rhythm of the movements.

11. Stretching activities can occur during the warm-up and then in the cool-down, but stretching activities should be performed while the muscles are still warm.

12. Cooling-down time is necessary to help the body return to its normal resting state and should be part of the overall fitness package. The activity is continued, but at a lower intensity.

STRETCHING

13. Quiet, gentle background music could be used to help the children "unwind" and relax. Have child concentrate on his or her breathing.

14. Be aware of children's growth and development. Movement is needed for the development of bones and muscles; therefore, it is important that children experience developmentally-appropriate activities for their age group.

15. Be a positive role model by being enthusiastic and joining in whenever and wherever possible. Children learn by example. Encourage, praise, and provide constructive feedback; don't push or be overbearing.

16. Provide a variety of activities. Make the activity fun, challenging, interesting, and motivating. Vary the intensity so that children do not become fatigued.

17. Be aware of exercise "do's" and "don'ts." Never stretch "cold" muscles. Avoid ballistic movements when stretching. Avoid exercises that hyperextend any joint areas. Encourage children to use their own body weight to develop strength.

18. See fitness as the BIG picture. That is, physical fitness is only one integral part of the total health and well-being package that also includes good nutrition, mental health (thinking), emotional health (attitude), quality sleep, relaxation, and "play" time. The key is to achieve a "balance" of all these health-related components!

19. Establish exercise/activity as a "habit." Establish an activity routine schedule, but within this schedule be flexible and realistic as you may not have the time or opportunity to do activity with the children at the same time each day.

20. Develop in children a "knowing attitude"; that is, get the children used to being active, used to doing exercises, and in the know of *why* exercise is so good for everyone!

STRATEGIES TO ENCOURAGE THE RELUCTANT CHILD

➤ Try to discern *why* a child is reluctant to do an activity: Is she or he overweight? Is she or he insecure? Does the child have low self-esteem, a fear of failure? Does the child feel unsafe—and does not want to get physically or emotionally hurt? Does the child have poor coordination?

➤ Create a safe, fun, positive learning environment free of any physical threat, ridicule, bullying, put-downs.

➤ Provide immediate feedback, given out at the "time of doing." Use words of praise and encouragement that are meaningful: "You ran all the way without stopping—that's terrific!"

➤ Don't be overprotective. Establish consistency and firmness.

➤ Try to create situations that guarantee success within a short period of time.

➤ Keep within the limits of the child's abilities. Don't force the child to do the activity; instead, encourage the child to be responsible for her or his own activity involvement.

➤ From time to time, offer some kind of incentive or reward. The instant reward is praise and encouragement. Set a goal that is followed by a reward: "If you can try to run for two minutes non-stop, then you can have free play with your favorite piece of equipment at the end!"

➤ Provide a variety of activity experiences that will sustain children's interest.

➤ Have the children create activities that the whole class can do together. Include a description and even a drawing with the "title" of the activity.

➤ Don't confuse a child's *needs* with the child's *wants*. Young children do not have the knowledge or experience to know what is good for them. You need to impose your knowledge of the importance of exercise on the child and the benefits of regular play activity.

WARMING-UP SIGNALS

The following fitness signals continue to reinforce listening skills, alertness, reaction, and spatial and body awareness through enjoyable and beneficial activity.

1. *Home.* Using your right hands, shake hands with 5 different children, then return Home and shake all over like a wet dog coming out of the water.

SHAKE HANDS   1.   WET DOG

2. *Scrambled Eggs!—Walking.* Walk forward, looking carefully where you are going. "Iceberg!"

   ➤ Stretch *tall* toward the sky.

   ➤ Walk quickly; walk slowly; quickly–slowly. "Iceberg!"

   ➤ Stretch *wide*! "Dead Bug!" Quickly lie on your back and wiggle your hands and feet in the air!

   2.
   STORK STAND

   ➤ Walk with big steps; walk with baby steps; walk with feet close together; walk with feet far apart. "Iceberg!" "Stork Stand!" (balance on one foot)

   ➤ Walk happily; walk angrily; walk frightened; creep quickly. "Iceberg!"

   ➤ Curl up into a ball, then slowly, very slowly uncurl and stretch tall.

   3.

   ➤ Walk in a straight line; walk in a zigzag pattern; walk in a figure-8.

   ➤ Walk in a circle. "Iceberg!" Touch 3 body parts to the ground.

3. *March!* March to music and clap your hands in time. "Iceberg!" March in place! March in a big circle, March in a rectangle. March backward. March together with a partner.

4. Try *combinations of signals* and watch the action!

   ➤ "Scrambled Eggs!—Running!" "Hit the Deck!" "Clear the Deck!"

   ➤ "Scrambled Eggs!—Slide-stepping" "Iceberg!" "Hit the Deck!"

   ➤ "Scrambled Eggs!—Skipping" "Clear the Deck!"

   ➤ "Scrambled Eggs!—Leaping" "Hit the Deck!" "Pencil Stretch!"

   ➤ "Scrambled Eggs!—Hopping" "Iceberg!" "Shake-Shake-Shake!"

" HIT THE DECK! "   SLIDE - ICEBERG!

4.

WARMING-UP FITNESS GAMES

1. ***Six Corners.*** Use markers positioned at 6 locations in a rectangular area or hexagonal shape. With a marking pen, number the markers 1 through 6 as shown in the diagram. On signal "Corner!" players run to a corner of their choice and stay there jogging on the spot. Throw a large dice and see which number comes up. Players caught in the corner with that number must come to the center of the play area and do stretches; the other players continue the game. When only 6 players remain, each player must run to a different corner! Who will be the last player left?

2. ***Here, Where, There.*** Listen carefully to the word I will say. If you hear the word "Here," walk quickly toward me; "Where," walk on the spot; "There," walk quickly away from me. Repeat this activity, having children move in other ways, such as: skipping, running, jumping, slide-stepping, hopping.

3. ***Follow-the-Leader.*** Find a partner and stand together in a Home space one behind the other. Take turns being the leader and the follower, changing on the whistle signal. Think of lots of different ways that you can move. How many different body parts can you warm up?

4. ***Let's Pretend You Are . . . .*** (Remember to watch where you are going!)

   ➤ a 747 jet taking off down the runway, lifting off, and then flying
   ➤ a lawn mower cutting the grass
   ➤ a jet-ski slicing through the water
   ➤ a hawk swooping down on a small critter
   ➤ a hockey player scoring a goal
   ➤ a figure skater spinning
   ➤ a shadow-boxer punching into the air and "dancing" with the feet
   ➤ a karate-kid, kicking with feet and slashing with hands
   ➤ a hummingbird flitting from flower to flower
   ➤ a prancing horse
   ➤ a snake wriggling along the ground

STRENGTHENING SIGNALS

Good muscular strength is needed to carry out daily work and play—taking out the garbage, bringing in the groceries, chopping the wood, raking the leaves, hanging and swinging on the playground apparatus, throwing a football, swinging a baseball bat, swimming in the surf . . . and even dealing with unforeseen emergencies!

By improving the child's muscular strength, the strength of bones, ligaments, and tendons are also increased. Young children's bones are still growing and therefore need low-impact exercises or activity. The more weight-bearing activities they can experience, the better. Keeping the activities enjoyable and at the developmentally-appropriate age level will ensure proper strength development, decrease the chance of injury, prevent poor posture and back injury, and improve the child's performance.

1. *Critter Walks.* Begin in your Home space. Show me how you can move like the following "critters" (animal walks):

   ➤ **Crab Walk.** Walk on all fours with face upward.

   ➤ **Kangaroo.** Jump with hands held up in front.

   ➤ **Puppy Walk.** Walk on all fours.

   ➤ **Bunny Hop.** On all fours, first move hands forward, then feet. Continue in this way.

   ➤ **Seal Walk.** Move along using your forearms and dragging your feet behind.

   ➤ **Inchworm Crawl.** Begin in front support position (on hands and feet, facing downward). Walk hands away from feet, then walk feet up to hands. Continue to "inch" along in this way!

   ➤ **Bucking Bronco.** Take your weight on your hands and kick your legs gently up into the air. How high can your legs go?

   ➤ **Critter Walk.** Make up your own critter walk!

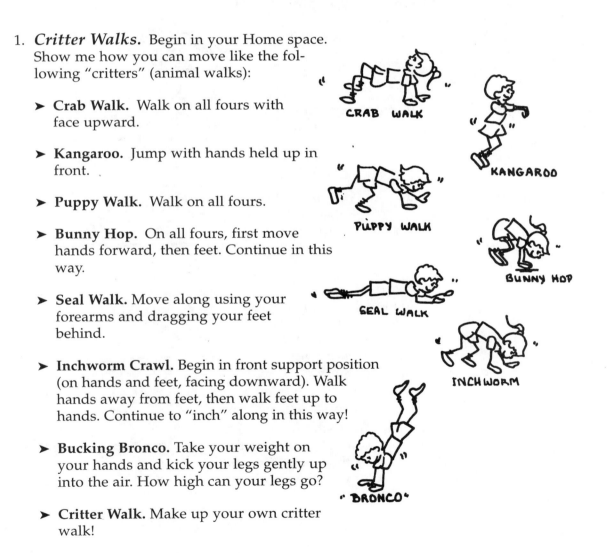

2. ***Ankle Taps.*** Begin in hook-lying position, and curl up to tap inside of ankle with opposite foot. Return to hook-lying and repeat with other hand and ankle.

3. ***Seat Waddles.*** In long-sit position, move forward and backward by using only seat muscles.

4. ***Hand Walkers.*** In front support position, walk hands 4 steps in front, walk hands 4 steps back, walk hands to the right side, then to the left side. Repeat.

5. ***Compass.*** From a front-support position, walk hands around in a circle while keeping feet in the same spot.

6. ***Fire Hydrants.*** In all-fours position, with hips square and right knee bent, raise right leg to side and lower it again. Repeat 8 times. Change legs and repeat another 8 times.

7. ***Thigh Lifters.*** Begin in half-hook/half-long sit position. Raise and lower extended leg 8 times, alternatively pointing (away) and flexing foot (pointing toes toward you). Reverse leg positions and repeat.

8. ***Ankle Builders.*** In hook-sit position, start with one leg and point foot away; flex foot by pointing the toes toward you; circle it one way, then circle it the other way. Repeat with the ankle of the other foot.

COOLING-DOWN ACTIVITIES

Cooling-down after active play is as important as warming-up large muscle groups and should never be omitted from the lesson. The following activities serve as a gradual decrease in activity level to allow the body to recover from effort and reduce the effects of fatigue. A cooling-down passive activity (such as walking or some simple activity requiring only moderate effort) and stretching improve the recovery of the muscles, heart, and other tissues through the removal of waste products. This quieter period of time can also be used to review the learning that has taken place, to provide extra practice in concentration and attentiveness; and/or to provide individual recognition for some positive aspect ("Legends of the Day"). Some ideas for cooling-down activities are presented here, followed by 15 different stretching suggestions.

1. *Puppets.* You are a puppet and I will pull certain strings to make you move, such as: raising and lowering your right arm; lifting your left knee; making your head bend forward and gently back; stamping your feet, shaking you gently all over; then making you floppy so that you "plop" gently to the ground.

2. *Pockets.* In partners, move in and out of each other's shapes, filling in the empty spaces. For example, the first partner forms a shape; second partner forms a shape around the first partner by filling the empty spaces created by the first partner's shape. First partner then moves to form a shape around the second partner. Continue in this way. Encourage "flowing" movements.

3. *Pink Panther.* Use the theme music, if possible. Select two children to be the "Pink Panthers." The rest are "Sleepers." Find a Home space in the play area and get into back-lying position, with arms folded across the chest and eyes closed. When the music starts, the Pink Panthers—keeping hands behind their backs—prowl around the area and bend to talk to sleeping players. Panthers are encouraged to be clever and humorous as they try to get a sleeping player to wake up. If the sleeping player moves in any way, he or she is automatically awakened and becomes a Pink Panther helper to try to wake up other Sleepers. The challenge is to see which sleeping player(s) can last the length of the song and become the best concentrator(s) of the day!

4. *Barnyard Chatter.* Name each team after farm animals, such as pigs, cows, ducks, chickens, and sheep, and have each animal find a Home space. Ask each team to practice the sounds of its animal; for example, pigs "oink"; cows "moo." On signal "Barnyard Chatter," close your eyes, put your hands up in front of you as bumpers, and carefully walk around making the sounds of your animal. When you find someone who sounds like you, hold hands, and continue to listen for and find other members of your team. Which team can collect its members the quickest and cross-leg sit in a circle? Remember, no peeking—play fair! *Variation:* Use another theme, such as the colors of the rainbow—Red, Orange, Yellow, Green, Blue, Indigo, and Violet.

5. *Balance Feathers.* Take a balance feather to your Home space and quietly explore balancing the feather in the palm of the hand; back of the hand; each finger; one hand; other hand; other body parts such as elbows, shoulders, knees, head.

6. *Gotcha.* Everyone sit in a large circle in cross-leg sit position near to the person on either side. Hold right thumb up. Keep left hand flat and over the thumb of the person on your left. (See illustration.) Wait for signal "Gotcha!" It may be heard when you least expect it. On signal "Gotcha!" try to grab the thumb of the person on your left while at the same time, trying to pull your own thumb away from being caught.

   ➤ Repeat with your eyes closed. Listen carefully for the signal.

   ➤ Reverse so the left thumb is up and the right hand is flat over the thumb of the person on your right.

   ➤ Repeat with eyes closed.

7. **Tap Heads.** Find a Home space and hook sit. Rest your head on your hands and close your eyes. Think of something very pleasant like playing at the beach on a warm sunny day. Shhhhh . . . be quiet. As I walk around I will tap you on the head. Quietly get up and follow behind me or join the end of the line. Who will be the last one to be tapped? We will finish in a long "snake" and make our way back to the classroom.

7.

8. **Changing Motions.** Everyone long-sit in a big circle facing the center. Follow my motions as you clap your hands, tap your feet, nod your head, etc. Now you will have a turn at being leader, exept for one player who will step out of the circle and stand with back to the rest of the class. This player is IT and must try to guess within 3 tries who the leader is. (Secretly choose one of the children to be the leader. This leader must change the movements without IT being able to detect what is happening.

LEADER   8.

9. **Tall to Small.** This is a team-building activity. Have teams scatter throughout the play area and do a "Scramble Eggs—Walk." On signal "Tall to Small," each team must carefully but quickly find its members and arrange itself to stand from tallest to smallest.

➤ Do again, but this time, give the signal "Small to Tall."

➤ Repeat, and have teams arrange themselves alphabetically, using first names.

➤ Arrange themselves by "Birthdays!"

➤ Combine two groups and play the game.

➤ Try this as a whole-class activity and watch the fun!

9.

10. *Healthy Habits.* Have class in stand tall position on one endline of play area facing the opposite end line. Tell them that you are going to ask them a series of questions about their "habits." Discuss what a habit is and how habits are formed; how healthy habits can lead to a healthy lifestyle in general. Emphasize that they must answer honestly. The rules are simple: If you answer "Yes," then take one giant step forward; if you answer "No," then take a step backward; if you are unsure or don't know, stay on your spot. Your goal is to reach the other endline. Some suggestions follow:

➤ Did you brush your teeth before coming to school?

➤ Did you floss your teeth before going to bed last night?

➤ Did you eat breakfast this morning before coming to school?

➤ Did you drink a glass of milk yesterday?

➤ Did you eat a piece of fruit (or more than one fruit) yesterday?

➤ Did you eat some vegetables with your dinner last night?

➤ Did you eat *no* junk food at all yesterday?

➤ Did you give your Mom or Dad (or significant other) a hug today?

➤ Did you walk or bike to school this morning?

➤ Do you wash your hands each time before you eat?

11. *Legends of the Day.* Use this self-esteem builder at the end of every lesson. Have class gather in a listening circle or in teams. Recognize a child (children) from each team or from the class as the "legend(s) of the day" and have them stand up facing the class. Tell the class why you think each person is so special: perhaps for cooperating so well with others; playing fairly throughout the game or activity; sharing equipment; being kind and cheerful; helping others; helping you; or trying hard to improve at a skill. The class responds by giving these legends a big "round of applause" by clapping hands while moving them clockwise in a big circle. Ensure that each child in the class receives a "legend of the day" experience at various opportunities throughout the school year. You may wish to give each "legend" a certificate or sticker.

STRETCHING SIGNALS

Stretching is one of the most important, yet most neglected, fitness activities that should be done almost every day of your life. Research has clearly indicated that children need to experience stretching activities on a daily basis. Often this is not the case. Most young children are flexible, but they quickly lose this ability if they do not stretch regularly. The benefits of stretching include an increased range of motion of joints; improved flexibility of muscles and joints; improved coordination and overall body management; prevention of injuries such as muscle strains and pulls; and development of overall body awareness.

Children with movement difficulties need to be taught to stretch from an early age, as they are more injury- and accident-prone. Teaching the young child how to fall safely or recover from a falling position has a strong carry-over value for the rest of his or her life. We have presented several different, interesting, and fun ways of getting kids to stretch and keep stretching. In fact, we suggest that *you* do these yourself on a daily basis!

1. ***Good Morning Stretch!*** (Pretend you are still in bed and just beginning to wake up. Lying on your back, stretch as wide as possible. Do this slowly. Stretch like a pencil. Yawn! Smile a "good morning" smile!

2. ***Nodding Heads.*** Stand tall. Gently and slowly nod your head as if saying "Yes!" Now gently nod your head as if saying "No!"

3. ***Shrugs!*** Stand tall. Shrug your shoulders as if saying "I don't know!"

   ➤ **Rolls!** Now gently roll your shoulders backward, then forward.

4. ***Sky Reaches.*** Stand tall. Stretch one arm up toward the sky, then stretch the other arm. Continue.

5. ***Propellers!*** Gently circle arms forward.

   ➤ **Squeeze!** Gently close and open your hands.

6. ***Wingers!*** Start with arms bent and parallel to ground, hands at chest level and closed. Gently pull arms backward, squeezing shoulder blades together, and continue to open sideways holding the stretch. Repeat from beginning.

7. ***Belly Button Circles.*** Pretend your belly button is the center of the circle. Trace 3 circles in one direction, then 3 circles in the opposite direction. Repeat.

8. ***Side Stretcher.*** Standing tall, slowly reach down one side of body, "walking" fingers as far down as you can go. Walk fingers back up to starting position, and then walk fingers down the other side.

9. ***Periscope!*** Lie on your back, arms at sides and legs straight. Bring one leg straight up and gently press it toward you for 10 seconds. Repeat with the other leg.

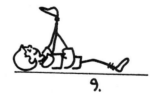

10. ***Finger Stretcher.*** In stand tall position, interlock fingers of both hands, then gently straighten arms, pushing the palms of your fingers outward. Hold this stretch for 5–10 seconds; relax. Now stretch in this position with arms overhead.

11. ***Butterfly Stretch.*** In sitting position, place the bottoms of your feet together. Holding ankles with your hands, let your arms gently push along the inside of knees. Hold for 10 seconds.

12. ***Foot Artist.*** In sitting position, lean back on hands for support. Lift one leg and draw circles in the air with your pointed toes. Now draw circles in the opposite direction. Repeat using the other foot. Use your foot to trace your favorite letter; favorite number.

13. ***Calf Stretch.*** Stand facing a wall with hands flat against wall for support. Point both feet to wall. Keep the front leg bent and the back leg straight, while pressing the heel of the back foot to the floor. Reverse leg positions and repeat.

14. ***Sprinter Stretch.*** Begin in all-fours position. Move one leg forward until the knee of this front leg is directly over the ankle. Extend the other leg back.

15. ***Quad Stretch.*** In stand tall position with hand support on nearby wall, bend one leg gently back until heel of foot is touching back of upper leg. Hold for 10 seconds. Repeat with other leg.

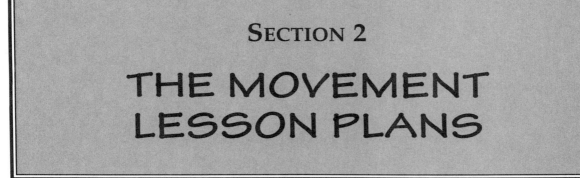

SECTION 2

THE MOVEMENT
LESSON PLANS

BLANK VERSO

HOW TO USE THESE INTRODUCTORY LESSON PLANS

ORGANIZATION

Each lesson is based on a 30-minute activity experience divided into 5 segments—Warming-Up/Fitness Signals, Motor Memory, Spatial Awareness, Body Awareness, and Closing Activities—with each segment lasting around 5–6 minutes. The segments build sequentially and progressively, with age- and developmentally-appropriate activities and simple games, from one lesson plan to the next. Each lesson has an "opening" or warming-up activity and a "closing" or cooling-down activity. The equipment required is given for each lesson.

WARMING-UP/FITNESS SIGNALS

Discuss with the children why signals are important to learn and do (develop and improve listening skills, alertness, spatial awareness, fitness benefits), and give examples of how these can be applied to everyday living Be patient, yet insist that children respond immediately to the signal and praise them for doing so.

MOTOR MEMORY

Motor memory relates to the child's ability to visually and auditorily copy single movements, movement patterns, and rhythm patterns. Start with one movement and then increase the number (one movement for each age year). First have the child remember the moves in any order, then in the correct sequence.

SPATIAL AWARENESS

Children have to learn to cope with near (personal) and far (general) space; otherwise, many of the fundamental movement skills—such as throwing, catching, and striking—will be more difficult to master.

Personal space, as the name suggests, is the immediate space within reach of a child's body parts. The child who continually bumps into things or knocks objects off the table may very likely be displaying poor personal spatial skills. Also at this time the different *stance positions* in personal space—*square, side on,* and *diagonal*—are introduced.

The second type of spatial orientation is that of *general* space, the area in which a child (or children) and objects may move. Children who display poor evasive skills,

33

who have difficulties in predicting the path of a ball or judging distances, are really displaying deficiencies in general space orientation. Within the understanding of space we have knowledge of directions such as "up and down"; levels of space such as "high and low"; distance relationships such as "near and far"; and temporal aspects such as judging the speed of objects moving through space.

BODY AWARENESS

It is essential that children have an understanding of their own body. They need to know body parts and where they are in relation to each other, as well as an internal knowledge of sidedness (that is, left and right sides of the body) even though they might not be able to name them. Eventually children should be able to respond to the directional language of left and right so that they are combining their knowledge of their body with spatial concepts. It is important that children also know and can respond to the movement language associated with body image.

CLOSING ACTIVITIES

These **quiet activities** focus on stretching, concentration, and cooperation. At this time what the children have learned is recapped through asking the appropriate questions and having the children provide the feedback. The closing time presents an ideal moment for recognition of individual performance ("Legends of the Day"). A child from each team should be selected, or, if children are not in teams, individual child(ren) can be selected to receive this special self-worth recognition. Keep a record of the children you have selected so that eventually *all* children will be given this "self-esteem builder" opportunity.

A note regarding the content of the first 10 lessons of each level presented: The content may vary in the developmentally appropriate activities that are taught at each level; however, the *foundation concepts* and the *signals* will be the same for the three levels to provide *consistency* of class management and organization and *continuity* from one level to the next. Thus, a year 2 Teacher will be able to "jump in" at Level 2 without having to revert to Level 1 teaching.

You will also note that Level 1 foundation movement lessons have been designed to be repeated over two lessons to ensure that children have learned the content well; to allow for ample time to teach through the materials; to provide for repetition to reinforce certain concepts; and for the teacher to get to know the children well and establish a good rapport.

FOUNDATION MOVEMENT
Lessons 1 and 2, Level 1

ORGANIZATION: Identify the play area by setting up cone markers around the perimeter. As a general rule, space cone markers every 10 feet (3 meters) apart, using about 15 markers for a play area that is 60´ by 30´ (20m by 10m). Try to use different polygonal figures such as square, rectangle, pentagon, hexagon, octagon. The younger the children, the more cone markers you will need to use to designate clearly the boundaries. Throwing rings or beanbags could be used as Home space markers if these are available.

EQUIPMENT REQUIRED:

> 15–30 cone markers
>
> Equipment or objects in teaching environment
>
> 1 throwing ring (or beanbag) per child

WARMING-UP/FITNESS SIGNALS

1. Pick up your ring. Carry it to a Home space and place it gently on the ground. This is your **Home.** Check that you cannot touch anyone or anything. This is your first signal, "Home!" (Show hand signal.) Whenever you hear this signal, find your Home and "Stand Tall" in it.

2. Now leave your Home and touch 5 different cone markers with 5 different body parts. Can you remember where your Home (ring) is? Return to your Home and stand tall, crossing right arms/legs over left. Go!

3. You are standing in a **"Corkscrew."** Show me how you can sink your corkscrew to the floor. Now you are in "Cross-leg Sit" position. Show me how you can return to standing tall without undoing your corkscrew.

4. I am going to give you 3 important rules to remember:

   ➤ Don't hurt yourself!

   ➤ Don't hurt anyone else!

   ➤ Don't hurt the equipment!

5. Now take a good look at the boundaries of the play area that are marked out by cone markers. We are going to play the game "Touch!"

➤ Touch a cone marker on a sideline with your elbow.

➤ Touch a cone on an endline with your knee.

➤ Run to the other sideline and touch the cone with your shoulder.

➤ Run to the opposite endline and touch a cone with your foot.

5.

ENDLINE

➤ Go Home! and corkscrew with left arms and legs crossed.

➤ Sink your corkscrew to cross-leg sit. Now try to stand tall.

6. The next signal that you will learn is called "Scrambled Eggs!" (Show hand signal.) You will move in and out of each other without "touching" anyone else, and in a certain way. Listen carefully to how you will move. "Scrambled Eggs—Walking!"

6.

7. *Iceberg!* (hand signal) is your stopping signal. When you hear this word, stop immediately by "jump stopping." Land on your feet at the same time, knees bent, hands out for balance. Let's practice this.

7.

8. *"Scrambled Eggs—Walking!" "Iceberg!"*

➤ "Scrambled Eggs—Happy Walking!" (Walk quickly while pumping with your arms.) "Iceberg!" "One!" Stand on one foot and hold your balance.

➤ "Scrambled Eggs—Walking Tip-Toes!" "Iceberg!" "Three!" (Touch the floor with any three body parts.)

HAPPY WALKER
8.
ONE!

MOTOR MEMORY

1. Copy hand movements: opening and closing; finger isolations.

2. Copy touching movements to different body parts.

➤ Touch your elbow to your knee.

➤ Touch your ankle to your hand.

➤ Touch your hand to opposite knee.

3. Play "Simon Says."

2.

SPATIAL AWARENESS

1. Have child in standing tall position, feet shoulder-width apart, facing one wall of the room (or side of the play area). Demonstrate the square (facing), side-on, back-to-the-wall positions. Have child copy you, then repeat using other walls (sides) as focal points. (You could trace child's feet on paper, cut out footprints, and position in the different stance positions for child to stand on.)

2. Using objects in a room, have children move to music. When the music stops, ask children to position in relation to an object or piece of equipment or another person: e.g., stand *behind* something; sit *in front of* the chair; kneel *beside* the table; stand *back to back* with someone.

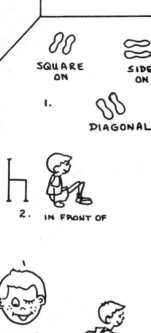

BODY AWARENESS

1. Point to the body parts that I call out first with eyes open, then with eyes closed.

2. Ask questions such as: "What body part do you . . . Smell with? Talk with? Hear with? Blink with? Clap with? Point with? Wave with? Jump with?"

3. Move to music; when music stops, jump stop and touch the body part that I name. (Vary the way the child moves.)

CLOSING ACTIVITIES

1. ***Good Morning Stretch!*** (Pretend you are still in your bed and just beginning to wake up. Lying on your back, stretch as wide as possible. Do this slowly. Roll over. Stretch like a pencil. Yawn! Smile a "good morning" smile!

2. ***Nodding Heads.*** Stand tall. Gently and slowly nod your head as if you are saying "Yes!" Now gently nod your head as if you are saying "No!"

3. ***Shrugs!*** Stand tall. Shrug your shoulders as if you are saying "I don't know!"

4. ***Legend(s) of the Day!***

FOUNDATION MOVEMENT
Lessons 3 and 4, Level 1

ORGANIZATION: Identify the play area by setting up cone markers around the perimeter. As a general rule, space cone markers every 10 feet (3 meters) apart, using about 15 markers for a play area that is 60´ by 30´ (20m by 10m). Signals taught in Lesson 1 are further reinforced, with new listening and movement signals introduced.

EQUIPMENT REQUIRED:

15–30 cone markers

Equipment or objects in teaching environment

WARMING-UP/FITNESS SIGNALS

1. Run to touch each corner cone of the play area, then find your Home. Check for good spacing. "Pencil Stretch" in back-lying position. Slowly curl up into a ball. Count to 5 as you uncurl and pencil stretch. Count to 5 as you curl into a ball.

2. When you see my hand in the air like this (one hand/arm raised overhead), this is your signal to be "Quiet!" Quickly cross-leg sit and "Stop–look–and listen," giving me your full attention.

3. *Scrambled Eggs—Walking!*

   ➤ Walk with big steps; walk with baby steps; walk with feet close together; walk with feet far apart.

   ➤ **Iceberg! Dead Bug!** Quickly lie on your back and wiggle your hands and feet in the air!

   ➤ Walk in a circle; walk in a triangle; "Iceberg!"

   ➤ Get onto your hands and feet and walk like a puppy.

4. "Quiet." Now we are going to learn a new signal called *Clear the Deck!* (Show hand signal.) Move quickly to stand *outside* one of the sides of the marked play area. Clear the deck again! Now move to stand *outside* another side. Continue in this way. (Vary the way children move: walking, jogging, skipping, sliding.)

38

5. ***Scrambled Eggs—Marching!*** Be a happy marcher: Lift your knees high and swing your arms. "Hit the Deck!" (hand signal). This is your signal to drop to the floor, quickly getting into front lying position.

MOTOR MEMORY

1. Copy my body movements:

   ➤ hands on head, wiggle-wiggle, stamp-stamp

   ➤ kick-kick, punch-punch, slash-slash

   ➤ start low and gradually get bigger and bigger

   ➤ start high and gradually get lower and lower

2. Show me how you can copy my clapping rhythms. (If possible, use a drum to bring out the rhythm.)

SPATIAL AWARENESS

Let's Pretend You Are . . . (Remember to watch where you are going!)

➤ a 747 jet taking off down the runway, lifting off, and then flying

➤ a lawn mower cutting the grass

➤ a jet-ski slicing through the water

➤ a hockey player scoring a goal; a figure skater spinning

➤ a shadow-boxer punching into the air and "dancing" with the feet

➤ a karate-kid, kicking with the feet and slashing with the hands

➤ a prancing horse

➤ a snake wriggling along the ground

BODY AWARENESS

1. Listen carefully as I ask you to move just a certain body part at a time; turn your head from side to side; wiggle your nose; snap your fingers; open and close your hand; blink your eyes; clap your hands; stamp your feet; lift one knee, then the other: shake your arms.

BLINK!

1.

SNAP FINGERS

KNEE LIFT

2. Now show me how you can touch a body part to objects in the environment: head to ground; elbow to chair; knee to table; and so on.

2.

CLOSING ACTIVITIES

1. *Finger Stretcher.* In stand tall position, interlock your fingers of both hands, then gently straighten your arms, pushing the palms of your fingers outward. Hold this stretch for 5–10 seconds; relax.

   ➤ Stretch in this position with arms overhead.

   ➤ Stretch with your hands behind your back.

1.

2. *Periscope!* Lie on your back, arms at your sides and legs straight. Bring one leg straight upward and gently press it toward you for 10 seconds. Then repeat with the other leg.

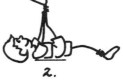

2.

3. *Foot Artist.* In sitting position, lean back on hands for support. Lift one leg and draw circles in the air with your pointed toes. Now draw circles in the opposite direction. Repeat using the other foot. Use your foot to trace your favorite letter; favorite number.

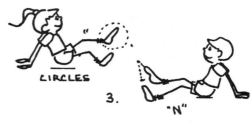

CIRCLES

3.

"N"

4. *Legend (s) of the Day!*

ORGANIZATION: Identify the play area by setting up cone markers around the perimeter. As a general rule, space cone markers every 10 feet (3 meters) apart, using about 15 markers for a play area that is 60´ by 30´ (20m by 10m). Children are introduced to new formation signals and starting positions. Be patient, but insist that children immediately respond to these signals. Practice!

EQUIPMENT REQUIRED:

> Cone markers
> 1 hoop per child
> 3 sponge balls

WARMING-UP/FITNESS SIGNALS

1. *Here, Where, There.* Listen carefully to the word I will say. If you hear the word "Here," walk quickly toward me; "Where," walk on the spot; "There," walk quickly away from me. Repeat this activity, having children move in other ways, such as: skipping, running, jumping, slide-stepping, hopping. Between these signals, call out "Hook Sit"and gently lean back. Put your hand on your tummy muscles and feel them tightening. "All Fours," face-up, and Crab Walk (arm/leg strengthener).

2. *Listening Line.* (*Hand signal:* Arms stretched out sideways as you stand near and face line. Use the boundaries of the play area.) Immediately run and stand in a long line where I am pointing. Face me and space yourself arm's length apart. Now take *giant steps* across to the opposite side and stand on a listening line once there. How many giant steps did you take? Return to your listening line, again counting the number of steps.

3. *Listening Circle.* (*Hand signal:* Point with index finger to the floor near you while circling the other index finger overhead.) Run quickly and safely to cross-leg sit in the circle that I am pointing to and face me. Give me your full attention.

MOTOR MEMORY

1. ***Airplane Signals.*** You are an airplane. Show me how you can "Clear the Deck!" "Propellers!" Gently circle arms forward as you fly in general space. "Clear the Deck again!" "Scrambled Eggs—Flying!" (by running only on the lines of the court) "Hit the Deck!" "Clear the Deck!" "Iceberg!" "Flying." Land gently on your boundary line (runway).

1.
"PROPELLERS"
FLYING

"HIT THE DECK"

2. Everyone collect a hoop. Drive your hoop like a car to your Home and have some free play with it.

3. ***Hoop Pattern Jumping.*** Start from inside your hoop. Jump out to the front, jump out to the back; jump to the right side, jump to the left. Jump in and out all round your hoop.

2.
CARS

3.

SPATIAL AWARENESS

1. ***Traffic Lights.*** Place your hoop around your waist. This is your car. Rev up the engine (bouncing on the spot).

   ➤ **"Scrambled Eggs—Green Light!"** Travel, but watch where you are going so that you do not bump into anyone.

   ➤ **"Red Light."** Jump stop on the spot.

   ➤ **"Yellow Light."** Jog on the spot.

YELLOW
LIGHT

GREEN LIGHT

1.

RED
LIGHT

2. ***Traffic Cop Tag.*** Select three players to be the Traffic Cops, each holding a medium-sized sponge ball. The Traffic Cops give chase to the other players, trying to tag them with their ball. A tagged player becomes a *sign post* and jogs in place. Observe play until there are 15-20 sign posts, then use the "Iceberg!" sign to stop the play. Select new Traffic Cops and continue the tagging game.

TRAFFIC COP

2.

BODY AWARENESS

1. *Simon Says.* When you say "Simon Says," child responds by doing the task; when you ask child to do a task without first saying "Simon Says," child does not respond. How good a listener can each child be? "Simon says. . . wiggle your fingers." "Stamp your feet!" "Simon says . . . clap your hands." "Blink your eyes."

WIGGLE FINGERS 1.   STAMP FEET   BLINK EYE

2. *Hokey Pokey.* (This is the traditional simple folk dance.)

   "You put your right foot in; you put your right foot out;

   You put your right foot in and you shake it all about.

   Do the Hokey Pokey, and turn yourself around.

   That's what it's all about."

   (Continue with left foot, right hand, left hand, head, bottom, etc.)

RIGHT   LEFT   2.

CLOSING ACTIVITIES

1. *Pencil Stretch.* In back-lying position, stretch as long as you can make yourself. Hold for 10 seconds. Roll over to front-lying position and hold pencil stretch.

1.

2. *Butterfly Stretch.* In sitting position, place the bottoms of your feet together. Holding at the ankles with your hands, let your arms gently push along the inside of the knees. Hold for 10 seconds.

2.

3. *Side Stretcher.* Standing tall, slowly reach down one side of your body, "walking" your fingers as far down as you can go. Walk your fingers back up to starting position, and then walk your fingers down the other side.

4. *Legend(s) of the Day!*

4.

3.

ORGANIZATION: Identify the play area by setting up cone markers around the perimeter. As a general rule, space cone markers every 10 feet (3 meters) apart, using about 15 markers for a play area that is 60′ by 30′ (20m by 10m). More organization and formations signals are introduced.

EQUIPMENT REQUIRED:

> 15–30 cone markers
> Large throwing dice
> "Alphabet Arms" chart
> Cassette/CD player; music

WARMING-UP/FITNESS SIGNALS

1. *Move with Me.* Find a Home space and march in place to the music. March forward; march back to Home. March around in a circle. March in place, clapping your hands in time to the music.

   ➤ Little bounces in place; bounce around in a circle. Pretend to jump a rope. Jump–jump–jump.

   ➤ Dance to the music.

2. *Listening Corner.* (*Hand signal:* Cross your arms to make the letter X, then point to the corner with your index finger.) Have children point to the corners. Run quickly and safely to knee-sit in this corner and face me. On my signal "2 Corners!," touch one corner with 1 hand and 1 foot, then the opposite corner with other hand and foot, and safely knee-sit.

3. *End Line.* (*Hand signal:* Arms outstretched to sides, with fingers of hand facing upward.) Run safely and quickly to stand on endline that I am pointing to and face me. Check for good spacing. On signal "Endline" quickly run to the opposite endline, jump-stop on the line, and jump-turn to face me!

4. *Lines.*

➤ Run to *Blue* line and knee sit. Run to the *Red* line and, in front support position, make a bridge.

➤ Walk along a *Black* line like a tightrope walker.

➤ Jog along the *Boundary* lines of the play area in a clockwise direction like a train. Chug-chug along as you go. On "Iceberg!" jump stop between the lines, then Hook sit and twirl yourself around like a spinning top.

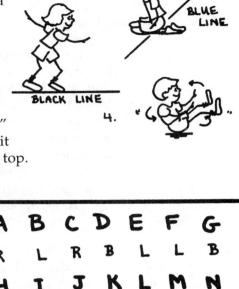

MOTOR MEMORY

Alphabet Arms. On a large piece of paper write the letters of the alphabet using upper-case letters. Underneath each letter write an L, R, or B. (See illustration.) Choose one color for the letters of the alphabet and another color for the movement letters. For "L," have child extend left arm to the side; for "R", extend right arm to side; for "B," extend both arms out in front. Have child say the letter and do the associated arm movement with that letter. Encourage child to progress at his/her own rate. Observe actions and the saying of the letters. Have children practice part by part, slowly, until they have mastered each part. Challenge children by asking them to do this activity backward, or from right to left.

VARIATIONS:

➤ Use upper-case; lower-case; different fonts.

➤ Randomly mix the letters and arm movements.

➤ Use shapes, pictures, and colors instead of letters for younger children.

➤ Use colored dots on the hands of young children instead of having them relate to the directions of left and right.

➤ Use different movements—but only 3 at the most. For example, fingers(S), clap hands(C), jump in place (J).

SPATIAL AWARENESS

1. *Four Corners.* Use markers positioned at the corners of a rectangular area. With a marking pen, number the markers 1 through 4 as shown in the diagram. On signal "Corner!" players run to a corner of their choice and stay there jogging on the spot. Draw one of the 4 numbers out of a hat. Players caught in the corner with that number must come to the center of the play area and do stretches; the other players continue the game. When only 4 players remain, each player must run to a different corner! Who will be the last player left?

1.

2. *Endline Cross Tag.* Use the endline signal to position children behind one of the endlines of the play area. Select 3 children to be the ITs who stand in the center of the play area, each holding a beanbag or sponge ball. On signal "Cross," players try to run across to the opposite end line without being tagged. If a player is tagged, he/she must jog on the spot. After 10 players have been caught, everyone goes free. Choose new ITs and play again.

2.

BODY AWARENESS

1. *Simon Says.* When you say "Simon Says," children respond by doing the task. When you ask children to do a task without first saying "Simon Says," children do not respond. How good a listener can each child be? "Simon says . . . click your left fingers." "Stamp your feet!" (Children continue clicking left fingers until they hear the next "Simon Says . . . ")

1.

2. *Busy Body Parts.* Call out a body part; for example, "knees." Child uses beanbag to touch partner's knee. Call out another body part; for example, "elbows." Now child must find a new partner and use beanbag to touch this body part.

2.

CLOSING ACTIVITIES

1. *Angels in the Snow.* Begin in wide sit position, then slowly sink to back lying position.

   ➤ Spread your arms/legs apart; bring together.

   ➤ Spread your legs apart, hold for 3 seconds, then bring legs together.

   ➤ Spread your arms out to the side and bring slowly together.

   ➤ Roll over into front lying position. Pretend your head weighs 500 pounds. Slowly move to stand tall with your head being the last to come up.

2. *Breathing.* Stand tall in your Home space. Take a deep breath and slowly blow it out. Do this again. One more time!

3. *Legend(s) of the Day!*

FOUNDATION MOVEMENT
Lessons 9 and 10, Level 1

ORGANIZATION: Identify the play area by setting up cone markers around the perimeter. As a general rule, space cone markers every 10 feet (3 meters) apart, using about 15 markers for a play area that is 60´ by 30´ (20m by 10m). The signals taught in previous lessons are further reinforced. A new organizational grouping signal is introduced.

EQUIPMENT REQUIRED:

15–30 cone markers

"Alphabet Arms" chart

Beanbag, flag, scarf, or tag belt per player

CD/Cassette player; quiet "mood" music

WARMING-UP/FITNESS SIGNALS

Refer to Strengthening Signals on page 21.

1. Try *combinations of signals* and watch the action!

    ➤ "Scrambled Eggs!—Jogging!" "Clear the Deck!" "Dead Bug!"

    ➤ "Home!" "Puppy Walk!" from one sideline to other

    ➤ "Scrambled Eggs!—Crab Walking" "Iceberg!" "Hit the Deck!"

    ➤ "Home!" "Inchworm!"

    ➤ "Scrambled Eggs!—Bouncing Ball" "Hit the Deck!" Roll . . . !"

    ➤ "Scrambled Eggs!—Duck Waddle" "Iceberg!" "Shake–Shake–Shake!" all over

2. *Group Signals—"2!"; "3!"; . . .*

    ➤ **"2's"** (*Hand signal:* Show 2 fingers in the air.) Find a partner and stand face-to-face. Give each other high tens.

    ➤ **"3's"** (*Hand signal:* Show 3 fingers in the air.) Form groups of 3, stand one behind the other, and hold on at the waist. Form a train as you move along. Stay together—don't let go!

    ➤ **"4's"** (*Hand signal:* Show 4 fingers in the air.) Form a circle, join hands, and face inwards. Circle clockwise; then circle in the opposite direction.

MOTOR MEMORY

Alphabet Arms. Create a new Alphabet Arms and have children perform the activity. (See Lesson 4 for variations on original Alphabet Arms.)

A	B	C	D	E	F	G

← MIX LETTERS →

D	G	A	E	C	B	F
R	L	B	B	R	L	R

SPATIAL AWARENESS

1. *Partner Tag.* Pair children and give each a tag belt to wear. One partner of the pair is IT to start. On the signal "Tag!" IT tries to tag the other partner. If successful, partners change roles. (Scarves or flags could be used instead of commercial tag belts.)

2. *Knee Box.* Quickly find a partner and stand face-to-face in your Home space. On signal "Knee Box" try to touch partner's knee without your partner touching yours. Remember to stay in your Home. When you hear "Knee Box" again, find a new partner to challenge!

2.

BODY AWARENESS

1. *Statues.* Working in pairs, create different Statues by taking your weight on different body parts.

2. *Busy Body Parts.* (Play in groups of 3.) Call out a body part; for example, "knees." Children touch each other's knees. Call out another body part; for example, "elbows." Now children form a new group of 3 and touch this body part. Continue in this way.

1.

2.

ELBOWS

CLOSING ACTIVITIES

1. *Mirrors.* Get into Home space. Slowly lead children to stretch through the body in different ways. Children "mirror" your movements. Quiet background music could be used to set the "mood."

2. *Walking Finger Stretch.* In long sit position, take your "walking fingers" (pointer and middle) and walk them down your leg, past your knee, toward your shoelaces. Grab your toes and gently hold for 5 seconds, then walk your fingers back. Repeat.

WALKING FINGERS 2.

3. *Side Stretcher.* Standing tall, slowly reach down one side of your body, "walking" your fingers as far down as you can go. Walk your fingers back up to starting position, and then walk your fingers down the other side. Repeat.

4. *Legend(s) of the Day!*

4.

ORGANIZATION: Identify the play area by setting up cone markers around the perimeter. As a general rule, space cone markers every 10 feet (3 meters) apart, using about 15 markers for a play area that is 60′ by 30′ (20m by 10m). The teamness concept is introduced in this lesson. (Refer to page 14.)

EQUIPMENT REQUIRED:

  15–30 cone markers

  Music; a cassette/CD player
  Chalkboard or large flip chart; markers

WARMING-UP/FITNESS SIGNALS

1. *Marching Signals!* March to music and clap your hands in time. "Hit the Deck!" "March in Place!" "Dead Bug!" "March in Place." Now march forward in a big circle. March, changing directions every 8 counts.

2. *Teams.* **Divide your class into teams of 5–6 children.** Establish the Team Line and introduce the Team Signal (hand signal). Then use cone markers to designate where each team will cross-leg sit in file formation: captain at the front; co-captain at the back; boy–girl or vice versa. Give each team time to select an appropriate Team Name and to create a Team Cheer.

   ➤ Now let's practice getting into teams. On my signal "Endline!" everyone leave your teams, touch the end line with two hands, then return to sit in your teams. Captains, look for your cone markers. (Repeat using other signals until children can easily fall into their teams.)

3. *Waves.* (Have team members turn to face you as you position to one side of the group as shown.) Stand tall and space yourselves arm's length apart, facing me.

51

MOTOR MEMORY

Directions, Patterns, and Pathways. Show these directions on the chalkboard or large flip chart. In the classroom ask children to draw these movements as an art project.

➤ *Directions:* Show me how you can move forward; backward; sideways.

➤ *Pathways:* Walk in a straight line like a tightrope walker; zigzag your way through my cone markers.

➤ *Patterns:* Walk in a giant circle; a triangle; a square; a figure-8 pattern.

SPATIAL AWARENESS

1. *Two-way/Four-way Traffic.* Have each team position on one side of the play area (30′ by 30′ [10m by 10m] square). Assign the teams numbers: "1, 2, 3, and 4." (See diagram.) Signal teams to move across the square in different ways and from a variety of starting positions.

➤ 1's and 2's cross to the opposite side; Then 3's and 4's cross.

➤ Repeat but cross by jogging.

➤ Walking—1's, 2's, 3's, and 4's all cross at the same time. Heads up—watch where you are going!

➤ Everyone begin in Cross-leg sit position. Listen carefully for your number: 3's and 4's cross as quickly as you can. Now 1's and 2's!

2. Play *Endline Cross Tag* (Lesson 4), but have half the children stand behind one endline; the other half behind the other endline, and the 3 ITs in the middle of the play area. Emphasize that everyone must watch where they are going at all times!

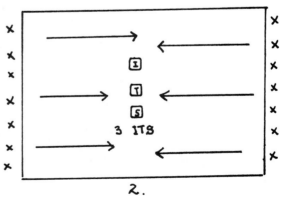

BODY AWARENESS

1. *Can you . . .* (Give specific directionality instruction [right and left] with body movements.)

   ➤ Wave with your right hand; left hand.

   ➤ Open and close your left hand; right hand.

   ➤ Balance on your right foot; left foot.

   ➤ Hop on your left foot; right foot.

   ➤ Lift your left arm; slowly lower.

   ➤ Raise and lower your right leg.

   ➤ Touch your right elbow to your right knee.

   ➤ Touch your left elbow to your left knee.

   ➤ Hold your left foot with your left hand.

   ➤ Hold your right foot with your right hand.

2. *Busy Body Parts.* Play this game as before (see Lesson 4, on page 38), but have players touch right or left body parts. For example, touch right knees; touch your left elbow to right elbow of other partner.

CLOSING ACTIVITIES

1. *Imagery—R-E-L-A-X!* Lie on a mat in back lying position and relax. Think of something that is very pleasant, that will bring a smile to your face. Listen to the quiet background music. Breathe slowly. Relax—let yourself just go.

   ➤ Now tense just your hands for a 3-second count, then relax. Tense again, relax.

   ➤ Tense your shoulders. Relax.

   ➤ Tense your face. Relax.

   ➤ Tense your legs and feet. Relax.

   ➤ Tense your seat muscles. Relax.

   ➤ Tense your stomach muscles. Relax.

   ➤ Tense all over!

   ➤ Let everything go limp. Relax! Smile!

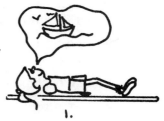

2. *Legend(s) of the Day!*

FOUNDATION MOVEMENT
Lessons 13 and 14, Level 1

ORGANIZATION: Identify the play area by setting up cone markers around the perimeter. As a general rule, space cone markers every 10 feet (3 meters) apart, using about 15 markers for a play area that is 60' by 30' (20m by 10m). The file formation is introduced in this lesson. Directionality is further explored.

EQUIPMENT REQUIRED:

Music with a steady 4/4 count

Cassette/CD player

1 light mat per child

Several pieces of equipment such as balance bench/beam, new line chairs, table, low hurdles, box horse, hoops

Tagging objects or tag belts

WARMING-UP/FITNESS SIGNALS

1. *Good Morning Workout.* (*Signal:* "Waves!") Do simple aerobic exercises to develop a warming-up effect and rhythm sense.

   ➤ light bouncing on the spot; for 8 counts

   ➤ jogging in place 8 counts; bouncing in place for 8 counts

   ➤ jogging in a circle for 8 counts; jogging in place for 8 counts

   ➤ shake–shake–shake all over!

   ➤ marching to music and clapping hands

   ➤ "Scrambled Eggs—Walking!" "Iceberg!"

2. *Listening Line!* Everyone turn to face this wall or direction. You are now in a long file or chain. The new signal for this is **"Snake."** Let's move as an Aerobic Snake. I will be at the head of the Snake; the last child is the tail of the Snake. Everyone else in between stays in the order that you are now standing. You are the links of the Snake. Walk to the music as we "Snake along." Follow me. Finish in one large circle and stretch to the sky!

MOTOR MEMORY

In the Jungle. Start in your Home space. Check for good spacing. Take children on a "safari" using different movements such as:

➤ stepping over tall grass (*big knee lifts*)

➤ moving under the bridge (*crawling on tummy*)

➤ wading across the stream (*giant steps*)

➤ jumping off a rock (*jumping into air from a squat*)

➤ sneaking up behind a tree to watch the zebras eating grass (*creeping*)

➤ crawling through a cave (*crawling on all fours*)

➤ walking across a suspended bridge (*along a line or rope*)

➤ sitting cross-legged in front of the fire playing African drums

SPATIAL AWARENESS

1. *Ship Ahoy! signals.* Let's turn the play area into a giant ship. Face square on to this wall (or boundary line). This is the "bow" of the ship. Your back is now facing the "stern" of the ship.

   ➤ As you face the bow, the right side of the ship is called "starboard"; left side, "port."

   ➤ Point as I call out these names. Turn to face each side of the ship as I call out the name: starboard; stern; port; bow.

Now add signals to this game:

➤ Jog to the *bow;* "Iceberg!" "Dead Bug!"

➤ Jump to the *stern*. "Periscope" (back lying position with one knee straight up into the air and hold).

➤ Walk to *starboard* on your tip-toes. "Rescue!" Quickly find a partner and grab each other's wrist of one hand and gently pull.

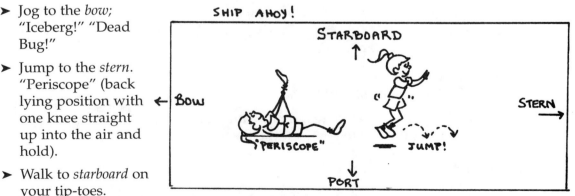

➤ March to *portside*. "Hit the Deck!" Now "Scrub the Deck." Continue in this way.

2. ***Pirate Tag!*** Stand at one end of the ship. Choose 3 players to be the Pirates who stand in the middle of the ship. On signal "Pirates Are Coming!" all other players must try to cross the ship without being tagged. If tagged, that player is "frozen" to the spot with legs wide apart and arms extended sideways. If a free player crawls through the frozen player's legs, then that player is unfrozen and free to go. After a while choose new Pirates and continue the game. Have Pirates use beanbags or some other suitable object to make the tag.

BODY AWARENESS

Using beanbags or folded socks, have child place or throw object according to certain spatial commands:

➤ Put beanbag on top of your head.

➤ Place it behind you.

➤ Put it on the side of you; put it on your other side.

➤ Put beanbag in front of you.

➤ Throw beanbag high.

CLOSING ACTIVITIES

Pick up a mat and take it to a Home space.

1. In back lying position, do the following:

➤ Bring your right leg up and hold it with both hands, gently pulling it toward your chest. Hold for 10 seconds. Then slowly lower.

➤ Bring your left leg up and gently pull it toward your chest. Hold for 10 seconds and slowly lower.

➤ Bring both legs up and hold each leg at your ankles with the hand on that side.

➤ Now roll over to front lying position. Stretch long and roll to the right; roll to the left.

➤ Slowly raise yourself to stand tall with your head being the last to come off the floor.

PENCIL

2. ***Legend(s) of the Day!***

FOUNDATION MOVEMENT
Lessons 15 and 16, Level 1

ORGANIZATION: Identify the play area by setting up cone markers around the perimeter. As a general rule, space cone markers every 10 feet (3 meters) apart, using about 15 markers for a play area that is 60' by 30' (20m by 10m). The circle formation signal is introduced.

EQUIPMENT REQUIRED:

> Cassette/CD player; music
> Tag belts, flags, or tagging objects
> 20–30 cone markers
> Whiteboard and whiteboard marking pens
> 1 Beanbag per child

WARMING-UP/FITNESS SIGNALS

1. ***Choo-Choo Train.*** (Use the Snake signal.)
   You are the Engine, the end child is the Caboose, and the children in between are the Cars. The train moves along the railway tracks (lines on the gym floor or boundary lines), weaving in and out of traffic cones. Use arm actions to simulate the wheels turning; make sounds of the train chugging along and horn blowing.

2. Use the following break signals to give children a change of pace, as well as develop overall body balance and coordination. (Refer to Break Signals on page 13.)

   ➤ "Thread the Needle"
   ➤ "Spinning Top"
   ➤ "Log Roll"
   ➤ "Rockers"

3. ***Circle Formation Break.***
   On signal "Sticky Popcorn!" children start "popping" (light bouncing) as they move into a popcorn ball. Challenge the children to see how long it will take them to form their "popcorn ball" (tight circle facing middle).

4. In circle formation, walk in a clockwise circle; "Iceberg!" Circle in counterclockwise direction. Do the action song: "If You're Happy and You Know It."

Add the following actions:

➤ If you're excited and you know it, jump up and down.

➤ If you're mad and you know it, stamp your feet.

➤ If you're sad and you know it, wipe your eyes.

➤ If you're dizzy and you know it, turn around.

➤ If you're sleepy and you know it, say good night.

MOTOR MEMORY

1. *Right and Left.*

➤ Touch an object with your left foot.

➤ Place a beanbag on the right side of you.

➤ Touch a cone marker on a sideline with your left elbow.

➤ Touch a cone on an endline with your right knee.

➤ Run to a sideline and touch a cone with your right shoulder.

➤ Run to the opposite endline and touch a cone with your left foot.

➤ Shake hands (right hands) with 5 different team members who are not on your team.

➤ Give low fives using only your left hand with 5 different classmates.

2. *The Figure-8 Eye.* On the whiteboard draw a large figure-8. Have children stand in their Home space and interlock their fingers, with the pointer fingers staying long and touching. The pointers become the drawing pencil. Say to the children: Trace a large figure-8 with your pointers and, without moving your head, let your eyes follow your pointers.

SPATIAL AWARENESS

Pirates Are Coming! Stand at one end of the ship. Choose three players to be the Pirates who stand in the middle of the ship. Pirates call out, "You may cross our ship if you are wearing (name a color or wearing apparel)." On signal "Pirates Are Coming!" all other players must try to cross the ship without being tagged. All those tagged become Pirates. Continue until everyone is caught. Have Pirates tag with an object in their hand (beanbag, deck ring).

WEARING "STRIPES"

BODY AWARENESS

Body Balances. Find your Home space. Show me how you make a:

➤ 3-point shape; 4-point shape; 5-point shape

➤ Make a long shape; a wide shape; a twisted shape; a round shape.

WIDE

TWISTED

LONG   ROUND

CLOSING ACTIVITIES

1. ***The Bus Trip.***

    ➤ The wheels on the bus go "round and round" (*gentle, slow arm circles*).

    ➤ The windshield wipers go "swish, swish, swish"(*move arms in a wiping action*).

    ➤ The horn on the bus goes "honk, honk, honk" (*open and close hands*).

    ➤ The brakes on the bus go "skireech, skireech, skireech" (*stamp feet*).

    ➤ The windows on the bus go up and down (*raise up on toes, then sink low*).

    ➤ The signal lights on the bus go "blink, blink, blink" (*slowly open and close eyes*).

    ➤ The headlights on the bus go bright, then dim (*slowly sink to the floor and pretend to go to sleep*).

2. ***Legend(s) of the Day!***

2.

FOUNDATION MOVEMENT
Lessons 17 and 18, Level 1

ORGANIZATION: Identify the play area by setting up cone markers around the perimeter. As a general rule, space cone markers every 10 feet (3 meters) apart, using about 15 markers for a play area that is 60' by 30' (20m by 10m). Signals are reinforced. Teamness concept is further developed.

EQUIPMENT REQUIRED:

Cone markers placed in a large circle or oval
Music; Cassette/CD player
3 different colored marking pens
Whiteboard, chalkboard, or flip chart
1 set of colored pinnies per team

WARMING-UP/FITNESS SIGNALS

Superstar Warm-up. Listen carefully for my signal as I turn you into Superstars!

➤ "Scrambled Eggs—Hockey Player!" Move in and out of each other dribbling the puck like a hockey player. "Iceberg!" Score a goal! Be a "Figure Skater"!

➤ "Homes—Skier!" In your Home space create different movements as a skier skiing down a mountain.

➤ "Activity Circle Clockwise—Racing Car Driver!" Show me how you move in and out of each other as a racing car driver. "Iceberg!"

➤ "Black Line—Karate Kid!" Run to a corner of the play area and perform karate kicks!

➤ "Corners—Basketball Player!" Find a corner and show me how you can move like a basketball player.

➤ Make up your own Superstar move (baseball pitcher; batter).

HOCKEY PLAYER

SKIER

RACING DRIVER

KARATE KID

BASKETBALL PLAYER

Motor Memory

The EYE Box. On a whiteboard or flip chart draw a large rectangular box as shown. Tell the class that this is an "Eye Box." Use a different colored marking pen to indicate the following locations in the box: top right, top middle, top left, bottom right, bottom middle, bottom left. Ask children to stand tall in a Home space. Make sure that they can all see the Eye Box. Call out different locations and have each child move only the eyes to those places. Remind them to keep the head still. Observe their actions and comment.

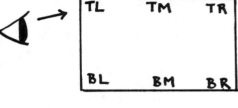

Spatial Awareness

1. *Colors Team Tag.* Give each team a set of colored pinnies to wear (red, green, blue, yellow). Select the Red team to be the tagging team and give each team member a tagging object. On signal "Red Tag," Red team members try to tag as many of the other players as they can in 15 seconds. A tagged player must jog on the spot. At the end of 15 seconds, count the number of tagged players. This is the Red team's score. Each team has a turn at being the IT team and is given the tagging objects. Which team will make the most number of tags?

2. *Islands.* Create several "islands" using hoops scattered throughout the play area. On signal "Scrambled Eggs—Jogging," move in and out of the islands without touching them. On signal "Islands!" quickly find an island and jump into it. You will need to share your island with others. Each time we "Scramble Eggs," I will take away one or two islands. Eventually the islands will become more and more crowded. You will have to cooperate in order to all fit into your island. Do so carefully!

BODY AWARENESS

Happy Being. Have each team sit together in a certain area near where you will talk about the "happy being."

HAPPY BEING

➤ On a chalkboard, whiteboard, or cardboard draw the outline of a "being" and use arrows to indicate different body parts. Have children call out the body parts as you point to each one in turn: head, eyes, mouth, ears, nose, neck, body, arms, hands, fingers, and so on. (See illustration.)

➤ Now ask each team to come up with 2 words that are positives (attributes) that they would like the "happy being" to have.

➤ Ask the captain and co-captain of each team to give you their positive words, and write them *inside* the body on the whiteboard.

➤ Then ask each team to think of 2 negative words. These words—the "emotional hurts"—will go on the *outside* of the body.

Ask children to think about how they can be a "happy being" for the whole day.

CLOSING ACTIVITIES

1. On signal "Robots," move around the play area like a robot. Slowly let your batteries run down until you come to a complete stop.

2. On signal "Raggedy Doll," show me how floppy you can be. Shake gently all over, then flop to the ground.

3. Now curl up into a tight ball. On signal "Sunrise," slowly open to make yourself as wide and "bright" as possible. On signal "Sunset," slowly curl up into a ball, sinking, sinking until you disappear.

4. *Legend(s) of the Day!*

WIDE
"Sunrise"   3. "Sunset"

4.

ORGANIZATION: Identify the play area by setting up cone markers around the perimeter. As a general rule, space cone markers every 10 feet (3 meters) apart, using about 15 markers for a play area that is 60' by 30' (20m by 10m). The shuttle formation signal is introduced, practiced, and then reinforced through relays.

EQUIPMENT REQUIRED:

Cone markers

Cassette/CD player; music

Carpet squares or floor tape

WARMING-UP/FITNESS SIGNALS

Grand Prix. Mark out a large oval area using cone markers. Ideally have one cone marker for each child in your class.

➤ You are racing car drivers, moving around a track. Everyone stand on the outside of a cone marker, rev up your engine, and wait for your start signal!

➤ When you hear the signal "Circle Up—Clockwise" (clockwise hand signal), race around the oval in a clockwise direction like the hands of a clock.

➤ The rule at this race track is that you pass on the *outside* only!

➤ On signal "Circle Up—Counterclockwise" (counterclockwise hand signal), travel in the opposite direction.

➤ On signal "Pitstop," stop where you are and do the task: "Bridge"; "Dead Bug!"; etc.

MOTOR MEMORY

Grid Patterns. Set up a grid pattern for each team as shown using floor tape. Have each team member in turn start in Square One. Walk into 2 squares straight ahead; take 3 jumps into the left squares; step one step backward; touch your right hand to the square on your right side; put your left foot in the square behind you; etc.

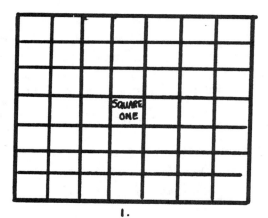

SPATIAL AWARENESS

1. *Partner Chase.* One partner stands tall; other partner cross-leg sits. On signal "Chase!" sitting partner tries to tag standing partner before signal "Iceberg!" is called. Then partners immediately stop and switch roles, waiting for the next "Chase!" signal to be called. Continue in this way.

2. *The Black Hole.* Give each team a "Star Wars" name such as Han Solo; Luke Skywalker; Chewbacca; C3PO; or R2D2. Select one team to be the IT team (Darth Vader and Storm Troopers) that stands in the middle of a circular area ("the black hole"). (See diagram.) The other teams "fly" around the outside of this circular area, saying "Whose spaceship are you?" Darth Vader can give several answers, but when he/she says "Yours!" the chase is on. Outside spaceships must fly to the safe zones (outside boundary lines of play area). If a spaceship is captured (tagged), that spaceship must join Darth Vader and his/her team.

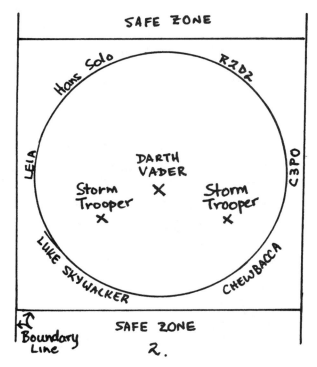

BODY AWARENESS

Human Shapes.

Partners:

➤ Make the letter O, T, L, C . . .

➤ Make the following numbers: 3, 6, 7, 11, . . .

Three's

➤ Make triangles, circles, squares, diamonds.

➤ Make different letters.

➤ Make different numbers.

➤ Make simple words.

TRIANGLE

CLOSING ACTIVITIES

1. *Shuttle Relays.* Shuttle formation. (See Formation Signals on page 9.)

   ➤ Run to opposite side giving high fives for the next player to go.

   ➤ Run to the opposite side passing a ball to the next player in line.

   ➤ Zigzag through the markers to the opposite line.

   ➤ Do different Animal Walks.

1. SHUTTLE RELAY "HIGH FIVES!"

2. *Legend(s) of the Day!*

2.

TEACHING SESSION
Lesson 21, Level 1

| MOVEMENT AREA: Locomotion |
| MOVEMENT: Running |

TEACHABLE POINTS:
1. Land on the forefoot when sprinting.
2. Plant foot along a narrow pathway.
3. Knees are up high at the front; feet are close to the buttocks at the back of the action.
4. Arms are bent at 90 degrees and work in opposition to legs.
5. Arms move back and forth in a straight line.
6. Hands are held in a relaxed position (as if holding an egg in each hand).
7. Head and upper body are stable and eyes look straight ahead.

EQUIPMENT REQUIRED: Marked courts and playing fields are useful, as the lines provide visual guidelines for the children to run along.

Music helps to establish a sense of rhythm

Several cones or witch's hats set boundaries

TEACHING GOALS:

☛ **Encourage children to move their body, arms, and legs in a straight line while running.**

☛ **Promote correct arm action.**

TEACHING PROGRESSIONS

1. Have the children walk along marked floor lines, keeping their feet close together on the lines.
2. Gradually have children increase the speed at which they are moving.
3. Practice marching. Emphasize lifting the knees and moving the arms vigorously and in opposition.
4. Create running lanes by placing cones in lines and spaced about 10 feet (3 meters) apart as shown. Assign children to lanes. Have each child, in turn, run through the lane over a distance of 60 feet (20 meters). Give the children a single cue each time before they commence running.

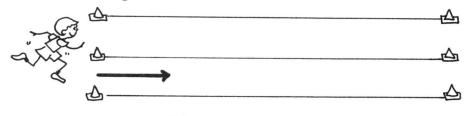

5. Technique—not speed—must be emphasized at this stage of running development.

> ➤ Head up, eyes looking forward.

> ➤ Keep your feet close to lines.

> ➤ Keep arms bent and relaxed.

ACTIVITIES

1. ***Scramble and Shake Hands.*** On the signal "Scramble," jog in and out of each other. On the signal "Shake," find a partner and shake hands. Have the children concentrate on certain locomotion teaching points when moving; for example, arms at right angles, and hands "holding eggs."

2. ***Here, Where, There.***

> ➤ "Here": run toward teacher.

> ➤ "Where": run on the spot.

> ➤ "There": run in the direction that the teacher is pointing.

3. ***Touch.*** Ask children to run and touch certain objects, such as wall, red line, basketball. Auditory memory skills can be practiced by increasing the number of instructions before children move.

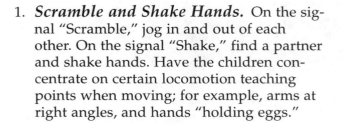

SHAKE HANDS
1.

"THERE"
2.

RED LINE   3.

MOVEMENT STATIONS
Lesson 22, Level 1

MOVEMENT AREA: Locomotion	
MOVEMENT: Running	

TEACHING GOALS:

➤ Encourage children to move their body, arms, and legs in a straight line while running.

➤ Promote correct arm action.

ORGANIZATION: Divide the class into 6 groups and assign each group to a station. Have groups rotate clockwise or counterclockwise to the next station after every 5 minutes of activity.

EQUIPMENT REQUIRED:

Several markers

Large open space

Variety of obstacles such as hoops, chairs, low hurdles, low bench or beam, low box horse, mats, boxes, and so on

MOVEMENT STATIONS

1. ***Obstacle Course Run.*** Create a running obstacle course that children move through as quickly and safely as possible.

2. ***Line Run.*** Children must complete runs along marked lines. Emphasis is on feet staying along the line. Start by walking and gradually increase speed to power-walking, and then jogging.

3. ***Bounding Run.*** Space markers or carpet squares 6 feet (2 meters) apart.
   Children practice bounding exercises,
   springing from one foot to the next.
   Adjust the markers according to the
   ability level of the children.

3.

4. ***Figure-8 Agility Run.*** Set up two
   identical agility patterns using the
   witch's hats as shown. Have children,
   in turn, run the pattern.

4.

5. ***Zigzag Run.*** Children zigzag run around obstacles, such as witch's hats, that
   are spaced 6 feet (2 meters) apart over a distance of 30 feet (10 meters).

5.

6. ***Stretching Station.***

   ➤ Quad Stretch
   ➤ Calf Stretch
   ➤ Butterfly Stretch
   ➤ Periscope

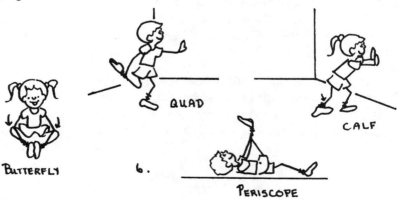

BUTTERFLY   **6.**   QUAD   CALF

PERISCOPE

| MOVEMENT AREA: Locomotion |
| MOVEMENT: Running |

TEACHABLE POINTS:

1. When sprinting, land on the forefoot.
2. Foot plant is along a narrow pathway.
3. Knees are up high at the front; feet are close to the buttocks at the back of the action.
4. Arms are bent at 90 degrees and work in opposition to legs.
5. Arms move back and forth in a straight line.
6. Hands are held in a relaxed position (as if holding an egg in each hand).
7. Head and upper body are stable and eyes look straight ahead.

EQUIPMENT REQUIRED:

Marked courts are useful, as the lines provide visual guidelines for the children
Music helps establish a sense of rhythm
Cones, hoops, carpet squares

TEACHING GOALS:

☞ Revise Lesson 1.
☞ Encourage correct knee action.
☞ Promote correct body alignment.

TEACHING PROGRESSIONS

1. Have children copy you running in slow motion in a straight line completing the knee lift, correct arm action, and leg lift behind the body. Emphasize head up and looking forward.

2. Have children jog on the spot with knees touching the hands which are held in front at waist height. Tell children to keep relaxed with head held up and looking forward. Repeat jogging along the line slowly; gradually increase the speed.

3. As children master this, slowly increase the speed, making sure that the action is completed along a line or piece of string on the ground. As the speed increases, so should the emphasis on starting to lean slightly forward, and landing on the fore-foot. Have the children change to different paces at your call: slow, medium speed, fast.

4. Have children relax hands, pretending to hold an egg in each hand. Moving feet in place, have child move his/her hands back and straight forward. Now have children jog along a line. Observe hand position and offer praise for good performance.

ACTIVITIES

1. *Islands.* Place carpet squares or hoops on the ground. Ensure they are well spaced. Every child except one (Pirate) has an island. When the music starts, everyone has to move around the islands. When the music stops, children must find an island. Of course, one will not and becomes the new Pirate. Use less islands so there are more pirates.

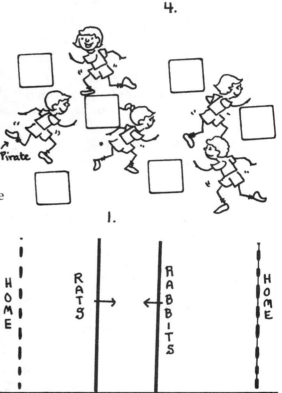

2. *Rats and Rabbits.* Split the class so that one half of the class are the Rats and the other half are the Rabbits. Have the children stand facing away on designated lines as shown. Call out a name "Rats." This is the signal for the Rats to give chase to the Rabbits who must try to safely run back to their Home (as shown). If a Rabbit is tagged by a Rat, the Rabbit must join the Rat group. Continue in this way. Try tricking the groups by calling out "Rrrr . . . Rodents!" If anyone moves, he/she must sit out and lose one turn. Use tag belts which must be pulled to make the "tag." Have the groups take different starting positions: cross-leg sitting; "Dead Bug"; front lying; back lying; all-fours; knee-sitting; front support.

3. *Simon Says.* Play the game but use only locomotion running skills. Jog in place; run fast on the spot; jog slowly; walk with giant strides; march; lift knees high. Remember, only do the movement when you hear the words "Simon Says . . ." and then the action!

MOVEMENT STATIONS
Lesson 24, Level 1

MOVEMENT AREA: Locomotion
MOVEMENT: Running

TEACHING GOALS:

➤ Revise Lesson 1.
➤ Encourage correct knee action.
➤ Promote correct body alignment.

ORGANIZATION: Divide the class into 6 groups and assign each group to a station. Have groups rotate clockwise or counterclockwise to the next station after every 5 minutes of activity. The emphasis is to keep all activities either teacher- or parent-directed. This prevents wasting time through having to explain new activities each session.

EQUIPMENT REQUIRED:

Several markers

Large open space

Variety of obstacles such as hoops, chairs, low hurdles, low bench or beam, low box horse, mats, boxes, and so on

MOVEMENT STATIONS

1. *Obstacle Course Run.* Create a running obstacle course that children must complete 3 times in a selected time.

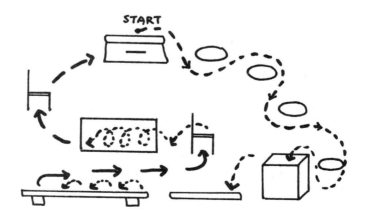

2. ***Triangle Run.*** Set up 3 markers in a triangular pattern, spaced 15 feet (5 meters) apart. Mark them 1, 2, and 3 as shown. Set up 2 identical patterns. Each child, in turn, starts at the first marker, runs around the second, back around the first, then around the third, and back around the first marker. This circuit must be completed twice.

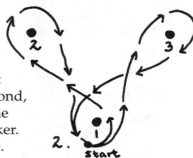

3. ***Rectangle Run.*** Mark out a rectangle that is 15´ by 30´ (5m by 10m). Child *runs* the *lengths* of the rectangle and *walks* the *widths*. Repeat, running in the opposite direction. Repeat by power-walking the widths.

4. ***Changing Speed.*** Space 4 markers at 30 feet (10 meters) apart, over a distance of 120 feet (40 meters). Each child in turn runs quickly to the first marker; slowly to the second; quickly to the third; and slowly to the fourth. Reverse direction and repeat.

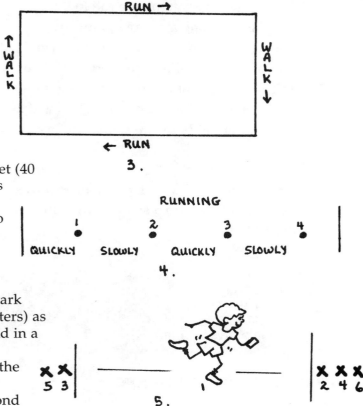

5. ***Shuttle Run.*** Use cones to mark off a distance of 30 feet (10 meters) as shown. Have half of team stand in a file behind one line facing the other half standing in a file at the opposite line. First child runs across, gives a beanbag to second child who runs across to hand beanbag to third child, and so on. Continue in this way.

6. ***Stretching Station.***

   ➤ Quad Stretch
   ➤ Calf Stretch
   ➤ Butterfly Stretch
   ➤ Foot Artist

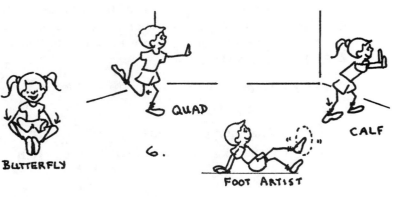

| MOVEMENT AREA: Locomotion |
| MOVEMENT: Running |

TEACHABLE POINTS:

1. When sprinting, land on the forefoot.
2. Foot plant is along a narrow pathway.
3. Knees are up high at the front; feet are close to the buttocks at the back of the action.
4. Arms are bent at 90 degrees and work in opposition to legs.
5. Arms move back and forth in a straight line.
6. Hands are held in a relaxed position (as if holding an egg in each hand).
7. Head and upper body are stable and eyes look straight ahead.

EQUIPMENT REQUIRED:

Marked courts are useful, as the lines provide visual guidelines for the children
Music helps establish a sense of rhythm
Cones, hoops

TEACHING GOALS:

- ☛ Revise arm action, knee action, and linear movement.
- ☛ Increase stride length.

TEACHING PROGRESSIONS

1. Have children hold an object, such as a beanbag or small weight in each hand. Observe hand/arm movements as children jog along a line.

2. To increase stride length, place 10 markers at even intervals and have the children place a foot at each marker while running. Gradually increase the distance between the markers. (Do not increase the distance to the point where the action looks uncomfortable.)

3. *On Your Toes* signals.

   ➤ Run on your toes.
   ➤ Run clapping your hands
   ➤ Run stiffly like a wooden man.

➤ Run in place, drop to the ground, stand up, and run.

ACTIVITIES

1. ***Witch Tag.*** Mark off a large circular playing area with cone markers, with a 12-foot (4-meter) diameter circle inside, marked off using floor tape or flat rope. Choose one of the children to be the "The Witch" who stands in the middle of the large circle. The Witch's children run around the outside of the large circle, calling out "Whose children are you?" Witch answers in varying ways, such as Santa Claus's, the President's, the Prime Minister's, etc. But when Witch answers "Yours," Witch gives chase and tries to tag the children before they can reach the safety of the boundary lines. Those tagged become Witch's helpers and the game continues in this way.

   ➤ Use tag belts to ensure safety in making the tag.

   ➤ Have outside children move with different locomotor movements.

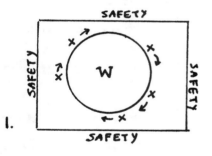

2. ***Three Elbows.*** Scatter objects on the ground in a marked area; for example, carpet squares, bean-bags, hoops, small mats, low bench or beam, large balls, jump ropes. The children run in and out of the objects to music. When the music stops, a number is called out along with a body part: "3, Elbows!" The children must then quickly, but safely, run to touch 3 of the objects with an elbow.

3. ***Traffic Lights.*** Hold up different colors to represent traffic lights: *Red*—jump-stop in place; *Green*—jog along the lines on the floor or in a straight line; *Yellow*—jog in place (or light bounces in place); *Round-about*—jog around in a circle clockwise.

MOVEMENT STATIONS
Lesson 26, Level 1

MOVEMENT AREA: Locomotion
MOVEMENT: Running

TEACHING GOALS:

☞ Revise arm action, knee action, and linear movement.

☞ Reinforce stride length.

ORGANIZATION: Divide the class into 6 groups and assign each group to a station. Have groups rotate clockwise or counterclockwise to the next station after every 5 minutes of activity. The emphasis is to keep all activities either teacher- or parent-directed. This prevents wasting time through having to explain new activities each session.

EQUIPMENT REQUIRED:

Several cone markers, hoops   8 Bases

Cassette/CD player   6 Beanbags

Assessment Recording Sheets

MOVEMENT STATIONS

1. *Friendly Races.* Mark off a 50-yard (50-meter) distance. Have children pair off and race each other to the finish line. Then they challenge someone else. Emphasize that they choose to race someone who is about the same size.

2. *Assessment.* Observe and record performance of running. (See Book 1, *Ready-to-Use Fundamental Motor Skills & Movement Activities for Young Children*, for Recording Sheet.)

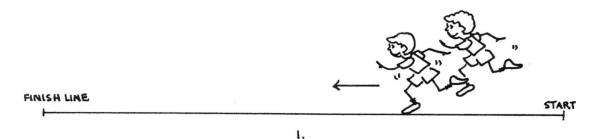

FINISH LINE   ←   START

1.

3. ***Music Run.*** Create a tape using popular music with varying tempos. Change the tempo every 20 seconds; provide rest breaks (such as stretch breaks) or breathing breaks before picking up the tempo again. Suggest 3 minutes of activity; 3 minutes of passive movement. Children keep in time to the music as it changes tempo from quick, to jogging tempo, to walking or marching tempo. Move on the spot or in general space, watching where you are going. When the music stops, you stop by jump-stopping!

4. ***Baseball Diamond Run.*** Set up 4 bases in the shape of a diamond as shown. Start with bases spaced 15 feet (5 meters) apart. Set up 2 identical courses. Use arrows to show direction of movement (one course, run clockwise; other course, counter-clockwise). Children take turns running the bases with a foot tag at each base.

5. ***Shuttle Run.*** Use cones to mark off a distance of 30 feet (10 meters) as shown. Place beanbag (#1) on the start line and two beanbags (#2, #3) on the other line. Set up 2 identical courses. Each child, in turn, runs to the opposite line, grabs beanbag #2, carries it to the start line, sets this bag down, grabs beanbag #1, runs back to the opposite line, places #1 on the line, grabs #3 and runs back across the start line.

6. ***Stretching Station.***

   ➤ Quad Stretch

   ➤ Calf Stretch

   ➤ Sprinter Stretch

   ➤ Butterfly Stretch

MOVEMENT AREA: Body Control
MOVEMENT: Jumping and Landings (Horizontal)

TEACHABLE POINTS:

Jumping for Distance

1. Head up with eyes looking forward.
2. Arms extend behind the body as the knees, hips, and ankles bend.
3. At the same time, body leans slightly forward.
4. Legs extend vigorously and forcefully; at the same time, arms extend forward and upward vigorously.
5. Body remains leaning slightly forward.

Landing

1. Land on balls of both feet and then roll back onto flat feet.
2. Ankles, knees, and hips bend to absorb force. Feet should be shoulder-width apart.
3. On landing, lean slightly forward at the hips.
4. Arms held out in front or to side of body to assist balance.
5. Head should be up and the eyes looking forward to stop falling forward.

EQUIPMENT REQUIRED:

Cone markers   1 short rope per child

1 hoop per child   Music with a steady 4/4 beat; cassette/CD player

TEACHING GOALS:

- ☞ Hold head up on landing.
- ☞ Promote leg drive.
- ☞ Coordinate use of the arms in the jump.
- ☞ Bend knees on landing.

TEACHING PROGRESSIONS

1. Have the children mirror your actions as you complete the following movement. Stand swinging the arms back and forth as the knees bend and straighten.

2. Instruct children to jump in different directions over a rope stretched out along the ground: jump forward over the rope; backward; from side to side.

3. *Jumping Signals.*
   - ➤ Bounce gently like a ball in your Home place.
   - ➤ Jump rope pantomime the action of rope jumping.
   - ➤ Jog forward for 4 counts; slow jump 4 counts in place; jog backward for 4 counts; quick jump in place.
   - ➤ Run in place, drop to the ground, jump up high, run in place.
   - ➤ Quarter jump-turn right; quarter jump-turn left.

BOUNCING   ROPE JUMPING

ACTIVITIES

1. *Hoop Challenges.*
   - ➤ Jump forward in and out of your hoop.
   - ➤ Jump backward in and out of your hoop.
   - ➤ Jump sideways in and out of your hoop.
   - ➤ Jump out the front, back in; out the back, jump in; out the right side, back in; out the left side, back in. Repeat.
   - ➤ Walk 5 giant steps away from your hoop, jump turn to face your hoop, and run to land with both feet in your hoop.
   - ➤ Spring out of your hoop and land as far away from it as you can.
   - ➤ Create your own hoop challenge!

RUN   JUMP   LAND

1.

2. *Hoop Relay.* Place children in teams of 4 in shuttle formation, with 2 children at either end of marked course 10 yards (or 10 meters) apart. Children in turn use the hoop like a jump rope to travel across to the opposite side, hand the hoop over to the next teammate in line, and join the end of that line.

MOVEMENT STATIONS
Lesson 28, Level 1

MOVEMENT AREA: Body Control
MOVEMENT: Jumping and Landing (Horizontal)

TEACHING GOALS

➤ Hold head up on landing.
➤ Promote leg drive.
➤ Coordinate use of the arms in the jump.
➤ Bend the knees on landing.

ORGANIZATION: Divide the class into 6 groups and assign each group to a station. Have groups rotate clockwise or counterclockwise to the next station after every 5 minutes of activity. The emphasis is to keep all activities either teacher- or parent-directed. This prevents wasting time through having to explain new activities each session.

EQUIPMENT REQUIRED:

Several hoops   6 small mats
Low box horse, balance bench, or balance beam   1 large mat
Chalk or floor tape   Assessment Recording Sheet

MOVEMENT STATIONS

1. *Jumping/Landing Circuit.* Create a jumping/landing circuit by marking circles (using chalk or floor tape) on mats positioned at different angles and distances for children to jump and land on. Jump from low box horse onto a mat as far as possible.

2. *Assessment.* Observe and record performance of Jumping/Landing for Distance. (See Book 1, *Ready-to-Use Fundamental Motor Skills & Movement Activities for Young Children*, for Horizontal Jump Recording Sheet.)

3. ***Beanbag Run Course.*** Set up 2 identical courses as shown. Each runner, in turn, runs to opposite cone marker, picks up beanbag, and places it on top of cone marker for the next player to pick up.

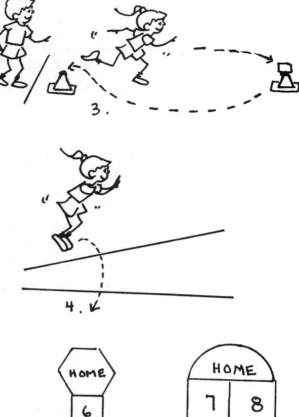

4. ***Jump the Stream.*** Place 2 long ropes as shown. Children take turns jumping across the "stream" from its narrowest point to its widest.

5. ***Hopscotch.*** Using the 2 hopscotch patterns shown, children play the game. *Variation:* Have children create their own hopscotch pattern that can be drawn with chalk on the playground, and play the game with a partner.

6. ***Hoop Jumping Course.*** Create 2 different courses by taping or securing the hoops on the floor in a pattern. Hoops should be close enough to jump off 2 feet from 1 hoop to the other. Children, in turn, jump through the course.

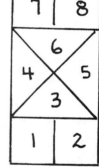

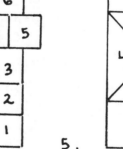

MOVEMENT AREA: Body Control
MOVEMENT: Jumping and Landing (Vertical)

TEACHABLE POINTS:

Jumping for Height

1. Head up with eyes looking forward.
2. Arms extend behind the body as knees, hips, and ankles bend.
3. At same time, body leans slightly forward at hips.
4. Legs and arms extend forcefully.
5. Arm action is synchronized with leg action.
6. Body extends upward.
7. Arms extend upward.
8. Head up with eyes looking upward.

Landing

1. On landing, head is up and eyes look forward.
2. On landing, lean slightly forward at the hips.
3. Arms held out in front or to side of body to assist balance.
4. Land on balls of both feet and then roll back onto flat feet.
5. Ankles, knees, and hips bend to absorb force.
6. Feet should be shoulder-width apart.

EQUIPMENT REQUIRED:

Cone markers
Soft surface on which to land
1 hoop per child
Floor or wall tape

TEACHING GOALS:

☞ Revise previous lesson points.
☞ Use legs and arms to maximize upward springing.
☞ Use arms to assist balance on landing.
☞ Encourage guided discovery on balance techniques.

TEACHING PROGRESSIONS

1. Ask children to jump upward *without* using their arms to help them. Now do this again using arms to jump upward. Which way is better? Ask them how their arms help them to jump upward. Swing arms backward, then upward.

    ➤ How do your knees help you to jump upward? Bend your knees as arms swing backward, then straighten as arms swing upward to give you force.

2. Now jump upward and land with feet together, knees bending. Repeat, landing with feet apart—about shoulder-width apart, knees bending.

    ➤ Which way is better to improve balance on landing? (Land with feet apart, knees bending.)

    ➤ Why should you bend your knees on landing? (Knees bend to absorb the force of landing.)

3. *Practice:* Jump upward as high as possible from Home place. Hold your landing and check that knees are bent, arms are out for balance, and head is forward. Repeat, reaching for the sky.

ACTIVITIES

1. ***Ghost in the Box.*** On signal "Ghost in the Box!" children jump upward from their "box" (hoop) and say "Boo!" Then they run to touch a boundary line, run Home, and jump back in their box. Repeat.

2. ***Wall Touch.*** Children find a free space near a wall, jump upward and reach for a mark on the wall. Challenge them to reach beyond the mark.

MOVEMENT STATIONS
Lesson 30, Level 1

MOVEMENT AREA: Body Control
MOVEMENT: Jumping and Landing (Vertical)

EQUIPMENT REQUIRED:

> Hoops, large mats, medium box horse
>
> Several long and short ropes, elastic bands, deck rings
>
> Ball in sock suspended from support
>
> Large cones
>
> 6 chairs
>
> Deck ring with rope
>
> Assessment Recording Sheet

STAR JUMP

HURDLE LEAP

MOVEMENT STATIONS

1. *Jumping/Landing Circuit.* Create a jumping/landing circuit that consists of 3 stations each requiring different landing tasks:

   ➤ Star jumping from medium box horse onto a mat.

   ➤ Leaping over a low obstacle such as a rope or hurdle and landing with 2 feet.

   ➤ Jump-turning from a springboard onto a mat, and land facing the opposite direction.

2. *Sockeroo Jump.* Jump upward to hit an object (ball in a long sock suspended from a support or tree).

3. *Assessment.* Observe and record performance of the vertical jump. (See Book 1, *Ready-to-Use Fundamental Motor Skills & Movement Activities for Young Children,* for a Recording Sheet.)

84

4. *Hoop Jumping.* In pairs, one partner holds the hoop horizontally just off the floor. Other partner jumps into and out of the hoop. Partner gradually holds hoop higher. Then partners switch roles.

5. *Elevator Jump.* Place one long rope stretched between 2 chairs as shown in the diagram. Children take turns jumping over the rope from its lowest height to its highest height.

   ➤ If possible, set up 2–3 stations at varying heights.

6. *Jump the Ring.* One child swings a deck ring attached to a short length of rope in a circle along the ground. The other children try to jump the ring each time it passes under their feet.

TEACHING SESSION
Lesson 31, Level 1

MOVEMENT AREA: Body Control
MOVEMENT: Static Balance

TEACHABLE POINTS:

1. Head is up and eyes are focused straight ahead of a fixed point.
2. Feet are flat on the floor with toes extended.
3. All body parts are kept straight and still.
4. Knees are kept slightly flexed.
5. Arms can be used to assist in balancing.

EQUIPMENT REQUIRED:

Several hoops

Music; CD/cassette player

Carpet squares, enough for every pair (both large square pieces and smaller square pieces)

TEACHING GOALS:
☞ Keep head up and eyes focused.
☞ Keep feet flat on the floor.

TEACHING PROGRESSIONS

1. Have children sit on the floor and try to lift legs off the floor while balancing on bottom. Use hands for support, if needed.

2. From all-fours position (4-point balance position), have the children do a 3-point balance on hand and knee combinations.

3. Explore 3-point balances; for example: knee–foot–hand; hand–hand–foot.

4. Try a 1-foot balance with hands on hips; hands on head; arms out to side. Repeat balance on other foot. Repeat balance with eyes closed.

ACTIVITIES

1. ***Statues.*** Have children move in different ways to music. When the music stops, call out a number "1, 2, 3 . . ." Children jump-stop immediately and perform a balance on "1" part; on "2" parts; and so on.

2. ***Balancing Challenges.*** Children move around in a large marked area to music. Hoops are placed around the area. When the music stops, you call a number that indicates to the children that they must form a group of that size in a hoop—all supporting each other as they stand on one leg.

3. ***Shrinking Islands.*** Pair off the children and give each pair a carpet square that they carry with them as they move around to music. When the music stops, they quickly place the carpet square on the floor and both stand on it. The last pair to do this task must run once around the play area, then rejoin the game. *Variation:* Start with large pieces of carpet squares, then change to smaller pieces so that partners will have to carefully balance together.

MOVEMENT STATIONS
Lesson 32, Level 1

> **MOVEMENT AREA: Body Control**
> **MOVEMENT: Static Balance**

TEACHING GOALS:
- ☛ Keep head up and eyes focused forward.
- ☛ Keep feet flat on the floor.

EQUIPMENT REQUIRED:

> Partner balancing cards—1 per pair
> Balance boards
> Several dome markers or blocks of wood
> Elastic bands
> Individual and partner challenges cards
> Large rope
> Assessment Recording Sheet

MOVEMENT STATIONS

1. ***Balancing Challenges.*** Children perform balancing challenges. (See page 89.) Enlarge each challenge onto individual cards and have the children complete the balancing positions.

2. ***Static Balance—Assessment.*** (See Book 1, *Ready-to-Use Fundamental Motor Skills & Movement Activities for Young Children*, for a recording sheet.)

3. ***Partner Balancing Challenges.*** (See page 89.) Enlarge each challenge onto individual cards and have the children work in pairs to complete the balancing positions.

   ➤ *Challenge:* Try Buddy Walker or Gym Skis.

4. ***Obstacle Run Course.*** Set up an obstacle course and have children take turns going through the course. As soon as one runner is at halfway point, the next runner can begin.

5. ***Elastics Jump.*** Secure elastic bands on the legs of two chairs that are spaced 12 feet (4 meters) apart, as shown. Children explore different ways of jumping over the elastic band. If possible, set up 3 mini-stations and vary the jumping height.

6. ***Large Rope Balance.*** Using a large rope, the children together explore different ways of balancing cooperatively.

88

BALANCING CHALLENGES

PARTNER BALANCING CHALLENGES

TEACHING SESSION
Lesson 33, Level 1

MOVEMENT AREA: Body Control
MOVEMENT: Dynamic Balance

TEACHABLE POINTS:

1. Feet are flat on the floor with toes extended.
2. Feet remain slightly bent.
3. Hips, back, and shoulders remain straight.
4. Arms are extended out to the sides for balance.
5. Head is up and upper body remains steady.
6. Eyes are focused and looking straight ahead at a fixed point.

EQUIPMENT REQUIRED:

Firm even surface
Hoops/carpet square, mats
Several cone markers

3 small sponge balls
Floor tape or floor lines

TEACHING GOALS:
☛ **Keep head up and eyes focused.**
☛ **Keep feet flat on the floor.**

TEACHING PROGRESSIONS

1. Have children walk forward; walk backward along the line with arms out to the side.
2. Combine forward and backward walking.
3. Have children walk sideways along the line.
4. Combine these 3 types of walking together.
5. Have children perform the above activities with hands on hips.
6. Have children walk heel to toe forward with hands on hips. Repeat walking backward.
7. Have children walk heel to toe, forward then backward with arms out to sides.

SIDEWAYS   BACKWARD   FORWARD
4.

6.

ACTIVITIES

1. ***Balance Tag.*** This tag game is played by traveling only on the lines of the floor. Choose 3 ITs who each hold a small sponge ball to tag with and give chase to others. A tagged player must step off the lines and hold a balance for 5 seconds. Then the player can rejoin the game. Change ITs frequently.

2. ***Balancing Tugs.*** With a partner, each take up a balance on your right foot, with left hand holding left foot behind. Using a right hand wrist hold, try to pull each other off balance.

   ➤ Repeat, balancing on left foot.
   ➤ Repeat, using a left-hand wrist hold.
   ➤ Challenge someone else.

3. ***Heel–Toe Crossing.*** Split the class into groups of 5-6. For each group, mark a long line on the floor (4 yards/meters) using floor tape. Have each group position in shuttle formation as shown. Children must walk heel–toe along the line to the opposite side. When a walker has reached the opposite side and signals "Heel–Toe," then the next walker can begin. If a walker comes off the line, he or she must start over again.

   ➤ Count the number of crossings your group will make before the "Stop" signal is given.

3.

MOVEMENT STATIONS
Lesson 34, Level 1

> **MOVEMENT AREA:** Body Control
>
> **MOVEMENT:** Dynamic Balance

TEACHING GOALS:

☛ Keep head up and feet flat on the ground.

☛ Keep upper body quiet (relatively still).

EQUIPMENT REQUIRED:

Long ropes
Wooden blocks or dome markers
Balance boards (Duck Walkers™)
Foam stilts or bucket steppers
2–3 balance benches or beams
Assessment Recording Sheet

MOVEMENT STATIONS

1. *Snake Walk.* Place several long ropes on the ground in a snaking pattern. (Floor tape or dome markers can also be used.) Have the children walk forward and backward along the rope, then sideways, and finally heel to toe.

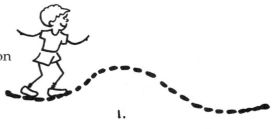

2. *Balancing Challenges.* Set up a balancing course as shown. Print tasks on a large sheet of posterboard.

   ➤ Balance on one leg on the mat for a count of 5. Balance on other leg.

   ➤ Balance on one leg on 2 dome markers/blocks of wood as shown; then balance on 1 dome marker/wooden block.

   ➤ Repeat these tasks except with eyes closed.

   ➤ Explore other ways of balancing on the dome markers or wooden blocks using different body parts.

3. ***Dynamic Balance—Assessment.*** Observe and record performance of dynamic balance (See Book 1, *Ready-to-Use Fundamental Motor Skills & Movement Activities for Young Children,* for a recording sheet.)

4. ***Balance Walk Challenges.*** Explore using foam stilts or foam bucket steppers to travel.

5. ***Balance Board Challenge.*** Use commercial (Duck Walker) or homemade boards and try to balance as you rock side-to-side; walk like a duck.

6. ***Balance Bench Challenges.*** Put the following tasks on large posterboard or whiteboard:

   ➤ Walk forward along the bench to the other end.

   ➤ Walk backward along the bench to the start.

   ➤ Walk heel–toe along the bench.

   ➤ Run carefully forward along the bench and jump off, gently landing.

   ➤ Carefully jump your way along the bench.

   ➤ Explore other ways of moving along the bench.

| MOVEMENT AREA: Locomotion |
| MOVEMENT: Hopping and Leaping |

HOPPING TEACHABLE POINTS:

1. Hop-start on one foot and land on the same foot (both on forefoot).
2. Swinging leg remains bent and moves back and forth during the hop—in opposition to the support leg—assisting in the forward movement.
3. Hopping leg bends to absorb the landing force.
4. Arms move in opposition and nonsupport leg assists in forward movement.
5. Head remains stable with the eyes looking forward.
6. Movement should be smooth and in balance.

LEAPING TEACHABLE POINTS:

HOPPING

1. Head remains up with eyes looking forward during the action.
2. Arms assist and are synchronized in opposition to the legs.
3. Take off is on one foot; landing is on the opposite foot.
4. Landing is on the forefoot.
5. Knees bend slightly to absorb force on landing.
6. Balance is maintained on landing.

EQUIPMENT REQUIRED:

Firm even surface or carpeted play area
Cone markers
1 low hurdle per team

LEAPING

TEACHING GOALS:
☛ **Maintain good balance.**
☛ **Landing correctly.**
☛ **Show good leg drive.**

TEACHING PROGRESSIONS

Hopping is an extremely fatiguing movement and should be used in conjunction with other movements. The duration should be short when hopping, with adequate rest between efforts. Encourage hopping with the nondominant leg.

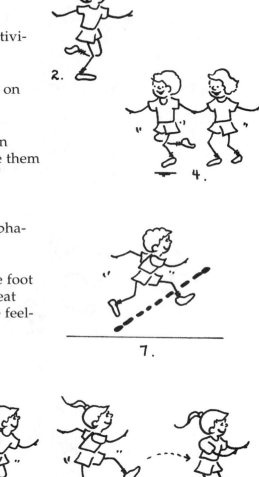

1. Demonstrate the correct hopping action to the children, emphasizing the teaching goals.

2. Have children practice single-leg balance activities. Balance on one foot, then on the other.

3. Have children jump from two feet and land on one foot. Repeat, landing on the other foot.

4. In pairs, one at a time, ask children to hop in place with support from their partner. Have them concentrate on knee action and support leg position.

5. Demonstrate the correct leaping action, emphasizing the teaching goals.

6. Have children run forward and leap off one foot into the air, landing softly on two feet. Repeat leaping off the other foot. Try to convey the feeling of "flying" through the air!

7. Have children leap over a line or stretched rope, landing on opposite foot. Explore leaping over the line with one foot; then leap using the other foot.

8. Have children leap in a straight line over a set distance. Count the number of leaps taken.

ACTIVITIES

1. *Hopping Mad.* Place hoops randomly throughout the play area. Use 3 hoops less than the total number of children in the class. Call out the signal "Scrambled Eggs—Hopping!" Children must hop to a hoop and jump inside. Anyone caught outside of a hoop must do "3" of something (e.g., 3 jump turns; 3 jumping jacks; 3 inchworms). Use music to enhance children's movements and enjoyment.

2. *Hopping Relay.* Divide the class into 4 teams. Mark out a start line and a turning line with cone markers. Have each team set up in file formation, facing a cone marker as shown. On signal "Hop-away!" each team member, in turn, hops with the preferred foot to the turning cone, then hops back with the nonpreferred foot to the starting line. Emphasize that children do not change legs mid-journey.

3. *Leaping Relay.* Divide the class into 4 teams and have each team set up in shuttle formation 30 feet (10 meters) apart from each other. Set up a low hurdle in the middle among each team as shown. On signal "Leap Away!" each team member, in turn, travels across to the opposite group, leaping over the obstacle.

MOVEMENT STATIONS
Lesson 36, Level 1

MOVEMENT AREA: Locomotion
MOVEMENT: Hopping and Leaping

TEACHING GOALS:
- ☛ Maintain good balance.
- ☛ Landing correctly.
- ☛ Show good leg drive.

EQUIPMENT REQUIRED:

2 long ropes
Cone markers
Floor tape or chalk for hopscotch station
Ball in nylon stocking, suspended
Assessment Recording Sheet

MOVEMENT STATIONS

1. *Alligator Leap.* Place 2 long ropes at an angle to each other as shown, about 1 meter at the narrow end and about 3 meters at the wide end. Children, in turn, attempt to leap across the "river" which is full of alligators. With each successful leap, child attempts to leap across the wider part.

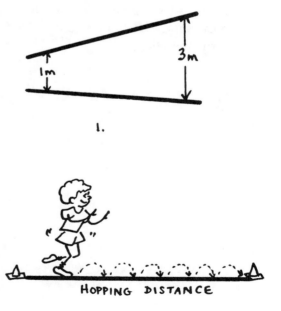

2. *Hopping Sprint.* Use markers to determine a certain traveling distance. Have children, in turn, hop through this distance. Emphasize arm action.

   ➤ Use your preferred foot to hop; then hop using other foot.

3. *Hopping—Assessment.* Observe and record performance of hopping. (See Book 1, *Ready-to-Use Fundamental Motor Skills & Movement Activities for Young Children,* for a recording sheet.)

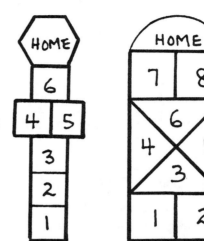

4. **Hopscotch Station.** Use floor tape or chalk lines to create hopscotch pattern(s).

5. **Leap and Tap.** Suspend a ball in a nylon stocking from a tree or other suitable fixture. Children take turns leaping up to tap the ball. Gradually increase the height of the ball.

5.

6. **Leaping—Assessment.** Observe and record performance of leaping. (See Book 1, *Ready-to-Use Fundamental Motor Skills & Movement Activities for Young Children*, for a recording sheet.)

TEACHING SESSION
Lesson 37, Level 1

MOVEMENT AREA: Object Control
MOVEMENT: Receiving a Rolled (Large) Ball

TEACHABLE POINTS:

1. Eyes are focused on the ball source and track the ball along the ground.
2. Child moves to get the body behind the ball.
3. Fingers are spread and face downward ready to receive the oncoming ball.
4. Preferred leg is in front and knees bent to get down to the ball.
5. Child takes the ball cleanly in the hands.

EQUIPMENT REQUIRED:

Firm even surface
1 large soft ball per person

TEACHING GOALS:

☞ Keep head up and eyes focused.
☞ Maintain correct body and hand position.

TEACHING PROGRESSIONS

1. Demonstrate how to roll the ball: hold the ball in both hands; feet shoulder-width apart.

   ➤ Swing arms back on your favorite side (right side for right-hander).

   ➤ Step forward with the opposite foot and swing your rolling hand forward and through.

   ➤ Release the ball downward with your favorite hand as you follow through.

   ➤ Practice rolling the ball against the wall.

   ➤ Cue words: "Ball"—"Swing back"—"Step forward"—"Swing through."

2. Demonstrate the receiving position. Have children copy you.

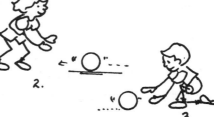

3. Have children practice moving down into the receiving position from standing still to bending at the knees. Repeat, going down on one knee. Let them decide which is more comfortable.

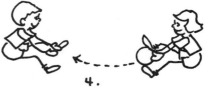

4. Children sit on the ground in pairs, facing each other. Instruct children to roll the ball toward each other, emphasizing that they keep eyes fixed on the ball. Check for hands in the correct position to receive the ball.

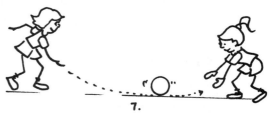

5. Now repeat activity 4 in kneeling position. Repeat with one knee up, the other down.

6. Repeat activity 4 in a standing position. At this stage, emphasize the importance of bending from the knees to reach down to the ball.

7. Repeat activity 6, gradually increasing the distance between the partners.

ACTIVITIES

1. ***Rolling Stunts.*** Find a Home space and stand tall holding your ball. Always roll your ball into an open space.

   ➤ Roll the ball ahead of you and try to jump back and forth over the ball.

   ➤ Roll the ball ahead of you. Run after it to get in front and field the ball.

   ➤ Keep the ball rolling. Change its direction, but don't let it touch any of the other rolling balls.

   ➤ Roll the ball in a figure-8 between your legs.

   ➤ Create a rolling stunt of your own.

2. ***Roller Ball Relay.*** Form groups of 4 and position in shuttle formation. Roll the ball in turn across to the player on the opposite side, then go to the back of your file. Count the number of crossings your group can make in a certain time.

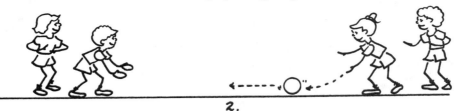

MOVEMENT STATIONS
Lesson 38, Level 1

MOVEMENT AREA: Object Control
MOVEMENT: Receiving a Rolled (Large) Ball

TEACHING GOALS:

☞ Keep head up and eyes focused.

☞ Use correct body and hand position.

EQUIPMENT REQUIRED:

12 bowling pins or plastic jugs
6-8 small traffic cones
Variety of balls
3 cardboard boxes
Assessment Recording Sheet

MOVEMENT STATIONS

1. ***Guard the Goal.*** Working in pairs, set up a goal area as shown using 2 traffic cones. One player is the Roller; the other player, the Goalie. The Roller stands about 10 feet (3 meters) away and rolls the ball toward the Goalie trying to score a goal. Goalie may use only hands to stop the ball. After 5 attempts, change roles.

2. ***Circle Pattern Roll.*** In your group sit in a circle with legs crossed. One player starts with the ball and rolls it across the circle to a player who is not on either side of them. Each player in turn does the same. When the ball returns to the first player, the pattern begins again.

   ➤ How many times can this pattern be repeated before moving to the next station?

3. **Bowling Challenge.** Set up two 6-pin bowling stations as shown. (Plastic jugs or small traffic cones could also be used.) In turn, players take 2 tries to knock over as many pins as possible. Organize your station so that there is a Bowler, a Setter-up, and a Ball Returner.

3.

4. **Receiving a Rolled Ball— Assessment.** Observe and record performance of receiving a rolled ball. (See Book 1, *Ready-to-Use Fundamental Motor Skills & Movement Activities for Young Children*, for a recording sheet.)

4

5. **Jump the Ball.** Play each game with 3 players. Two players stand facing each other, spaced 5 giant steps apart. The third player stands in the middle. The 2 outside players roll the ball back and forth to each other. The middle player tries to jump or leap over the ball. After 5 jumps, change roles until everyone has had a turn in the middle.

5.

6. **Box Rolling Targets.** For each pair, set up a large open box or bin on its side as shown. Children take turns rolling the ball into this target.

6.

MOVEMENT AREA: Object Control
MOVEMENT: Bouncing and Catching Large Ball with 2 Hands

TEACHABLE POINTS:

1. Keep in a balanced position with the feet comfortably spread.
2. Arms bend to receive oncoming ball at waist height.
3. Ball is caught on its sides, with the fingers spread.
4. Arms bend at the elbows to provide "give" as the ball is taken.
5. Push the ball down with both hands by extending arms downward; do not "pat" the ball.
6. Eyes are focused on ball at all times.

EQUIPMENT REQUIRED:

Firm even surface
1 large ball per child
1 hoop per child
Several cone markers

TEACHING GOALS:
☛ Keep head up and eyes focused.
☛ Push, do not pat, the ball.

TEACHING PROGRESSIONS

1. Ideally have children each with a large ball. Ask children to find a Home space and cross-leg sit with the ball in their lap. Feel the ball with the finger pads, not the whole hand on the ball. Do this with eyes opened; the eyes closed.

2. Demonstrate the action of bouncing and catching the ball with two hands. Emphasize having fingers relaxed and spread; feet apart and balanced; and eyes on ball.

3. In kneeling position have them bounce the ball with two hands, using cue words: "bounce–catch, bounce–catch"; then "bounce–bounce–catch"; etc.

4. Repeat task #3 in standing position. Observe that ball is *pushed* to the ground, not dropped. Emphasize that arms remain extended, fingers relaxed and spread, eyes on ball. Insist that ball is caught in the hands, not trapped against the body.

5. Now bounce the ball in a hoop. Try "bounce–catch, bounce–catch" pattern; then "bounce–bounce–catch"; and so on. *Challenge:* How many bounces can you make in a row?

6. Bounce the ball in front; to one side; to the other side. Bounce the ball as you walk in a straight line. Bounce the ball on one spot as you walk in a circle around the ball.

ACTIVITIES

1. ***Loose Ball.*** Mark a large area and divide it into two halves. Select two children to be the Taggers and have them stand on the endline in the half where the other children will be bouncing their balls. Everyone else finds a Home space in this half. On signal "Bounce!" everyone begins bouncing their ball. As soon as Taggers see someone lose control of the ball, they call out "Loose Ball." Everyone must grab their ball and quickly but safely run to the opposite endline of the other half area. Those tagged become Helpers. Who can last the game without being tagged?

2. ***Bouncing Relay.*** Divide the class into 4–5 even teams and have each team stand in file formation behind a cone marker. Have captains place a ball in a hoop 5 yards (meters) in front of each team as shown. The aim of the relay is for each child in turn to run to the hoop, bounce the ball 3 times (or a designated number of times), place the ball back in the hoop, and run back to tag the next team member.

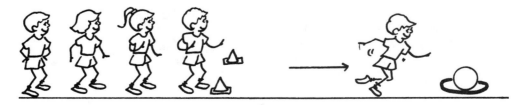

MOVEMENT STATIONS
Lesson 40, Level 1

MOVEMENT AREA: Object Control

MOVEMENT: Bouncing and Catching Large Ball with 2 Hands

TEACHING GOALS:

☞ Keep eyes focused, arms outstretched, and fingers spread.

☞ Catch and bounce the ball; do not drop or pat it.

EQUIPMENT REQUIRED:

15 hoops
Cone markers
Variety of balls per station
Beanbags
Objects for obstacle course—chairs, mats, hoops, rope, box
Music; cassette/CD player
Assessment Recording Sheet

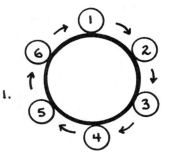

MOVEMENT STATIONS

1. ***Hoop Circle Bounce.*** Place hoops in a circle (one for each child) as shown in the diagram. Prepare a tape with music that plays in 20-second intervals, then 10-second drumbeats. The children bounce the ball in their hoop until they hear the music stop and drumbeats sound. When this happens, they move clockwise to the next hoop and start bouncing when the music starts.

2. ***Figure-8 Bounce.*** Set up 2 identical figure-8 courses using cone markers as shown. Children take turns 2-hand bouncing ball in a figure-8 pattern around cone markers.

3. ***Long Jump (for Distance).*** Create 2 identical stations as shown. Have children take turns jumping as far forward as possible from a standing position. Use beanbags to mark each jump.

105

4. ***Bouncing Ball with 2 Hands—Assessment.*** Observe and record performance. (See Book 1, *Ready-to-Use Fundamental Motor Skills & Movement Activities for Young Children,* for a recording sheet.)

5. ***Wall Roll & Receive.*** With a partner, take turns rolling the ball at the wall and receiving it.

6. ***Obstacle Course.*** Have several objects available, such as chairs, mats, hoops, bench, low box, rope, and cones. Have each team set up its own course to travel on, over, under, through, around, in, and out.

TEACHING SESSION
Lesson 41, Level 1

> **MOVEMENT AREA:** Object Control
>
> **MOVEMENT:** Catching a Large Ball (hands/body)

TEACHABLE POINTS:

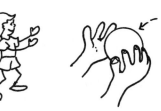

1. Keep in a balanced position with the feet comfortably spread.
2. Arms with elbows bend into the stomach.
3. Fingers spread, ready to receive the oncoming ball (ready position).
4. Hands move to receive ball
5. Ball is caught with the hands.
6. When ball meets the hands, arms bend at the elbows to cushion the impact of the ball.
7. The ball is hugged into the body
8. Eyes are focused on the ball.

EQUIPMENT REQUIRED:

1 large ball per pair
Cone markers
Firm even surface
Music; cassette/CD player
Hoops/carpet squares

> ### TEACHING GOALS:
> ☛ Keep head up and eyes focused.
> ☛ Take the ball and hug it into body.

TEACHING PROGRESSIONS

Soft Gator® balls are ideal for teaching this catching skill.

1. Demonstrate the "catching" action yourself. Emphasize having hands the right distance apart, fingers relaxed and spread, feet apart and balanced, and eyes watching the ball.

2. In pairs have the children bounce the ball to each other.

3. Have the children bounce the ball against a wall. Let it bounce once off the wall and catch it.

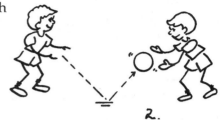

4. In pairs the children move around inside a marked area. When the music stops, they must listen as you call the number of catches they must complete.

ACTIVITIES

1. ***Wall Relay.*** Divide the class into teams of 5–6. The teams stand 2 yards (meters) from the wall. Each team member is 1 yard (meter) behind the child in front. The first team member throws the ball against the wall and catches it on the first bounce. That player then runs to the back of the line. The rest of the team moves forward and the ball is passed to the front child for the next turn.

2. ***Beat the Ball.*** Divide the class into groups of 6–7. The children are placed in a large circle with one of the team members in the middle of the circle with the ball. The middle child tosses the ball to a team member who then throws the ball around the circle back to the original thrower. The outside players must try to beat the middle player who runs around the circle and back to the middle.

MOVEMENT STATIONS
Lesson 42, Level 1

MOVEMENT AREA: Object Control
MOVEMENT: Catching a Large Ball (hands/body)

EQUIPMENT REQUIRED:

2 different colored medium-sized balls 2 balance boards
Targets such as a box, a bin, plastic container 4 wooden blocks
Large cone markers 2 short ropes
6 balls of various sizes for rolling and catching Assessment Recording Sheet
Floor tape or colored chalk for hopscotch patterns

MOVEMENT STATIONS

1. ***Catch up.*** (Use 2 different colored balls.) The children are in a large circle. The first ball is thrown around the circle. Once the first ball has been thrown to the third child, the next ball is introduced. The aim is for the second ball *not* to catch the first.

2. ***Semi-Circle Bounce.*** Have the children form a semi-circle with one child, the leader, in front. Leader bounces the ball to each child in turn and back again to the first child. Then Leader goes to the end of the semi-circle and the first child becomes the new Leader. Continue in this way.

3. ***Rolling Targets.*** For each pair in group,
set up a different target to roll the ball into,
or between, or knock over as shown. Children
take turns performing these tasks.
Encourage them to switch target tasks
with other pairs.

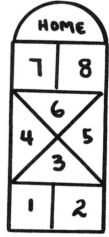
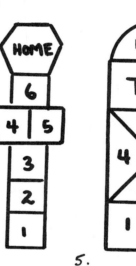

3.

4. ***Catching a Large Ball (Hands/Body)—
Assessment.*** Observe and record performance.
(See Book 1, *Ready-to-Use Fundamental Motor Skills
& Movement Activities for Young Children*, for a
recording sheet.)

5. ***Hopscotch.*** Use floor tape or colored chalk
to mark out the hopscotch patterns shown
here. Children work in 3's to do the hopscotch
activity.

5.

6. ***Balancing Challenges.*** Children work in
pairs, completing balancing challenges that
consist of 3 tasks each requiring different
landing tasks (3 attempts/task). Partner assists
in balance, if necessary.

➤ Balance and rock on balancing board; feet
apart, feet together, one foot in front of
other.

➤ Balance on one leg, if possible, for
the count of 5 on ground; on 1 dome
marker or block of wood.

➤ Walk heel to toe along a line or rope.

6.

TEACHING SESSION
Lesson 43, Level 1

MOVEMENT AREA: Object Control
MOVEMENT: Catching a Large Ball (hands only)

TEACHABLE POINTS:

1. Keep in a balanced position with the feet comfortably spread.
2. Arms, with elbows bent and fingers spread, must be ready to receive the oncoming ball (ready position).
3. Ball is caught with the hands, not the arms.
4. Hands (with fingers spread) and the arms move to meet the ball.
5. When ball meets the hands, arms bend at the elbows and cushion the impact of the ball.
6. Fingers face upward for a high ball; downward for a low ball.
7. Eyes are focused on the ball.

EQUIPMENT REQUIRED:

Firm even surface
Cone markers
Large soft balls

TEACHING GOALS:

☞ **Keep head up and eyes focused.**
☞ **Use correct hand and finger position.**

1.

TEACHING PROGRESSIONS

1. Demonstrate the correct technique for catching.

2. Ask children to throw the ball into the air, let it bounce, then catch it. Practice catching it high; practice catching it low. Emphasize keeping eyes on the ball and watching it land right in the hands.

2.

3. Now have children toss ball into the air and catch the ball before it bounces. How many catches in a row can they make? Catch the ball high. Catch it at waist level. Catch the ball low.

4. Set up children in pairs to practice bouncing and catching the ball to each other at a distance of about 3 giant steps apart.

5. In pairs have the children stand approximately 3 giant steps apart. When both children catch the tossed ball, they take a step backward; if unsuccessful, a step forward.

ACTIVITIES

1. *Semi-Circular Leader Ball.* Divide the class into 4 teams. Each team has a Leader who stands at the center of the semi-circle line as shown. On the "Go!" signal, the Leader throws the ball to the child on the left side of the semi-circle. This child receives the ball and throws it back to the Leader. This process continues until Leader has passed the ball to the last player of the semi-circle and back again to the first player. The first player then becomes the new Leader; the rest of the team move to their right and the original Leader joins the semi-circle on the far right. Each child has a turn at being Leader. The winning team is the one that completes the rotation first and sits down.

2. *Sky Ball.* Divide children into groups of 5–6 and have each group form a circle. One child stands in the middle of the circle with a ball and calls a child's name. The ball is then thrown up into the air in the circle; the child whose name was called must attempt to catch the ball on the full or first bounce. If successful, he/she becomes the middle child. Make an effort to assist children having difficulties.

Variation: Form one large circle. Stand in the center and toss the ball upward calling out one of the children's name. If he/she makes an unsuccessful catch, he/she must run around the circle, back to place.

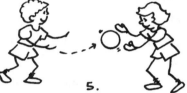

MOVEMENT STATIONS
Lesson 44, Level 1

MOVEMENT AREA: Object Control
MOVEMENT: Catching a Large Ball (hands only)

TEACHING GOALS:

☞ **Keep eyes focused.**

☞ **Use correct hand and finger position.**

EQUIPMENT REQUIRED:

Large balls
9 beanbags
6–7 hoops
Cone markers
6 throwing rings
Assessment Recording Sheet

MOVEMENT STATIONS

1. ***Ring Toss & Catch.*** Explore tossing and catching throwing rings: toss with one hand, catch with two hands; toss with one hand, catch with one hand. Toss and catch with a partner.

2. ***Wall Bounce & Catch.*** Have children stand near wall and toss ball to wall. Let it bounce, then catch. Practice catching with no bounces off wall.

3. ***Alley Races.*** Set up alleys using cone markers with start and finish lines as shown. Have children challenge a partner and race him/her over a set distance (50 yards [meters]). Challenge a different partner each time.

4. ***Catching a Large Ball (Hands Only)—Assessment.*** Observe and record performance. (See Book 1, *Ready-to-Use Fundamental Motor Skills & Movement Activities for Young Children,* for a recording sheet.)

5. ***Beanbag Shuttle Run.*** Use cones to mark off a distance of 30 feet (10 meters) and have group set up in shuttle formation as shown. First player carries beanbag across to second player and tosses it to him/her from a marked throwing line. Second player makes the catch, then runs across to toss beanbag to third player. Continue in this way.

6. ***Hoop Jumping Challenges.***

   ➤ Working in pairs, each with a hoop, place hoop on ground and practice running and landing in hoop.

   ➤ In pairs, one partner holds the hoop horizontally just off the floor. Other partner jumps into and out of the hoop. Partner gradually holds hoop higher. Then switch roles.

   ➤ Use hoop as a skipping rope and skip in place or travel in station area.

6.

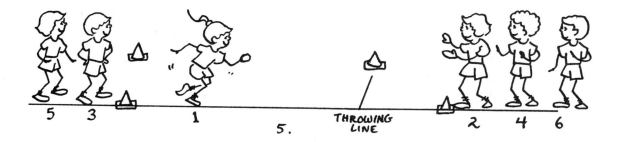

5.   THROWING LINE

5   3   1   2   4   6

MOVEMENT AREA: Object Control
MOVEMENT: Underhand Throwing

TEACHABLE POINTS:

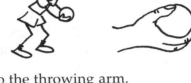

1. Stand square to the target.

2. Keep a *balanced* position with the feet comfortably spread.

3. Transfer weight from back to front foot during the throw by stepping forward with the foot opposite to the throwing arm.

4. Hold ball in the fingers.

5. Good arm extension in the wind-up; then in the throw and follow-through.

6. Release the ball in front of the body.

7. Follow-through toward the target.

8. Eyes are focused on the target.

EQUIPMENT REQUIRED:

Firm even surface
Hoops for wall targets
Beanbags
Cone markers

TEACHING GOALS:

☞ **Keep head up and eyes focused.**
☞ **Use good wind-up and follow-through.**
☞ **Use correct transfer of weight.**

TEACHING PROGRESSIONS

1. Demonstrate and explain the correct technique for the underarm throw, emphasizing the Teaching Goals.

   Use a line formation for the following activities.

2. Using a square stance with feet shoulder-width apart, have children rock back and forth moving weight from the front foot to the back foot, and back to the front.

3. As #2, but have children swing arm down and back in time with weight shifting from front to back. Count "one and two." "One" is on the way back; "and" is the pause; "two" is forward. Try to get a rhythm into the count.

" ONE - AND - TWO "

3.

4. Children stand with feet shoulder-width apart facing a wall. Ask children to step forward with the opposite foot as hand swings through. Emphasize good follow-through. Repeat several times.

5. Repeat activity 4 using a beanbag and the cue words: "down, back, swing through—step and throw up and out." Emphasize holding beanbag in fingers and stepping through with the opposite foot to throwing hand.

6. Have children throw at wall. Start with a large target; gradually decrease the size of target and increase the distance away. This emphasizes accuracy.

6.

ACTIVITY

1. ***Toss and Catch Tag.*** Pair off children. Have one child collect a ball. Then the pair find a free Home space. On signal "Toss," partners walk around the play area, tossing the ball back and forth to each other. On signal "Tag!" partner with the ball becomes IT and gives chase to the other partner. On signal "Toss!" partners once again toss the ball back and forth to each other as they walk around the play area. Continue in this way.

MOVEMENT STATIONS
Lesson 46, Level 1

MOVEMENT AREA: Object Control

MOVEMENT: Underhand Throwing

EQUIPMENT REQUIRED:

> 21 beanbags, 3 boxes of varying sizes
> Floor or wall tape
> Cone markers
> Plastic bottles or bowling pins
> Carpet squares, balance beam or bench, mini-trampoline, hoops
> Variety of balls (different sizes and shapes)
> Assessment Recording Sheet

MOVEMENT STATIONS

1. *Underhand Low Target Tossing.* Place 3 boxes of varying sizes near a wall. Use floor tape to mark off different distances as shown. Children, in pairs, take turns to underhand throw a beanbag into the box. Each one has 3 beanbags to target toss. Keep score. Switch to different target after a certain time.

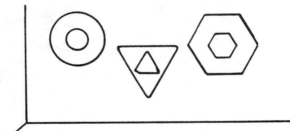

2. *Wall Target Tossing.* Create 3 different targets using wall tape as shown. Children, in pairs, take turns to underhand toss a beanbag at the target. Each thrower has 3 beanbags attempts. Switch to different targets after a certain time.

3. *Underhand Throwing—Assessment.* Observe and record performance. (See Book 1, *Ready-to-Use Fundamental Motor Skills & Movement Activities for Young Children*, for a recording sheet.)

4. ***Lawn Bowling.*** Set up pins (or plastic bottles) as shown in the diagram. Use a different pattern for each of the 3 setups.

> ➤ Children, in pairs, take turns rolling the ball toward the bowling pins (plastic bottles) to knock them down.

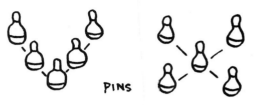

PINS

5. ***Obstacle Movement Tasks.*** Set up an obstacle course that has 6 checkpoints. At each checkpoint there is a task to be done before moving on to the next one. Children take turns completing the course. As soon as one child gets to the third checkpoint, the next child can go.

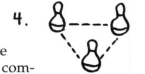

Small Balls

Checkpoints:

> ➤ Bounce ball 5 times in hoop.
> ➤ Toss and catch beanbag 5 times.
> ➤ Hop along the path from one cone marker to the next.
> ➤ Walk carefully along a balance beam; jump off and land on mat.
> ➤ Bounce 5 times on a mini-trampoline. Then jump off and land carefully on mat.
> ➤ Stand on carpet and hold a 5-second balance with your nonpreferred foot.

6. ***Underhand Throwing Free Play.*** Have a variety of balls available for partners to explore throwing back and forth to each other. Emphasize good catching, throwing form, and safety.

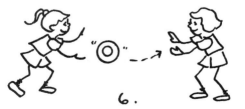

MOVEMENT AREA: Object Control
MOVEMENT: Catching a Beanbag and Other Similar Objects

TEACHABLE POINTS:

1. Keep in a balanced position.

2. Body is positioned behind the beanbag.

3. Arms reach for ball; fingers spread and curved ready to receive the oncoming beanbag.

4. Hands adjust for the size of the beanbag.

5. Arms bend at the elbows and give when the ball meets the hands.

6. Fingers face upward for a high ball; downward for a low ball.

7. Fingers wrap around not "clap," the ball.

8. Eyes are focused on the ball.

EQUIPMENT REQUIRED:

Firm even surface	Hoops
Beanbags	Carpet squares
Tennis balls; other small balls	Throwing rings
	Cone markers

TEACHING GOALS:
☞ Keep eyes focused and tracking object.
☞ Use correct hand position.
☞ Do not clap at object.

TEACHING PROGRESSIONS

1. For each object, demonstrate the "catching" action. Emphasize having hands the correct distance apart; fingers relaxed and spread; feet apart and balanced; eyes watching the object.

2. With children in pairs, have one child move into the "ready stage" for catching the beanbag. The other child, holding the beanbag, very slowly moves it toward the partner. Emphasize eyes on beanbag and getting hands in the correct position.

3. Demonstrate the correct hand position for high and low catches. Repeat activity calling out "high," "low," "middle." The beanbag is moved at this height.

4. Have the children explore throwing and catching a beanbag. Observe for correct hand, fingers, and arm positioning and control.

➤ Catch beanbag high; catch beanbag low; catch beanbag softly.

➤ Clap and catch beanbag; touch a body part before catching beanbag.

➤ Toss and catch beanbag with preferred hand; repeat with other hand.

➤ Toss and catch beanbag from one hand to the other hand.

5. Repeat #4 tasks using a tennis ball or small ball.

6. Repeat #4 tasks using a throwing ring.

7. *Challenge:* Who can make the most number of tosses and catches without dropping the object? Count fairly!

8. In pairs children underhand throw an object to each other.

9. In pairs the children stand approximately 2 yards (meters) apart. When both children catch the beanbag, they take a step backward; if unsuccessful, a step forward.

➤ Repeat using the other objects.

ACTIVITIES

1. *Toss and Catch Tag.* Pair children. Have one child collect a beanbag, tennis ball, or deck ring, and then the pair find a Home space. On signal "Toss," partners walk around the play area tossing the object back and forth to each other. On signal "Tag!" partner with the object becomes IT and gives chase to the other partner. On signal "Toss!" partners once again toss the object back and forth to each other as they walk around the play area. Continue in this way.

2. ***Beat the Catches.*** Divide the class into 4 teams. Use cone markers to mark out two fields of play opposite each other so that you can control both games as shown. Game consists of a throwing/running team and a fielding team. The first runner must underhand throw the beanbag as far as possible into the field of play. The fielding team must run to the beanbag, quickly form a circle, and toss the beanbag to each player in the circle. In this time, the runner tries to complete as many circuits of the running area before the circle toss is completed. He/she scores 1 point for passing each cone marker as shown in the diagram. Each member of the team has a turn; then the two teams exchange positions.

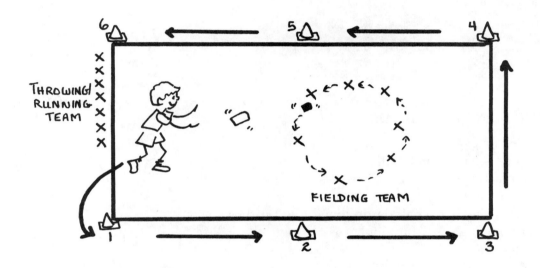

MOVEMENT STATIONS
Lesson 48, Level 1

MOVEMENT AREA: Object Control

MOVEMENT: Catching a Beanbag

TEACHING GOALS:
- ☞ Keep eyes focused and tracking object.
- ☞ Use correct hand position.
- ☞ Do not clap at object.

EQUIPMENT REQUIRED:

> Beanbags
> Tennis balls, small balls
> 6 plastic bottles, 2 long benches
> Cone markers
> Hoops, bench, chair, large cones, low hurdles
> 1 large mat, medium high box horse
> Floor tape
> Assessment Recording Sheet

MOVEMENT STATIONS

1. ***Individual Catching Challenges.*** Children use different objects to catch such items as beanbags, tennis balls, and small balls to do the following tasks. Repeat 5 times.

   - ➤ Throw and catch with two hands (beanbag).
   - ➤ Bounce and catch with two hands (large ball).
   - ➤ Throw and catch with one hand (beanbag).
   - ➤ Toss, bounce, and catch tennis ball with favorite hand.
   - ➤ Toss small ball to wall, let bounce once, and catch.

2. ***Make the Catch.*** Mark off 3 sets of catching distances as shown. Have children work in pairs using a beanbag. Start at the shortest catching distance line. When each partner has made 3 successful catches, then the pair can move to the second catching distance line. Then the third.

   - ➤ When the task is completed, find a new partner and begin again.

3. ***Pin Knock-Away.*** Using a small ball (tennis ball), underhand throw at 3 pin targets (plastic bottles) spaced apart on a bench to knock them off the bench. Have 2 different throwing lines as shown. If possible, set up two targets to maximize participation. Each child takes two throws and counts the number of pins knocked over. This is his/her score.

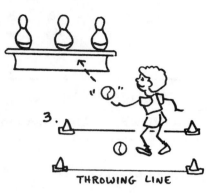

4. ***Catching—Assessment.*** Observe and record performance in catching a small object. (See Book 1, *Ready-to-Use Fundamental Motor Skills & Movement Activities for Young Children*, for a recording sheet.)

5. ***Jumping Jacks.*** Children explore jumping off a medium high box horse onto a large mat. Emphasize bending at the knees, pushing off, and keeping head up.

   ➤ Jump upward spreading arms and legs, landing carefully with bent knees, and feet shoulder-width apart.

   ➤ Jump backwards.

   ➤ Jump as far as you can.

   ➤ Jump quarter turn.

   ➤ Jump half turn.

   ➤ Make up your own safe jump.

6. ***Obstacle Course Run.*** Use several obstacles to create a course that children must run through. See the illustration for a sample obstacle course.

MOVEMENT AREA: Object Control
MOVEMENT: One-Handed Striking

FEET POSITION

TEACHABLE POINTS:

1. Keep in balance with feet comfortably apart.
2. Keep knees bent through the movement.
3. Take a side-on position when hitting.
4. Transfer the weight forward by stepping into the swing.
5. Take a big back-swing.
6. Follow-through in the intended direction.
7. Keep eyes focused and head steady throughout the movement.

EQUIPMENT REQUIRED:

Firm even surface
Small wooden bat per
child
Cone markers or T-ball
stands
1 balloon per child

TEACHING GOALS:

☛ Use side-on body position.
☛ Take a big back-swing.
☛ Follow-through in direction of target.

TEACHING PROGRESSIONS

2.

1. Demonstrate the stance and swinging action.

2. Have children get into the side-on stance. Move weight from front foot to back foot and back again on your signal.

3. Now add arm swing that starts with a small back swing and slowly increases. Make the action rhythmical, counting "one and two." "One" is the back swing; "and" is the pause at the top; and "two" is the downswing and follow-through.

"ONE   AND   TWO"

4. Have child hit a balloon to him- or herself using front and back of hand.

5. Hit a balloon back and forth with a partner.

6. Repeat #5 and #6 using a small wooden bat. Tell children to hold the bat by "shaking hands" with it.

ACTIVITIES

1. ***Partner Balloon Keep-Up.*** Cooperating together, partners try to keep the balloon in the air as long as possible before it touches the ground. Count the number of hits made before balloon touches ground, then start counting all over again!

2. ***Partner Balloon Bat Keep-Up.*** Play as for #1 but use wooden bats.

3. ***T-Ball Play.*** Each child has a large soft ball positioned on a cone marker or a "tee." Child stands side on to the ball and strikes the ball with an open hand toward a wall. Tee should be positioned about 3 giant steps from wall.

MOVEMENT STATIONS
Lesson 50, Level 1

MOVEMENT AREA: Object Control
MOVEMENT: One-Handed Striking

EQUIPMENT REQUIRED:

> 2 suspended balls in stockings
> 6–7 balloons and wooden bats
> 3 large cone markers
> 3 large balls
> 2 long jump ropes
> 2 boxes, 2 hoops, 2 bins
> Assessment Recording Sheet

MOVEMENT STATIONS

1. *Totem Tennis.* Children take turns striking a suspended ball in a stocking with an open hand.

   > ➤ If possible, set up two totem tennis areas.

2. *Bat the Balloon.* Each child has a balloon and a wooden bat in a Home space. Practice striking the balloon with the bat.

3. *T-Ball Strike.* Children, in pairs, take turns striking—with the open hand—a ball positioned on a large cone marker as shown. Suggest that ball be hit toward a wall so that it can be easily retrieved.

126

4. ***Single-Hand Striking—
Assessment.*** Observe and record
performance in single-handed
striking of an object. (See Book 1,
*Ready-to-Use Fundamental Motor Skills
& Movement Activities for Young
Children,* for a recording sheet.)

5. ***Underarm Target Throwing.***
Underarm throw into boxes and
hoops placed at different distances.
Use beanbags to throw into hoops;
use small balls (tennis balls) to throw
into boxes.

6. ***Long Rope Jumping.*** Have two
Turners and the rest as Jumpers.
Switch turner after awhile, or have
parent helper as the Turner. Jumpers
perform the following tasks:

   ➤ Start in the center and try to jump
   the turning rope as long as you
   can.

   ➤ Run in front door (at the top of the
   rope turn as the rope turns toward
   you); jump 5 times; run out.

   ➤ Create your own long rope jump stunt!

> **MOVEMENT AREA:** Object Control
>
> **MOVEMENT:** Two-Handed Striking

TEACHABLE POINTS:

1. Eyes are focused on the ball, head steady throughout movement.
2. Knees are bent through the movement.
3. Body is moved to the side-on position.
4. Weight is transferred forward by stepping into the swing.
5. Good shoulder turn occurs in back swing.
6. Nonpreferred arm remains relatively straight in back swing.
7. Hit starts with the hips rotating toward the target.
8. Good extension in the follow-through is evident.

EQUIPMENT REQUIRED:

For each group of 3: a batting tee or large cone, a medium-sized ball, children's bat, beanbag marker, base
Rolled-up newspaper

> **TEACHING GOALS:**
> - ☛ Use side-on body position.
> - ☛ Step into the swing.
> - ☛ Keep eyes focused on the ball.
> - ☛ Follow-through around the body in line of direction.

TEACHING PROGRESSIONS

1. Demonstrate the stance, hand positioning, and swinging action. Then have children get into a side-on stance and shift weight from front foot to back foot and back again to front foot on your signal.

2. Now add arm swing that starts with a small action backward, then slowly increases as the arms swing through around the body. Make the action rhythmical by counting "one and two." "One" is the back swing; "and" is the pause at the top; and "two" is the swing through.

3. Practice this action with a small children's bat or rolled-up newspaper.

4. Form groups of 3. Each group has a medium-sized ball, bat, and large cone marker or T-ball equipment. Children take turns at striking the ball off the tee. The batter attempts to bat the ball 3 times off the tee; other two children are the fielders.

5. Repeat #4 using a smaller ball.

ACTIVITIES

1. ***Batting Challenge.*** Children work in groups of 3. Each child gets 3 hits off a batting tee or high cone to see how far he/she can hit the ball. Two fielders use beanbags to mark the distance. Ensure each group has its own area and will not interfere with other groups.

2. ***Bat and Run.*** Children in groups of 4: one batter, one catcher, and two fielders. Set up safe areas for each group play as shown in the diagram. Batter hits the ball off the tee, then runs to the base and back, before fielding team can field the ball and pass it to the catcher who is positioned just behind the tee box as shown. Each batter gets 3 hits and keeps his/her score.

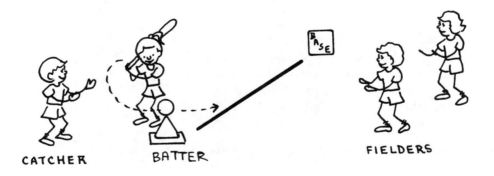

MOVEMENT STATIONS
Lesson 52, Level 1

MOVEMENT AREA: Object Control

MOVEMENT: Two-Handed Striking (stationary ball)

TEACHING GOALS:
- ☛ Use side-on body position.
- ☛ Step into the swing.
- ☛ Keep eyes focused on the ball.
- ☛ Follow-through around the body in line of direction.

EQUIPMENT REQUIRED:

5 medium-sized balls

2 large cone markers or 2
   T-ball sets

2 modified cricket bats

2 long jump ropes

6–7 balance feathers

Assessment Recording Sheet

MOVEMENT STATIONS

1. **Tee-Ball.** For each group of 3, set up a medium-sized ball on a large cone marker or proper T-ball equipment. One player bats; others field the ball. Children take turns striking the ball with a bat toward an open field. After 3 bats, a new batter takes a turn.

2. **Roll and Strike.** Children are in 3's and find a Home space. Each threesome has a medium-sized ball and a modified cricket bat. One player is the striker; the second, the roller; and the third, the fielder. (See diagram.) Players change roles after striker has hit the rolled ball 3 times.

3. **Bull in the Ring.** Group forms a circle with one player, the Bull, in the middle. Group tries to hit Bull below the waist with a soft, medium-sized ball. Ball can be rolled, bounced, or thrown. Bull tries to last for 5 attempts, then another player comes in the ring.

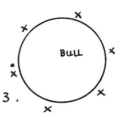

4. ***Two-Handed Striking—Assessment.*** Observe and record performance in two-handed striking of a stationary ball. (See Book 1, *Ready-to-Use Fundamental Motor Skills & Movement Activities for Young Children*, for a recording sheet.)

5. ***Balancing Feathers.*** Children explore balancing a peacock feather on different body parts: open palm, back of hand, different fingers, elbow shoulder, chin . . . .

5.

6. ***Long Rope Jumping.*** In groups of 3 have two rope turners and a jumper. (Parents could be turners!) Switch turners after jumper completes the following tasks:

➤ Start in the center and try to jump the turning rope 5 times. Then run out front door.

➤ Run in front door (at the top of the rope turn as the rope turns toward you); jump 5 times; run out.

➤ Run in front door, jump, and turn in place.

➤ Run in front door; jump as long as you can!

➤ Create your own long rope jump stunt!

6.

MOVEMENT AREA: Object Control
MOVEMENT: Kicking a Large Ball (distance)

TEACHABLE POINTS:

INSTEP OF FOOT

1. Keep in balance.
2. Nonkicking foot placed near and to side of the ball.
3. Knee is bent on back swing (at least 90 degrees).
4. Kick with the instep (shoelaces) and contact at bottom of ball.
5. Arm opposite the kicking leg is away from the body assisting balance.
6. Follow through toward the target.
7. Eyes are focused on the ball.

EQUIPMENT REQUIRED:

Firm even surface

Marker cones or beanbags as markers

Large round playground or soccer balls

TEACHING GOALS:
- Keep head up and eyes focused.
- Place nonkicking foot near and to side of the ball.
- Bend knee on back swing (at least 90 degrees).
- Use sole of the foot to control the ball.

TEACHING PROGRESSIONS

1. Demonstrate the kicking action using a ball and emphasize the teaching goals. Demonstrate the kicking leg movement and explain the requirements: lift the kicking leg and hold the foot of the kicking leg behind your buttocks and then let it go to swing through to kick the ball. Keep the toes pointed as contact is made with the instep (shoelaces) of the kicking foot. Call "Hold it and let it go."

1.

2. Have children hold a one-legged balance. Then ask them to extend the kicking leg back, hold it, and let it swing through to kick an imaginary ball. Arm opposite the kicking leg is forward for balance.

3. Repeat, but have children step to an imaginary ball and swing kicking leg through. Emphasize that the kicking foot finishes by pointing toward the target on the follow-through. Observe arm position to see if it assists in balance. Have children repeat this kicking movement several times.

4. Again show children that contact with ball is made on the shoelaces (instep). Have children kick a stationary balloon or beachball near a wall. Observe that the kicking foot is swung forward and underneath the ball and that eyes stay focused on the ball.

5. Have children continue to kick toward the wall using a soccer ball or playground ball. Gradually step farther away from the wall to increase the kicking distance.

   ➤ Encourage them to stop or "trap" the rebounding ball by using a "sole-of-the heel trap." Demonstrate first, then ask them to stand near the ball and place foot on top of the ball, with the heel closer to the ground. Do this with the other foot.

   ➤ In pairs, have one partner roll the ball; the other partner traps the ball with the sole of the foot; then reverse roles.

6. Free kick with a partner. Gradually increase the distance. Observe kicking technique and trapping the ball.

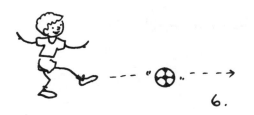

ACTIVITIES

1. *Mark the Kick.* Place the children in pairs with one ball. Give each child a marker. From a marked kick line, the children take turns kicking as far as they can. The partner marks the kick. The marker is only moved if the previous effort has been passed.

2. *Cumulative Kicking.* Use the end zones of a large marked field, or use cones to mark two end zones up to 50 yards (meters) apart. Place children into groups of 3. Each group has one ball and a marker. The aim of this game is for each member of the group to take turns at kicking the ball from where the previous kick stopped. The teams count how many kicks it takes to cross the field and return to the start.

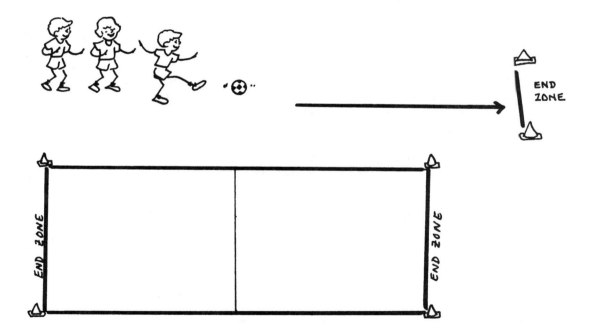

MOVEMENT STATIONS
Lesson 54, Level 1

MOVEMENT AREA: Object Control

MOVEMENT: Kicking a Large Ball (distance)

TEACHING GOALS:
- ☛ Keep head up and eyes focused.
- ☛ Place nonkicking foot near and to side of the ball.
- ☛ Bend knee on back swing (at least 90 degrees).
- ☛ Use sole of the foot to trap and control the ball.

EQUIPMENT REQUIRED:

9 playground balls
9 large cone markers
6 large balls; 6 beanbags; 6 small balls
6 lummi sticks; 3 deck rings; and 2 cone
   markers per pair
Tape machine and prepared tape
Assessment Recording Sheet

Targets such as, wall targets, hoops, plastic cones or bottles

Movement Stations

1. *Wall Kick and Trap.* Children pair off and face a wall. One partner kicks a playground ball at wall. Other partner tries to trap the ball with the sole of the foot as ball rebounds off the wall. Then this partner kicks the ball to the wall for other partner to trap. Continue in this way.

2. *Kicking Golf.* Set up 3 fairways with a "tee-off" and a "green" for each as shown. Have children pair off. Partners kick in turn, counting the number of kicks taken to kick the ball through the hole.

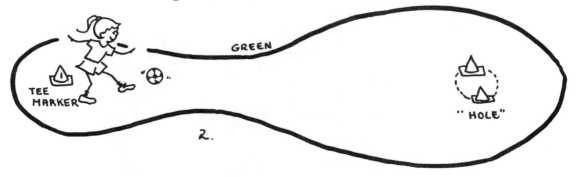

135

3. ***Ringette Play.*** Children pair off and use a lummi stick (12-inch [30-cm] piece of wooden doweling, 1-inch diameter) and deck ring.

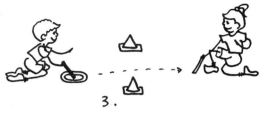

➤ Pass a deck ring back and forth to each other.

➤ Pass a deck ring between cone markers.

➤ Send the deck ring to knock over the cone marker.

4. ***Kicking for Distance—Assessment.*** Observe and record performance in kicking of a stationary ball. (See Book 1, *Ready-to-Use Fundamental Motor Skills & Movement Activities for Young Children,* for a recording sheet.)

5. ***Throwing Circuit.*** Create a throwing circuit that consists of 3 stations each requiring different throwing tasks, 3 attempts per task. Children work in pairs and take turns throwing and retrieving.

➤ Rolling a large ball into a box placed on the ground with the opening toward the thrower.

➤ Throwing a beanbag at a wall target or into a low target such as a hoop.

➤ Throwing a small ball at targets, such as plastic cones or bottles, to knock them over.

6. ***Musical Run.*** Make up a tape with music intervals, signals breaks, and relax or rest breaks that will last for 4 minutes. Children run around a marked area in time with the music. When the music stops, children stop and do the signal break such as:"Dead Bug," "Periscope," "Pencil Stretch, "Bounce in Place." On the "Relax" signal, children rest by hook sitting. Include several rest breaks so that children can go the distance!

MOVEMENT AREA: Object Control
MOVEMENT: Kicking a Large Ball (accuracy)

TEACHABLE POINTS:

1. Nonkicking foot is placed near and to side of the ball.
2. Kicking foot is turned so that the inside of the foot faces the ball.
3. Kicking leg is bent on the back swing.
4. Kicking foot remains firm at the ankle while kicking.
5. To assist balance, the opposite arm moves forward as kicking leg moves back.
6. Ball is contacted on the inside of the kicking foot.
7. Arm on same side as kicking leg swings away from the body assisting balance, as kicking leg swings through.
8. Follow-through toward the target.
9. Eyes stay focused on the ball during the movement.

EQUIPMENT REQUIRED:

Firm even surface
Cone markers
Large round playground balls

TEACHING GOALS:
- Keep head up and eyes focused.
- Follow-through toward target.
- Kick with the instep.
- Use inside of the foot to trap ball.

TEACHING PROGRESSIONS

1. Revise and demonstrate how to stop and control the ball:
   - ➤ sole-of-the-foot trap
   - ➤ inside-of-the-foot trap

   Have children practice trapping the ball in pairs. One partner rolls the ball toward other partner, who traps ball with either sole of the foot or inside of the foot. Encourage children to use either foot to make the trap.

2. Demonstrate the kicking action of pushing the ball with the inside of the foot. Have children practice this using either foot.

3. Now demonstrate stepping to an imaginary ball and swing kicking leg through, turning the kicking foot out to the side. Children practice this movement by kicking a stationary ball toward a wall. Use the inside-of-the-foot trap to stop and control the ball as it rebounds off the wall.

ACTIVITIES

1. *Kicking Relay.* Each group sets up in shuttle formation with opposite sides spaced 10 yards (10 meters) apart as shown. Use the inside-of-the-foot trap to travel the ball across to the opposite side.

2. *Triangle Pass.* Place the children into groups of 3. Use cones, spaced 10 yards (10 meters) apart to mark out this triangular area. Children pass around the triangle using the inside-of-the-foot kick and trap. *Variation:* Kick-pass ball around a square in groups of 4.

MOVEMENT STATIONS
Lesson 56, Level 1

MOVEMENT AREA: Object Control
MOVEMENT: Kicking a Large Ball

TEACHING GOALS:
- ☞ Keep eyes focused.
- ☞ Kick with the instep.
- ☞ Follow-through in direction of target.
- ☞ Use the inside of the foot to trap the ball.

EQUIPMENT REQUIRED:

Numbered cone markers
3 soccer balls
3 wall goals marked off with floor tape
3 plastic bottles or skittles
4 kicking balls
Assessment Recording Sheets

Dome markers
3 catchballs
3 hoops
3 large cone markers
3 beanbags
Several small cone markers

MOVEMENT STATIONS

1. *Spot Kicking.* Use cones or rope circles to designate 6 kicking spots around a goal area as shown. Each spot is worth so many points according to difficulty as indicated on cone. Children pair off, with one partner being the kicker; the other, the retriever. Kicker kicks from each spot to send ball through goal area; then the two change roles.

2. *Goal Kicking.* Use floor tape to mark out 10-foot (3-meter) square goals on a wall; or set up soccer goals as shown, one goal for every two kickers. Children are paired off and take turns trying to kick ball into goal. Mark off 3 kicking distances with dome markers and have kickers make 2 kicks from each marker.

3. ***Three-Pin Kick.*** For each group of 3, set up 3 plastic bottles or skittles (pins) near a wall in a triangular pattern as shown. Children take turns using the inside-of-the-foot kick to try to knock over the pins. Mark off 3 kicking distances as shown. Each kicker gets 2 kicks. Keep score.

4. ***Kicking for Accuracy—Assessment.*** Observe and record performance in kicking a stationary ball. (See Book 1, *Ready-to-Use Fundamental Motor Skills & Movement Activities for Young Children*, for a recording sheet.)

5. ***Catchball™ Play.*** Children pair off and practice throwing and catching using a catch-ball (which has 6 handles, of which 4 handles have a score on the end). Children can keep track of score.

6. ***Mini-Throw Golf.*** Set up 3 "fairways" using hoops as holes, marker cones as tees, and beanbags as the golf balls. Children underhand throw around the course and add their scores.

TEACHING SESSION
Lesson 57, Level 1

MOVEMENT AREA: Locomotion
MOVEMENT: Dodging

TEACHABLE POINTS:

1. When dodging, push off with the outside of the foot.

2. Keep eyes focused in which direction you want to move.

3. Keep head up and move into open spaces.

4. Bend at the knees to keep the body lowered in order to change direction quickly.

5. Use arms to help propel yourself into a new direction.

6. Move only as quickly as you can control, without falling over.

EQUIPMENT REQUIRED:

Marked courts are useful, as the lines provide visual guidelines for the children
Cone markers
Music with a steady 4/4 beat, CD or tape player

TEACHING GOALS:
☛ **Promote quick change of direction.**
☛ **Promote correct foot action.**

TEACHING PROGRESSIONS

1. Demonstrate the dodging action. Emphasize the teaching goals.

2. Have the children walk in a large marked area. On whistle blast signal, have the children make a quick change of direction. Slowly increase the speed of execution.

2.

3. Scatter markers throughout the play area. Have children walk up to a marker, then make a quick change of direction to either the right or left of the marker.

3.

141

ACTIVITIES

1. ***Artful Dodger.*** Find a partner and stand one behind the other. On the "Go" signal or when the music starts, the front partner, the Dodger walks in general space making quick changes of direction. The other partner, the Shadow, tries to follow as closely as possible to the Dodger without touching him/her. On the "whistle blast," both partners come to a jump stop and freeze. If Shadow can take one step forward and touch the Dodger, then the two partners change roles. Continue in this way. Use other locomotor movements such as running, slide stepping, and power-walking. *Variation:* Use music to start and stop action.

2. ***Heads or Tails.*** Children pair off and stand in a Home space. One partner is a "Head" with favorite hand on his/her head and the other hand free; other partner is a "Tail" with favorite hand on bottom, and the other hand free. On signal "Heads or Tails," children use free hand to tag an opposite player: "Heads" will tag "Tails"; "Tails" will tag "Heads." If tagged, you are transformed into the same mode as the player who tagged you. Continue in this way. On "Iceberg," everyone stops immediately. Count the number of "Heads" and "Tails."

3. ***Zigzag Relay.*** Place 5 cones 3 yards (meters) apart as shown. Split the class into teams of 6 and have each team stand in file formation behind a starting line, facing a set of cone markers. On signal "Zigzag!" each player in turn runs as quickly as possible through the zigzag course to the end cone, then returns by running straight back to his/her team to position behind the last team member. Continue until everyone has had a turn. Which team will be the first team in cross-leg sit position? *Note:* If there is an odd number of players on a team, have one member go twice.

MOVEMENT AREA: Locomotion
MOVEMENT: Dodging

TEACHING GOALS:
- ☞ Promote quick change of direction.
- ☞ Promote correct foot action.

EQUIPMENT REQUIRED:

Cone markers
Objects for obstacle course such as cones, mats, hoops, chairs, etc.
6 flags
3 beanbags
3 deck rings
3 elastic bands
2 balance benches
Assessment Recording Sheet

MOVEMENT STATIONS

1. ***Obstacle Dodge Course.*** Using a variety of obstacles as shown, set up a course for children to dodge in and out. As soon as one runner has reached halfway, the next runner can go.

2. ***Steal the Tail Tag.*** Each player has a tail tucked in at the back of the shorts except for one player who is IT. If IT successfully snatches a tail, then that player becomes the new IT. Continue to play in this way.

3. ***Beanbag Basketball.*** Children pair off and find a free space. One partner has a throwing ring, "the hoop"; the other partner has a beanbag critter, "the basketball." Partners stand 3 giant steps apart, facing each other. The shooter underhand-throws beanbag at hoop. The partner with hoop tracks the beanbag to make the catch. Switch roles after every 3 throws.

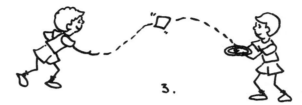

4. ***Dodging—Assessment.*** Observe and record performance of dodging ability. (See Book 1, *Ready-to-Use Fundamental Motor Skills & Movement Activities for Young Children*, for a recording sheet.)

5. ***Elastic Jumping Station.*** For each group of 2 or 3, set up elastic bands between two chairs as shown. Children explore a variety of ways of jumping over, in, and out of bands.

6. ***Balance Bench Challenges.*** Put the following tasks on large posterboard or whiteboard:

➤ Walk forward along the bench to the other end.
➤ Walk backward along the bench to the start.
➤ Walk heel–toe along the bench.
➤ Run carefully forward along the bench and jump off, gently landing.
➤ Carefully jump your way along the bench.
➤ Explore other ways of moving along the bench.

TEACHING SESSION
Lesson 59, Level 1

MOVEMENT AREA: Object Control
MOVEMENT: Overhand Throw (introduction)

TEACHABLE POINTS:

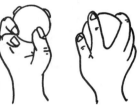

1. Stand side-on to target with head and eyes facing target.
2. Keep in a balanced position with the feet comfortably apart.
3. Hold ball in the fingers; wrist is cocked and nonthrowing arm points at the target.
4. Move throwing arm in a downward and backward arc.
5. Transfer weight onto back foot.
6. Bend elbow as throwing hand moves behind head.
7. Step front foot forward as weight transfers from back foot.
8. Rotate forward hips, then shoulders.
9. Forearm and hand lag behind upper arm.
10. Follow-through down and across the body.

EQUIPMENT REQUIRED:

Firm even surface
1 beanbag per child
Cone markers
5 skittles per group

TEACHING GOALS:
- ☛ Keep head up and eyes focused.
- ☛ Transfer weight.
- ☛ Use correct arm action.

TEACHING PROGRESSIONS

1. Demonstrate the overhand throw, emphasizing the teaching goals.

2. Children stand side on to a wall, feet closer together, and practice stepping to front foot. Use cue words: "one" is the lift (weight is shifted to the back foot); "and" is the pause; and "two" is the step with nonthrowing foot toward the target.

"ONE"   2.   "TWO"

3. Now have children hold a beanbag with the correct grip (in their fingers) and stand side on to the target. Nonthrowing arm points at the target. Practice overhand action without actually throwing beanbag using the cues: "Down as far as you can; back as far as you can; bend and throw."

➤ Practice the action first without a beanbag in your hand.

➤ Then practice overhand throwing the beanbag at the wall.

4. In pairs have the children overhand throw back and forth. Start close and gradually move farther away as the children begin to master the task. Be aware of catching ability. (If a child is experiencing difficulty in catching the ball, have the partner roll it back or hand it to him/her.).

ACTIVITIES

1. **Skittle Throw Race.** Divide the class into 4 groups and place each group around a large square with 5 skittles in the middle of each square. Each member has a beanbag. On "Go," the children attempt to knock down all their skittles before the other groups.

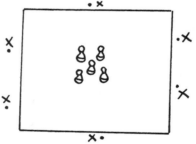

2. **Cumulative Throwing.** Use the end zones of a large marked field, or use cones to mark two end zones up to 50 yards (meters) apart. Place children into groups of 3. Each group has one ball. The aim of this game is for each member of the group to have turns at throwing the ball from where the previous throw landed. Each group counts how many throws it takes to cross the field.

MOVEMENT STATIONS
Lesson 60, Level 1

MOVEMENT AREA: Object Control
MOVEMENT: Overhand Throw (introduction)

TEACHING GOALS:
- ☞ Keep head up and eyes focused.
- ☞ Transfer weight.
- ☞ Use correct arm action.

EQUIPMENT REQUIRED:

Small balls, beanbags, markers, skittles
Music; cassette/CD player
2 hoops with ropes and weights
2 mini footballs
Fling-It™ Nets
6 flags
Floor tape
Partner Balance Cards (Lesson 32, Level 1)
Assessment Recording Sheet

MOVEMENT STATIONS

1. *Overhand Target Throw.* Set up 3 different wall targets as shown and three different throwing distances marked off using floor tape. Children pair off with each pair facing a target. Taking turns, partners overhand throw beanbags at targets. Each partner has 3 turns. Keep score.

2. *Hoop Target Throw.* Suspend a hoop from a basketball framework or other suitable fixture. Secure it with a rope and weight to the floor as shown. Children work in 3's and take turns throwing a small football through the hoop. If possible, set up two identical hoop targets. Use cone markers to set the throwing distances.

   Variation: Suspend a hoop in a grooved cone or between two chairs.

147

3. ***Partner Balances.*** (See Lesson 32, Level 1.) Enlarge these onto cards and have the children work in pairs to complete the balancing positions. *Challenge:* Try the Buddy Walker or Gym Skis.

3.

4. ***Overhand Throw—Assessment.*** Observe and record performance overhand throwing. (See Book 1, *Ready-to-Use Fundamental Motor Skills & Movement Activities for Young Children*, for a recording sheet.)

4.

5. ***Fling-It™ Play.*** Pair off with each pair having a Fling-It™ Net and ball. Find a Home space. Pairs work cooperatively to communicate and coordinate sending and receiving the ball in their net.

6. ***Tail Snatch.*** Each player in group has a tail tucked in the back of the shorts or a flag belt with two flags. Partners pair off and find a Home space, facing each other in the "Iceberg!" position with hands resting on the knees. On signal "Tail Snatch," partners try to grab each other's tails without any body contact. Play best 2 out of 3 tries to win; then challenge another player. Continue in this way.

6.

FOUNDATION MOVEMENT REVISION
Lesson 1, Level 2

ORGANIZATION: Identify the play area by setting up cone markers around the perimeter. As a general rule, space cone markers every 10 feet (3 meters) apart, using about 15 markers for a play area that is 60´ by 30´ (20m by 10m). Try to use different polygonal figures such as square, rectangle, pentagon, hexagon, octagon. Throwing rings or beanbags could be used as Home markers if these are available.

EQUIPMENT REQUIRED:

> 15 cone markers
> Equipment or objects in teaching environment
> 1 throwing ring (or beanbag) per child

WARMING-UP/FITNESS SIGNALS

1. Get a ring, carry it to a Home space, and place it gently on the ground. This is your Home and the ring marks the spot. Check that you cannot touch anyone or anything in your Home space. This is your first signal, "Home!" (Show hand signal.) Whenever you hear this signal, find yourself a free space and "Stand Tall" in it.

2. Now leave your "home" and touch 6 different cone markers, with 6 different body parts. Can you remember where your Home (ring) is? Return to your home, and stand tall, crossing left arms/legs over left. Go!

3. This position is called the "Corkscrew." Sink your corkscrew to the floor. Now you are in "Cross-leg Sit" position. Can you return to standing tall without undoing your corkscrew?

4. I am going to give you 3 important rules to remember:

   ➤ Don't hurt yourself!
   ➤ Don't hurt anyone else!
   ➤ Don't hurt the equipment!

5. Let's play the game "Touch!"

   ➤ Touch a cone marker on a sideline with your right elbow.

   ➤ Touch a cone on an endline with your left knee.

   ➤ Run to the other sideline and touch the cone with your right shoulder.

   ➤ Run to the opposite endline and touch a cone with your left foot.

   ➤ Go Home and corkscrew with right arms and legs crossed.

   ➤ Sink your corkscrew to cross-leg sit. Now try to stand tall.

5.

ENDLINE

6. Show me what you will do when I give you the signal "Scrambled Eggs!—Power Walking! (Show hand signal.) Move in and out of each other, without "touching" anyone. Walk vigorously, pumping with your arms and using quick changes of direction.

6.

7. *Iceberg!* (Hand signal.) Remember this is your stopping signal! When you hear this word, stop immediately by "jump stopping." Land on your feet at the same time, knees bent, hands out for balance. Let's practice this.

8. *"Scrambled Eggs!—Walking!" "Iceberg!"*

   ➤ "Scrambled Eggs—Happy Walker!" (Walk quickly pumping with your arms. "Iceberg!" "One!" Stand on one foot and hold your balance.

   ➤ "Scrambled Eggs—Tip-toe Walker!" "Iceberg!" "Three!" Touch the floor with any three body parts.

   ➤ "Scrambled Eggs—Marching!" "Iceberg!" "Five!" Touch the floor with any five body parts.

7.

MOTOR MEMORY

1. Copy hand movements: Opening and Closing; Finger isolations: Shaking; Waving; Finger snapping; Hand clapping.

2. Copy touching movements to different body parts.

   ➤ Touch your right elbow to your left knee.

   ➤ Touch your left hand to your right ankle.

   ➤ Touch your elbows together.

   ➤ Touch the bottom of your feet together.

   ➤ Touch your right knee to your forehead.

3. Play "Simon Says."

SNAP!

CLAP!

WAVE!

1.

2.

SPATIAL AWARENESS

1. In standing tall position, feet shoulder-width apart, face this wall of the room (or boundary line of play area). You are now *square on*. Show me how you can be *side on* to this wall. Show me another way to be side on to this wall. Position so that your back is to the wall. Square up again. Turn to face a corner. You are now in *diagonal* stance.

2. Using objects in a room and each other, have children move to music. When the music stops, ask children to position in relation to an object or piece of equipment or another person: e.g., stand *square on* to something; position *side on* to the chair; stand *face-to-face* with someone; sit *back-to-back* with a partner.

BODY AWARENESS

1. Listen carefully. I will ask you to move only one certain body part at a time.

   ➤ Gently turn your head from side to side.

   ➤ Gently lift one knee up and touch it with the opposite hand; then lift up the other knee and touch it your opposite elbow.

   ➤ Clap your hands.

   ➤ Blink your eyes.

   ➤ Snap your fingers.

2. Now touch a body part to objects in the environment: knee to table; elbow to rope; head to wall; shoulder to basketball, etc.

CLOSING ACTIVITIES

1. *Good Morning Stretch!* Pretend you are still in your bed and just beginning to wake up. Lying on your tummy, stretch as wide as possible. Do this slowly. Now stretch like a pencil. Yawn! Smile a "good morning" smile!

2. *Shrugs!* Stand tall. Shrug your shoulders as if you are saying "I don't know!"

3. *Nodding Heads.* Stand tall. Gently and slowly nod your head as if you are saying "Yes!" Now gently nod your head as if you are saying "No!"

4. *Legend(s) of the Day!*

TEACHING SESSION
Lesson 2, Level 2

> **MOVEMENT AREA:** Locomotion
>
> **MOVEMENT:** Running

TEACHABLE POINTS:

1. Land on the forefoot when sprinting.
2. Plant foot along a narrow pathway.
3. Knees are up high at the front; feet are close to the buttocks at the back of the action.
4. Arms are bent at 90 degrees and work in opposition to legs.
5. Arms move back and forth in a straight line.
6. Hands are held in a relaxed position (as if holding an egg in each hand).
7. Head and upper body are stable and eyes look straight ahead.

EQUIPMENT REQUIRED:

Marked courts are useful, as the lines provide visual guidelines for the children.
Music helps establish a sense of rhythm
Cone markers
Hoops
Beanbags
Tennis balls

> ### TEACHING GOALS:
> - Use correct body alignment.
> - Promote correct knee action.
> - Promote correct arm action.

FAST – SLOW

TEACHING PROGRESSIONS

1. Have children copy you running in slow motion in a straight line along a line completing the knee lift. Use correct arm action and lift leg behind the body. Tell children to keep relaxed with head held up and looking forward. Repeat jogging along the line, slowly increasing the speed.

2. As children master this, slowly build the speed, making sure that the action is completed along a line or piece of string on the ground. As the speed increases, so should the emphasis on starting to lean slightly forward and landing on the forefoot. Have the children change to different paces at your call.

3. Have children hold an object, such as a beanbag or small weights, in each hand. Observe hand/arm movement as children jog along a line.

4. To increase stride length, place 10 markers at even intervals and have the children place a foot at each marker while running. Gradually increase the distance between the markers. (Do not increase the distance to the point where the action looks uncomfortable.)

3.

4.

ACTIVITIES

1. *Mr. Wolf.* The teacher or child is nominated as Mr. Wolf. The class follow behind and when Mr. Wolf raises a hand, the class asks, "What's the time, Mr. Wolf?" Mr. Wolf can answer with "Hopping time" or some other movement, in which case the children perform this movement until Mr. Wolf stops. When Mr. Wolf says, "Dinner Time," this is the signal for the children to run back to the safety zone before being tagged. Select a new Mr. Wolf each time. Stress safety when turning and running.

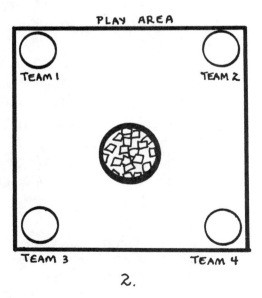

1.

2. *Robbers.* Split the class into teams of 4–5. Place enough beanbags in a center hoop for each team to have one beanbag per person. The teams each have its own hoop placed in the playing area as shown. On "Go," one team member must run to the center hoop and take only one beanbag back to his/her hoop. The player then tags the next person, who repeats the activity. When all beanbags are out of the center hoop, the teams must steal beanbags from other teams but only one at a time. Insist that only one robber from each team can be stealing at any one time. Teams are not allowed to prevent other robbers from taking a beanbag from their hoop.

3. *Simon Says.* Run fast, slow, large strides, high knees, etc.

PLAY AREA

TEAM 1   TEAM 2

TEAM 3   TEAM 4

2.

ORGANIZATION: Identify the play area by setting up cone markers around the perimeter. As a general rule, space cone markers every 10 feet (3 meters) apart, using about 15 markers for a play area that is 60′ by 30′ (20m by 10m). Organizational and movement signals are further reinforced.

EQUIPMENT REQUIRED:

>   15 cone markers
>   Equipment or objects in teaching environment

WARMING-UP/FITNESS SIGNALS

1. Run to touch each corner cone of the play area. Use a different body part each time. Now find a Home space. Check for good spacing. "Sky Reaches!" Stretch high into the sky; then slowly curl down into a ball. Count to 5 as you stretch tall again. Count to 5 as you curl into a ball.

2. When you see my hand in the air like this (one hand/arm raised overhead), this is your "Quiet!" signal. Stop–look–and listen, and give me your full attention.

3. *Scrambled Eggs!—Walking!*

   ➤ Walk like a giant; walk like a puppy; walk like a tight rope walker; walk like a penguin; walk like a . . . .

   ➤ "Iceberg!" "Dead Bug!" Quickly lie on your back and wiggle your hands and feet in the air!

   ➤ Walk backward in a straight line. "Iceberg!" "Stork Stand."

   ➤ Walk in a circle; walk in a figure-8. "Iceberg!" Touch 3 body parts to the ground.

4. *Clear the Deck!* (Hand signal.) Move quickly to stand *outside* on one side of the marked play area. Clear the deck again! Now move to stand *outside* another side. Continue in this way. (Vary the way children move: jump across, skip, run high, walk on all fours . . .)

5. ***Scrambled Eggs—Marching!*** Be a happy marcher, lifting your knees high and swinging your arms. "Hit the Deck!" (hand signal). This is your signal to drop to the floor, quickly getting into front lying position.

➤ "Scrambled Eggs—Kangaroo Jumping!" "Hit the Deck" "Dead Bug!"

➤ "Clear the Deck!"

MOTOR MEMORY

1. Copy my body movements:

➤ Knee sit, hands waving in air, jump up tall, wiggle-wiggle.

➤ Kick-kick, punch-punch, slash-slash.

➤ Start low and gradually get bigger and bigger.

➤ Turn around, jump in place, corkscrew down.

2. Copy my foot-stamping, knee-slapping, hand-clapping, finger-snapping pattern: stamp-stamp, slap-slap, clap-clap, snap-snap

3. Locomotion/rhythm sequencing:

➤ Walk forward 4 steps and clap (1-2-3-4 and clap).

➤ Walk backward 4 steps and clap (1-2-3-4 and clap).

➤ Walk in a circle for 4 counts, then stamp-stamp-stamp-clap.

➤ Repeat pattern.

SPATIAL AWARENESS

1. ***Let's Pretend You Are . . .*** (Remember to watch where you are going!)

➤ a 747 jet taking off down the runway, lifting off, and then flying

➤ a lawn mower cutting the grass

➤ a jet-ski slicing through the water

➤ a hawk swooping down on a small critter

➤ a hockey player scoring a goal; a figure skater spinning

➤ a shadow-boxer punching into the air and "dancing" with the feet

➤ a karate-kid kicking with the feet and slashing with the hands

➤ a prancing horse

➤ a snake wriggling along the ground

➤ a fish jumping out of the water

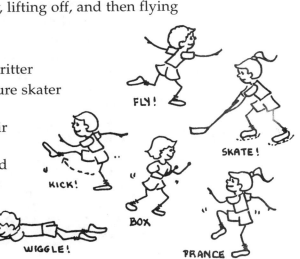

BODY AWARENESS

1. Listen carefully as I ask you to move just a certain body part at a time "Turn your head from side to side;" "wiggle your nose"; "snap your fingers"; "open and close your hand"; "blink your eyes"; "clap your hands"; "stamp your feet"; "lift one knee then the other"; "shake your arms."

2. Now show me how you can "touch a body part" to objects in the environment: "head to ground"; "elbow to chair"; "knee to table"; and so on.

CLOSING ACTIVITIES

1. *Finger Stretcher.* In stand tall position, interlock your fingers of both hands, then gently straighten your arms, pushing the palms of your fingers outward. Hold this stretch for 5–10 seconds; relax.

   ➤ Stretch in this position with arms overhead.
   ➤ Stretch with your hands behind your back.

2. *Periscope!* Lie on your back, bring one leg straight upward, and gently press it toward you for 10 seconds. Then repeat with the other leg.

3. *Foot Artist.* In sitting position, lean back on hands for support. Lift one leg and draw circles in the air with your pointed toes. Now draw circles in the opposite direction. Repeat using the other foot. Use your foot to trace your favorite letter; favorite number.

4. *Legend(s) of the Day!*

MOVEMENT STATIONS
Lesson 4, Level 2

> **MOVEMENT AREA: Locomotion**
>
> **MOVEMENT: Running**

TEACHING GOALS:

- ☞ Use correct body alignment.
- ☞ Promote correct knee action.
- ☞ Promote correct arm action.

EQUIPMENT REQUIRED:

Music; cassette/CD player
Cone markers
Relaxation tapes
1 set T-ball bases
5-6 Direction Cards; Counter Box
Assessment Recording Sheet

MOVEMENT STATIONS

1. *Friendly Races.* Mark off a 50-yard (50-meter) distance. Have children pair off and race each other to the finish line. Challenge someone else for the next race.

2. *Triangle Run.* Set up 3 markers in a triangular pattern, spaced 15 feet (5 meters) apart, marking them 1, 2, and 3 as shown. Set up 2 identical patterns. Each child in turn starts at the first marker, runs around the second, back around the first, then around the third, and back around the first marker. This circuit must be completed twice.

3. *Music Run.* (Create a tape using popular music, with varying tempos. Change the tempo every 20 seconds; provide "rest breaks"—such as the stretch breaks of "reaching for the sky" or "breathing breaks,"—before picking up the tempo again. Suggest 3 minutes of activity; 3 minutes of passive movement.) Keep in time to the music as it changes tempo from quick, to jogging tempo, to walking or marching tempo. Move on the spot or in general space, watching where you are going. When the music stops, you stop by jump-stopping!

157

4. ***Baseball Diamond Run.*** Set up 4 bases in the shape of a diamond as shown. Start with bases spaced 15 feet (5 meters) apart. Set up 2 identical courses. Use arrows to show direction of movement (one course, run clockwise; other course, counterclockwise). Children take turns running the bases with a foot tag at each base.

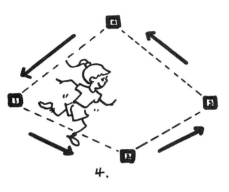

4.

5. ***Running Circuit.*** Children are to complete a running circuit. Each leg of the circuit is placed on a separate directions card located at each station. Children have to read the card. This also prevents children from following each other. Children who find it difficult to read may follow the diagram or ask another child or helper. *Example:* Run to the large tree at the end of the oval and collect a counter; then to the basketball courts and collect a counter; then to the flag pole and collect a counter; and so on. Suggest creating 5-6 circuit legs.

DIRECTIONS CARD

COUNTER BOX

5.

6. ***Stretching Station.***

   ➤ Calf Stretch

   ➤ Quad Stretch

   ➤ Sprinter Stretch

   ➤ Butterfly Stretch

7. ***Running—Assessment.*** Observe and record running performance. (See Book 1, *Ready-to-Use Fundamental Motor Skills & Movement Activities for Young Children*, for a Recording Sheet.)

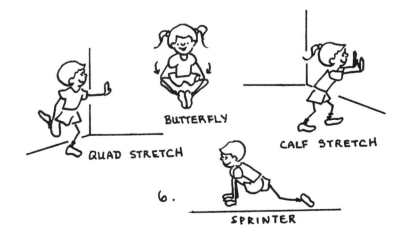

BUTTERFLY

QUAD STRETCH

CALF STRETCH

SPRINTER

6.

ORGANIZATION: Identify the play area by setting up cone markers around the perimeter. As a general rule, space cone markers every 10 feet (3 meters) apart, using about 15 markers for a play area that is 60´ by 30´ (20m by 10m). New formation signals and starting positions are revised. Be patient, but insist that children immediately respond to these signals. Practice!

"HERE!"

EQUIPMENT REQUIRED:

Cone markers

1 hoop per child

3 beanbags

WARMING-UP/FITNESS SIGNALS

HOOK SIT

1. *Here, Where, There.* Listen carefully to the word I will say. If you hear the word "Here," power walk quickly toward me; "Where," march on the spot; "There," jog quickly away from me. Repeat this activity, having children move in other ways, such as: skipping, running, jumping, slide-stepping, hopping. Between these signals, call out "Hook Sit," then lean back and pretend to climb a rope (tummy strengthener). "All Fours," face-up, and Crab Walk "dance" in your personal space (arm/leg strengthener).

2. *Listening Line.* (*Hand signal:* Arms outstretched sideways as you stand near and face line.) Use the boundaries of the play area.) Immediately run and stand in a long line where I am pointing. Face me and space yourself arm's length apart. Now take *giant steps* across to the opposite side and stand on a listening line once there. How many giant steps did you take? Return to your listening line, again counting the number of steps.

3. *Listening Circle.* (*Hand signal:* Point with index finger to the floor near you while circling the other index finger overhead.) Run quickly and safely to cross-leg sit in the circle that I am pointing to and face me. Give me your full attention.

159

MOTOR MEMORY

1. *Airplane Signals.* You are an airplane. Show me how you can . . . "Clear the Deck!" "Propellers!" (Gently circle arms forward.)

   ➤ Clear the deck again! Then do "Wingers!" Start with arms bent and parallel to ground, hands at chest level and closed. Gently pull arms backward, squeezing shoulder blades together, and continue to open sideways holding the stretch. Repeat from beginning.

   ➤ "Scrambled Eggs—Flying!" (run only on the lines of the court.) "Hit the Deck!" "Clear the Deck!" Land gently on your boundary line (runway).

2. Everyone collect a hoop. Drive your hoop like a car to your Home and have some free play with it.

3. *Hoop Pattern Jumping.* Start from inside your hoop, jump out to the front, jump out to the back; jump to the right side and jump to the left. Jump in and out all a round your hoop. Create a jumping pattern of your own!

SPATIAL AWARENESS

1. *Traffic Lights.* Place your hoop around your waist. This is your car. Rev up the engine (bouncing on the spot).

   ➤ "Scrambled Eggs!—Green Light." travel, but watch where you are going so that you do not bump into anyone.

   ➤ "Red Light." Jump stop on the spot.

   ➤ "Yellow Light." Jog on the spot.

2. *Traffic Cop Tag.* Spread 5 hoops throughout the play area. These hoops are the "safe zones." A player can stay in one of these Homes without getting tagged as long as she/he keeps her/his balance on one foot (without switching to the other foot). Select 3 Traffic Cops to be IT and give each a beanbag to hold. The Traffic Cops give chase to the other players, trying to tag them with their bean-bag. A tagged player becomes "glued to the spot" and must jog in place. Use the "Iceberg!" signal to stop the play. Select new Traffic Cops and continue the tagging game.

BODY AWARENESS

1. *Simon Says.* When you say "Simon Says," child responds by doing the task; when you ask child to do a task without first saying "Simon Says," child does not respond. How good a listener can each child be? "Simon says . . . wiggle your left fingers." "Stamp your feet!" "Simon says . . . click your right fingers." "Blink with your left eye."

WIGGLE FINGERS   STAMP FEET   BLINK EYE

1.

2. *Hokey Pokey.* This is the traditional simple folk dance.

   "You put your right foot in; you put your right foot out;

   You put your right foot in and you shake it all about.

   Do the Hokey Pokey, and turn yourself around.

   That's what it's all about."

   (Continue with left foot, right hand, left hand, head, bottom, etc.)

RIGHT   LEFT

2.

CLOSING ACTIVITIES

1. *Side Stretcher.* Standing tall, slowly reach down one side of your body, "walking" your fingers as far down as you can go. Walk your fingers back up to starting position, and then walk your fingers down the other side.

1.

2. *Butterfly Stretch.* In sitting position, place the bottoms of your feet together. Holding at the ankles with your hands, let your arms gently push along the inside of knees. Hold for 10 seconds.

2.

3. *Pencil Stretch.* In back-lying position, stretch as long as you can make yourself. Hold for 10 seconds. Roll over to front-lying position and hold pencil stretch.

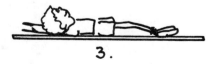

3.

4. *Legend(s) of the Day!*

4.

TEACHING SESSION
Lesson 6, Level 2

| MOVEMENT AREA: Locomotion |
| MOVEMENT: Dodging |

TEACHABLE POINTS:

1. When dodging, push off with the outside of the foot.
2. Keep eyes focused in which direction you want to move.
3. Keep your head up and move into open spaces.
4. Bend at the knees to keep the body lowered in order to change direction quickly.
5. Use your arms to help propel yourself into a new direction.
6. Move only as quickly as you can control, without falling over.

EQUIPMENT REQUIRED:

Marked courts are useful, as the lines provide visual guidelines for the children
Music helps establish a sense of rhythm
Cone markers
Hoops
Large balls

TEACHING GOALS:
- Promote quick change of direction.
- Promote correct foot action.

TEACHING PROGRESSIONS

1. Demonstrate the dodging action to the children, focusing on the teaching goals. Split the class into groups of 4–5 and place a parallel series of hoops or markers close enough together to allow the children to move forward while springing off alternate feet from one hoop to the other. (This is similar to the old army tire drill. See diagram.) Start slowly and gradually increase the speed of execution.

2. Have the children "Scrambled eggs—Walking!" in a large marked area. On whistle signal, have the children make a quick change of direction. Slowly increase the speed of execution.

3. Scatter markers throughout the play area. Children walk up to a marker and make a quick change of direction either right or left of the marker according to your signal!

ACTIVITIES

1. ***Heads or Tails.*** Have children pair up. One partner is a "Head" and has favorite hand on his/her head; other partner is a "Tail" and has favorite hand on his/her bottom. On signal "Heads or Tails," children use free hand to tag any opposite player: "Heads" will tag "Tails"; "Tails" will tag "Heads." If tagged, you are transformed into the same mode as the player who tagged you. Continue in this way. On "Iceberg" everyone stops immediately. Count the number of "Heads" and "Tails." *Variation:* Play again but this time add "Pockets" with one-third of the players having one hand in a pocket.

2. ***Artful Dodger.*** Children pair off and stand one behind the other. Use music to start and stop the action. Front partner is the "Dodger" who moves in general space, making quick changes of direction. The other partner is the "Shadow" who tries to follow as closely as possible to the Dodger without touching him/her. When music stops, everyone does an "Iceberg"—jump stops immediately. If the Shadow can take one step forward and touch the Dodger, then the two partners change roles. Continue in this way, each time calling out a different locomotor movement, such as jogging, power walking, skipping, slide stepping. . . .

ORGANIZATION: Identify the play area by setting up cone markers around the perimeter. As a general rule, space cone markers every 10 feet (3 meters) apart, using about 15 markers for a play area that is 60´ by 30´ (20m by 10m). More organization and formation signals are introduced.

EQUIPMENT REQUIRED:

Cone markers
Large throwing die
"Alphabet Arms" chart

WARMING-UP/FITNESS SIGNALS

1. *Follow-the-Leader.* Find a partner and stand together in a Home space one behind the other. Take turns being the leader and the follower, changing on my whistle signal. Think of lots of different ways you can move. How many different body parts can you warm up?

2. *Listening Corner.* (*Hand signal:* Cross your arms making the letter X, then point to the corner with your index finger.) Run quickly and safely to knee-sit in the corner I am pointing to, and face me. On signal "2 Corners!" touch 2 diagonal corners: first corner with your right elbow and left knee; diagonal corner with your left elbow and right knee.

3. *Endline.* (*Hand signal:* Arms outstretched to sides, with fingers of hand facing upward.) We will use this signal to play many of our tagging-type games. Run safely and quickly to stand on the endline that I am pointing to and face me. Check for good spacing.

4. *Lines.*

➤ Run to *Red* line and long sit.

➤ Run to the *Blue* line. In front support position, make a bridge over the line.

➤ Power walk along the *Black* line. In back support position, crab walk along the black lines.

➤ Jog along the boundary lines in a clockwise direction. On my whistle, change direction to counterclockwise. On "Iceberg!" jump-stop, then half hook sit. Lift your straight leg off the ground, alternately pointing and flexing foot 8 times; repeat with the other leg.

MOTOR MEMORY

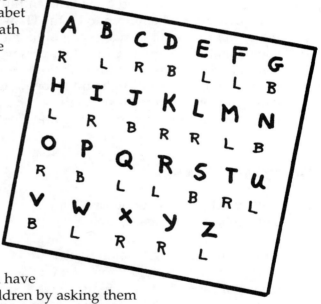

Alphabet Arms. On a large piece of paper write the letters of the alphabet using upper-case letters. Underneath each letter write an L, R, or B. (See illustration.) Choose one color for the letters of the alphabet and another color for the movement letters. For "L," have child extend left arm to the side; for "R," extend right arm to side; for "B," extend both arms out in front. Have child say the letter and do the associated arm movement with that letter. Encourage child to progress at his/her own rate. Observe actions and the saying of the letters. Practice part by part, slowly, until children have mastered each part. Challenge children by asking them to do this activity backward, or from right to left.

VARIATIONS:

➤ Use upper-case; lower-case; different fonts.

➤ Randomly mix the letters and arm movements.

➤ Use shapes, pictures, and colors instead of letters for younger children.

➤ Use different movements. For example, click fingers (C), stamp feet (S), turn around (T).

SPATIAL AWARENESS

1. *Six Corners.* Use markers positioned at 6 locations in a rectangular area or hexagonal shape. With a marking pen, number the markers 1 through 6 as shown in the diagram. On signal "Corner!" players have 10 seconds to run to a corner of their choice and stay there jogging on the spot. Throw a large dice and see which number comes up. Players caught in the corner with that number must come to the center of the play area and do stretches; the other players continue the game. When only 6 players remain, each player must run to a different corner! Who will be the last player left?

2. *Endline Cross Tag.* Use the endline signal to position children behind one of the endlines of the play area. Select 3 children to be the ITs who stand in the center of the play area, each holding a beanbag or sponge ball. On signal "Cross," players try to run across to the opposite endline without being tagged. If a player is tagged, he/she must jog on the spot. After 10 players have been caught, everyone goes free. Choose new ITs and play again.

BODY AWARENESS

1. *Simon Says.* When you say "Simon Says," child responds by doing the task; when you ask child to do a task without first saying "Simon Says," child does not respond. How good a listener can each child be? "Simon Says . . . stamp your feet!" "Click your right fingers." (Children must continue stamping their feet!)

2. *Busy Body Parts.* Call out a body part; for example, "knees." Child uses a beanbag to touch partner's knee. Call out another body part; for example, "elbows." Now child must find a new partner, and use the beanbag to touch this body part.

Variation: Touch more than one body part; for example, "elbows and knees."

CLOSING ACTIVITIES

1. ***Angels in the Snow.*** Begin in wide sit position, then slowly sink to back lying position.

    - ➤ Spread your arms/legs apart; bring together.
    - ➤ Spread your legs apart, hold for 3 seconds, then bring legs together.
    - ➤ Spread your arms out to the side and bring slowly together.
    - ➤ Let just your right side spread away from your body. Bring in. Now repeat with the other side.
    - ➤ Roll over into front lying position. Pretend your head weighs 500 pounds. Slowly move to stand tall with your head being the last to come up.

2. ***Rhythm Breathing.*** Take a big breath and slowly let it out. Do this again! As your hands come up through the middle of your body, slowly *breathe in*; then slowly *breathe out* as your hands circle downward. *Breathe in* as your hands come up through the middle again. Remember to do this slowly.

3. ***Legend(s) of the Day!***

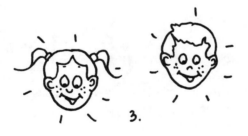

MOVEMENT STATIONS
Lesson 8, Level 2

MOVEMENT AREA: Locomotion
MOVEMENT: Dodging

TEACHING GOALS:
- ☛ Promote quick change of direction.
- ☛ Promote correct foot action.

EQUIPMENT REQUIRED:

Cone markers and other items for obstacle course
5–6 flags
4 large cone markers
Rectangle circuit movement cards
Stretching/strengthening poster
Assessment Recording Sheet

MOVEMENT STATIONS

1. *Zigzag Dodge Course.* Set up an obstacle zigzag course as shown. Children take turns moving through the course. As soon as one runner has reached halfway, the next runner can go.

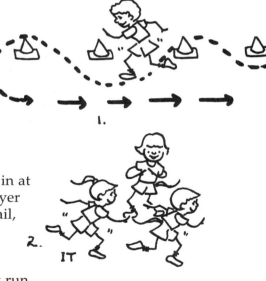

2. *Tail Tag.* Each player has a tail tucked in at the back of the shorts except for one player who is IT. If IT successfully snatches a tail, then that player becomes the new IT. Continue to play in this way.

3. *Figure-8 Agility Run.* Set up 2 agility run courses in a figure-8 pattern as shown. Children take turns running the course in as quick a time as they can.

   ➤ Children could race each other through the course.

4. **Dodging—Assessment.** Observe and record dodging performance. (See Book 1, *Ready-to-Use Fundamental Motor Skills & Movement Activities for Young Children*, for a Recording Sheet.)

5. **Rectangle Circuit.** Set up the rectangular circuit as shown in the diagram. On one side of rectangle, run the length; Puppy Walk the width; backward jog the length; Crab Walk the width. Children take turns to do circuit. When everyone has completed this circuit, then reverse direction and do new movements.

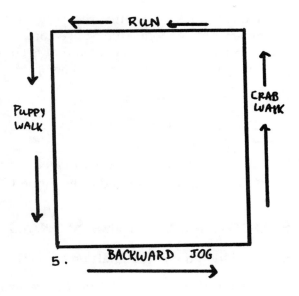

6. **Stretching/Strengthening Station.** Do the following stretches, holding them for a 10-second count:

Stretching

➤ Foot Artist

➤ Periscope Stretch

➤ Side Stretcher

Strengtheners

➤ Hand Walkers

➤ Ankle Taps

➤ Thigh Lifters

Display stretches and strengtheners on a wall chart.

ORGANIZATION: Identify the play area by setting up cone markers around the perimeter. As a general rule, space cone markers every 10 feet (3 meters) apart, using about 15 markers for a play area that is 60´ by 30´ (20m by 10m). The signals taught in previous lessons are reinforced. The organizational signal of "grouping" is extended.

EQUIPMENT REQUIRED:

15 cone markers
"Alphabet Arms" chart
1 flag, scarf, or tag belt per player
CD/Cassette player and quiet "mood" music

WARMING-UP/FITNESS SIGNALS

Refer to Strengthening Signals on page 21.

1. Try **combinations of signals** and watch the action!

   ➤ "Scrambled Eggs!—Skipping!" "Hit the Deck!" "Dead Bug!"

   ➤ "Home!" "Lame Dog Walk!" from one sideline to the other.

   ➤ "Scrambled Eggs!—Spider Walk" "Iceberg!" "Clear the Deck!"

   ➤ "Home!" 3 "Inchworms!"

   ➤ "Scrambled Eggs!—Giant Steps" "Hit the Deck!" Roll . . . !"

   ➤ "Scrambled Eggs!—Hopping" "Iceberg!" "Shake–Shake–Shake!" all over.

SPIDER WALK

LAME DOG WALK

1.

INCHWORM

2. *Group Signals—"2!"; "3!"; . . .*

   ➤ **"2's"** (*Hand signal:* Show 2 fingers in the air.) Find a partner and stand face to face. Give each other high tens; low tens; in between tens.

"2's"
"HIGH TENS"

   ➤ **"3's"** (*Hand signal:* Show 3 fingers in the air.) Form groups of 3 and stand back to back. Link elbows and sink to the floor. Now try to stand up without breaking your hold.

"3's"

   ➤ **"4's"** (*Hand signal:* Show 4 fingers in the air.) Form a circle, joining hands and facing inward. Circle walk clockwise for 8 counts; circle walk counterclockwise for 8 counts.

"4's"

MOTOR MEMORY

1. *Alphabet Arms.* Create a new Alphabet Arms and have children perform the activity.

2. *Memory Order Game.* Have children move to touch one object and then return to you to hear the next object to be touched. Now they must touch the first object, and then the second, before returning to you to hear what third object is to be touched. Children then move to touch the first object, the second, and then the third. Continue in this way. For example: Touch the red line with your elbow; the black line with your knee; the ball with your head.

SPATIAL AWARENESS

1. *Shadow Play.* With your new partner, stand one behind the other. Front partner leads, back partner follows like a "shadow." Listen for your moving signal (walk, jog, skip, hop, slide-step). Start on the music (whistle); stop when the music (whistle) stops. If the Shadow can take a step forward and touch partner, then change roles. Change partners on signal "New Partners!"

   ➤ Play Shadow Tag trying to tag your partner with a beanbag (or use tag belts).

2. *Knee Box.* Quickly find a partner and stand face-to-face in your Home space. On signal "Knee Box," try to touch partner's knee without your partner touching yours. Remember to stay in your Home. When you hear "Knee Box" again, find a new partner to challenge! Repeat this game, trying to grab each other's tag belts.

BODY AWARENESS

1. *Mirrors.* Find a partner, stand facing each other, and touch palm to palm. Show me how you can mirror each other's movements. Take turns changing roles on my signal "Mirrors!"

2. *Statues.* Working in pairs, create different Statues by taking your weight on different body parts.

CLOSING ACTIVITIES

1. *Belly-Button Circles.* Pretend that your belly button is the center of the circle. Trace 3 circles in one direction, then 3 circles in the opposite direction. Repeat.

2. *Side Stretcher.* Standing tall, slowly reach down one side of your body, "walking" your fingers as far down as you can go. Walk your fingers back up to starting position, and then walk your fingers down the other side.

3. *Partner Stretch.* Signal "2's—Home space"; "Mirrors." One partner leads the other to stretch through the body in different ways. Switch roles on signal.

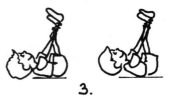

4. *Legend(s) of the Day!*

MOVEMENT AREA: Locomotion

MOVEMENT: Jumping and Landing for Distance (horizontal) and for Height (vertical)   *Revision*

TEACHABLE POINTS:

Jumping for Distance

1. Head up with eyes looking forward.
2. Arms extend behind the body as knees, hips, and ankles bend.
3. At same time, body leans slightly forward.
4. Legs extend vigorously and forcefully; at the same time, arms extend forward and upward vigorously.
5. Body remains leaning slightly forward.

Jumping for Height

1. Head up with eyes looking forward.
2. Arms extend behind the body as knees, hips, and ankles bend.
3. At same time, body leans slightly forward.
4. Legs and arms extend forcefully.
5. Arm action is synchronized with leg action.
6. Body extends upward.
7. Arms are extended upward.

Landing

1. Land on balls of both feet, then roll back onto flat feet.
2. Ankles, knees, and hips bend to absorb force.
3. On landing, lean slightly forward at the hips.
4. Arms are held out in front or to side of body to assist balance.
5. Head should be up and eyes looking forward to stop falling forward.

EQUIPMENT REQUIRED:

    1 hoop per child
    Even surface or carpeted area
    1 flag per child

TEACHING GOALS:

☞ Keep head up on landing.

☞ Bend knees on landing.

☞ Coordinate use of arms and legs in jump.

TEACHING PROGRESSIONS

1. Have children jump upward without using their arms. Do this again using arms. Which way is better?

2. Repeat #1, having children jump forward for distance.

3. How do knees help you to jump upward? Jump forward? Land?

4. Have children mirror your actions as you stand, swinging arms back and forth as knees bend and straighten.

5. Have children stand behind a line and jump as far forward as possible. Emphasize bending knees and using arms to swing forward. Remind children to land softly, bending at the knees and using arms to keep balance.

6. *Jumping Signals.*

   ➤ Bounce gently like a ball in your Home space. "Dead Bug!" "Bounce!"

   ➤ Pantomime the action of rope jumping.

   ➤ Jog in place; quarter jump-turn; jog in place; Quarter jump-turn the other way.

   ➤ "Scrambled Eggs—Jumping!"

BOUNCING   6.   ROPE JUMPING

7. *Hoop Jumping Challenges.*

   ➤ Jump in and out of hoop.

   ➤ Walk 5 giant steps away from hoop, jump-turn to face hoop, then run to land with both feet in the hoop. Repeat.

RUN   JUMP   LAND

ACTIVITIES

1. ***Clown in the Box.*** On signal "Clown in the Box!" children jump upward from their "box" (hoop), run to touch an object, then run Home to jump and land in their box. Repeat.

2. ***Frog in the Pond.*** Each "Frog" has a lily pad (hoop) and leaps from its lily pad into the pond, catching flies in the air. Select 2 players to be the "Hawks." All Frogs have a flag tucked into the back of their shorts. On signal "Ribbet!" Frogs must quickly but safely return to their pond before Hawks can swoop down and pull their tails. If caught, the players change places. The game continues in this way.

FOUNDATION MOVEMENT REVISION
Lesson 11, Level 2

ORGANIZATION: Identify the play area by setting up cone markers around the perimeter. As a general rule, space cone markers every 10 feet (3 meters) apart, using about 15 markers for a play area that is 60′ by 30′ (20m by 10m). The teamness concept is revised in this lesson. (Refer to page 14.)

EQUIPMENT REQUIRED:

> 15 cone markers
> Suitable music; cassette/CD player
> 1 Beanbag or softball per pair

WARMING-UP/FITNESS SIGNALS

1. *Marching Signals!* March to music and clap your hands in time. "Hit the Deck!" "March in place!" "Scrambled Eggs—Marching!" March backward. "Dead Bug!" Now march forward in a big circle. "Clear the Deck!" March in a square, changing directions every 8 counts.

2. Find your Home spot, facing square on to this wall.

   ➤ Jump turn to the right to face this wall (point).
   ➤ Jump turn again to face the back wall.
   ➤ Jump turn to face this wall (point).
   ➤ One more jump turn and you are facing the wall you started.

These are called "quarter jump turns." Show me how you can do quarter jump-turns in the opposite direction. Do half jump turns from facing the front wall to facing the back wall (jump through 180 degrees).

3. *Teams.* Divide your class into teams of 5–6 children. Revise the team signal (hand signal), then designate where each team will cross-leg sit in file formation. Captain is at the front; co-captain at the back; boy–girl or vice versa. Have each team select an appropriate Team Name and create a Team Cheer. Each team in turn gives its Team Cheer to the rest of the teams.

➤ Practice getting into your teams. On signal "Boundary Touch!" everyone must touch each boundary line of the play area, then quickly fall into your teams. Which team will do this the quickest?

176

4. *Waves.* Have team members turn to face you as you position to one side of the group as shown. Stand tall and space yourselves arm's length apart, facing me.

➤ Walk 4 steps forward; walk 4 steps back; walk 4 steps to the right; walk 4 steps to the left. Observe how children move in "waves."

MOTOR MEMORY

1. *Directions, Patterns, and Pathways.* Show directions on the chalkboard or large flip chart. In the classroom ask children to draw a movement collage as an art project.

➤ Move in the following *directions*: forward; backward; sideways.

➤ Move in the following *pathways*: straight line; zigzag; curved.

➤ Move in the following *patterns*: circle, triangle, rectangle.

➤ Try these patterns: figure-8; spiral; a letter.

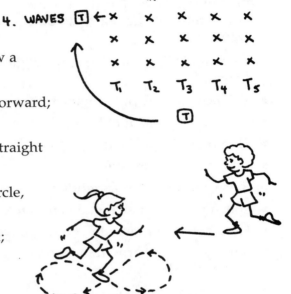

SPATIAL AWARENESS

1. *Two-way/Four-way Traffic.* Have each team position on a different side of the play area (30´ by 30´ [10m by 10m] square). Assign the teams numbers: "1, 2, 3, and 4." Signal teams to move across the square in different ways and from a variety of starting positions:

➤ 1's and 2's cross to the opposite side; then 3's and 4's cross by walking.

➤ Repeat but cross by slide-stepping.

➤ Jogging—1's, 2's, 3's, and 4's: all cross at the same time. Heads up—watch where you are going!

➤ Everyone begin in cross-leg sit position. Listen carefully for your number: 3's and 4's cross as quickly as you can. Now 1's and 2's!

2. Play **Partner Tag** with 3 pairs selected as the ITs. Once another pair is tagged, that pair becomes IT as well. Use beanbags or small soft balls as the tagging object. Remind the IT pairs to keep their inside hands joined and use only their outside hands to make the tag. Eventually there will be more IT pairs than free pairs—then watch the action!

Body Awareness

1. **Can you . . .** Give specific *directionality* instruction (right and left) with body movements.

   ➤ Open and close your left hand; right hand.

   ➤ Balance on your right foot; left foot.

   ➤ Wave with your right hand; left hand.

   ➤ Hop on your left foot; right foot.

   ➤ Lift your left arm; slowly lower.

   ➤ Raise and lower your right leg.

   ➤ Touch your right elbow to your left knee.

   ➤ Hold your left foot with your right hand.

   ➤ Raise your right arm in the air and your left arm out to the side.

2. **Busy Body Parts.** Play this game as before (see Lesson 4 on page 157), but have players touch right or left body parts; for example, touch right knees; touch your right elbow to left elbow of other partner.

Closing Activities

1. **Imagery—R-E-L-A-X!** Lie on a mat in back-lying position and relax. Think of something that is very pleasant, that will bring a smile to your face. Listen to the quiet background music. Breathe slowly. Relax—let yourself just go.

   ➤ Now tense just your hands for a 3-second count, then relax. Tense again, relax.

   ➤ Tense your shoulders. Relax.

   ➤ Tense your face. Relax.

   ➤ Tense your legs and feet. Relax.

   ➤ Tense your seat muscles. Relax.

   ➤ Tense your stomach muscles. Relax.

   ➤ Tense all over!

   ➤ Let everything go limp. Relax!

2. **Legend(s) of the Day!**

MOVEMENT STATIONS
Lesson 12, Level 2

MOVEMENT AREA: Locomotion
MOVEMENT: Jumping and Landing

TEACHING GOALS:

☞ Keep head up on landing.

☞ Bend knees on landing.

☞ Coordinate use of arms/legs in jump.

EQUIPMENT REQUIRED:

12 hoops
2 long ropes
1 rope and deckring
Box horse, bench, low hurdles, large mat
Floor tape or colored chalk
Assessment Recording Sheet

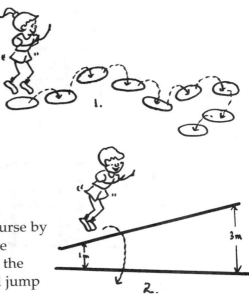

MOVEMENT STATIONS

1. *Hoop Jumping Course.* Make a jumping course by placing hoops on the ground in a pattern, close enough to jump off two feet from one hoop to the other. Together create other hoop patterns and jump through it.

2. *Jump the Stream.* Place two long ropes as shown in the diagram. Children take turns jumping across the "stream" from its narrowest point to its widest.

3. *Jump the Ring.* One child swings a deckring attached to a rope in a large circle along the ground. Children try to jump the ring each time it passes under their feet.

4. ***Jumping for Distance and Jumping for Height—Assessment.*** Observe and record performance. (See Book 1, *Ready-to-Use Fundamental Motor Skills & Movement Activities for Young Children*, for a Recording Sheet.)

5. ***Jumping and Landing Circuit.*** Create jumping and landing challenges such as:

   ➤ jump from low box horse onto a mat as far as possible

   ➤ walk along a bench, jump off to land in a hoop

   ➤ jump over low hurdles

   ➤ run, jump off favorite foot from a mark, and land on a mat

6. ***Hopscotch.*** Introduce 2–3 hopscotch patterns. Together create the rules for each game, then play the game.

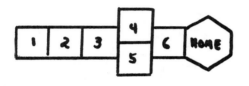

6.

5.

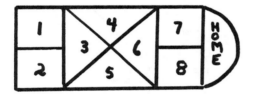

FOUNDATION MOVEMENT REVISION
Lesson 13, Level 2

ORGANIZATION: Identify the play area by setting up cone markers around the perimeter. As a general rule, space cone markers every 10 feet (3 meters) apart, using about 15 markers for a play area that is 60´ by 30´ (20m by 10m). The file formation is revised in this lesson. Directionality is further explored.

EQUIPMENT REQUIRED:

Music with a steady 4/4 count; cassette/CD player

1 light mat per child

Several pieces of equipment such as balance bench/beam, chairs, table, low hurdles, box horse, hoops

Tagging objects or tag belts

1 Beanbag per child

WARMING-UP/FITNESS SIGNALS

1. *Good Morning Workout.* (*Hand signal:* "Waves!") Do simple aerobic exercises to develop a warming-up effect and rhythm sense:

   ➤ Jog on the spot for 8 counts and finger snapping.

   ➤ Jog forward for 8 counts; light bouncing in place for 8 counts.

   ➤ Jog backward for 8 counts; light bouncing in place for 8 counts.

   ➤ March in a square with changes of direction every 4 counts.

   ➤ March in place to the music and clap hands in time for 8 counts.

   ➤ Kick legs out in front for 8 counts; kick legs to side for 8 counts.

   ➤ Wiggle, wiggle, wiggle—all over!

2. *Listening Line!* Turn to face this wall or direction. You are now in a long file or chain. This is the "Snake." Let's move as an Aerobic Snake. I will be at the head of the Snake, the last child is the tail of the Snake. Everyone else in between stays in the order that you are now standing. You are the links of the Snake. Jog to the music as we "snake along." Follow me. Finish in a big circle and have Snake do some "snaking" stretches and strengtheners (refer to pages 000 and 000).

181

Motor Memory

1. *In the Jungle.* Start in your Home space. Check for good spacing. Take children on a Safari using different movements such as:

➤ stepping over tall grass (*big knee lifts*)

➤ moving under the bridge (*crawling on tummy*)

➤ wading across the stream (*giant steps*)

➤ jumping off a rock (*jumping into air from a squat*)

➤ sneaking up behind a tree to watch the zebras eating grass (*creeping*)

➤ climbing up a tree to grab a swinging vine and splash into the water

➤ crawling through a cave (*crawling on all fours*)

➤ walking across a suspended bridge (*along a line or rope*)

➤ sitting cross-legged in front of the fire playing African drums

SUSPENDED BRIDGE

Spatial Awareness

1. *Square on, Side on, Diagonal.* Stand facing me in your Home space.

➤ You are now *square on*. Turn *side on* to me. *Square on*.

➤ Turn *side on* in a different direction.

➤ Turn your back to me. Now face me *square on*.

➤ Turn to face a corner of the play area that I point to. Now you are *diagonal on*.

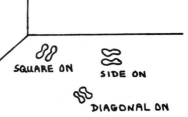

2. *Ship Ahoy! signals.* The play area becomes a giant ship. Face square on to this wall (or boundary line). This is the "bow" of the ship. Your back is now facing the "stern" of the ship.

➤ As you face the bow, the right side of the ship is called "starboard"; left side, "port." Point as I call out these names.

" STARBOARD - WALK BACKWARDS "

➤ Turn to face each side of the ship as I call out the name: starboard; stern; port; bow.

Now do the following Signals:

➤ Jump to the *bow*; "Iceberg!" "Dead Bug!"

" RESCUE! "

➤ Jog to the *stern*. "Periscope" (back lying positions with one knee straight up into the air and hold).

➤ Walk backward to *starboard!* "Rescue"— quickly find a partner and grab each other's wrists of one hand and gently pull.

➤ Hop to *port*. "Hit the Deck!" No "Scrub the Deck." Continue in this way.

3. ***Pirate Tag!*** Stand at one end of the ship. Choose three players to be the Pirates who stand in the middle of the ship. On signal "Pirates Are Coming!" all other players must try to cross the ship without being tagged. If tagged, that player is "frozen" to the spot but may use arms to touch other players crossing and thus free him-/herself. After a while choose new Pirates and continue the game.

BODY AWARENESS

1. In pairs, have one partner do one thing while other partner does the opposite. Example: one *in front of* something; the other *behind*; one *on* something; other *off*; move *over* something, while partner moves *under*; and so on.

2. Using beanbags or folded socks, have child place or throw object according to certain spatial commands:

   ➤ Put beanbag on top of your head.

   ➤ Place it behind you.

   ➤ Put it on the side of you; in front of you.

   ➤ Throw beanbag high.

   ➤ Throw beanbag square on to your partner.

   ➤ Throw beanbag to right side; to left side.

CLOSING ACTIVITIES

Pick up a mat and take it to a Home space.

1. In back lying position, do the following:

   ➤ Bring your right leg up and hold it with both hands, gently pulling it toward your chest. Hold for 10 seconds. Then slowly lower.

   ➤ Bring your left leg up and gently pull it toward your chest. Hold for 10 seconds and slowly lower.

   ➤ Bring both legs up and hold each leg at the ankles with the hand on that side. Spread your legs wide apart and hold. Then legs together and stretch. Slowly lower.

   ➤ Roll over onto your stomach and do a long pencil stretch.

   ➤ Roll to the right; roll to the left.

   ➤ Slowly raise yourself to stand tall with your head being the last to come off the floor.

2. ***Legend(s) of the Day!***

TEACHING SESSION
Lesson 14, Level 2

MOVEMENT AREA: **Body Management**
MOVEMENT: **Static Balance**

TEACHABLE POINTS:

1. Feet are flat on the floor with toes extended.
2. Keep the knees slightly flexed.
3. All body parts are kept straight and still.
4. Arms can be used to assist in balancing.
5. Head is up and the eyes are focused straight ahead on a fixed point.

EQUIPMENT REQUIRED:

Firm flat surface
Cone markers
Music; cassette/CD player
3 Beanbags

TEACHING GOALS:

☛ **Promote correct posture.**
☛ **Promote correct arm action to assist balance.**

TEACHING PROGRESSIONS

1. Demonstrate various forms of static balance emphasizing the teaching goals.

2. Have children explore different ways of making bridges. Use different body parts on which to balance. Ask individual children for demonstrations of their bridges. Have other children attempt these.

3. Place the children in pairs and have them find ways of combining and balancing on 2 body parts; 3 body parts; 4 body parts; even 5 body parts! Ask for demonstrations. Have other pairs attempt these.

4. In a marked area, have children move in different ways to music. When the music stops, have children stop and perform a balance on 1 part; on 2 parts; and so on.

ACTIVITIES

1. ***Connection.*** Children are in an open marked area. Using the signal "Scrambled Eggs" have the children move freely in this area using different methods of locomotion. On the signal they connect to the called body parts with another child, such as knee to knee, foot to foot.

FOOT-TO-FOOT

1.

2. ***De-Icer Tag.*** Choose 3 players to be ITs who give chase to moving Statues. Choose another player to be the "De-Icer." If a Statue is tagged, he/she becomes "frozen" and must stay in this fixed position until the De-Icer comes along and thaws out that player by touching the Statue with a magic "wand." Change ITs and De-Icer after every 2–3 minutes. *Variation:* Create a "frozen" position that a tagged player must take.

"DE-ICER"

3. ***Ship Ahoy!*** The play area becomes a ship with the front of the ship being the "bow"; the back, the "stern," the right side, "starboard," and the left side, "port." Create ship signals such as:

IT

2.

➤ Run to the bow. "Iceberg!" "Periscope" (back lying position with one foot in the air).

➤ Jump to the stern. "Bridge" (quickly find a partner and make a bridge with only each having one body part touching the floor).

➤ Power-walk to starboard. "Stork Stand" (stand on one foot, close eyes and count to five).

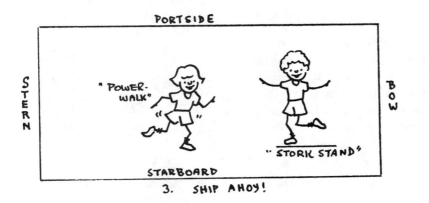

"PERISCOPE!"

"BRIDGE"

3. SHIP AHOY!

FOUNDATION MOVEMENT REVISION
Lesson 15, Level 2

ORGANIZATION: Identify the play area by setting up cone markers around the perimeter. As a general rule, space cone markers every 10 feet (3 meters) apart, using about 15 markers for a play area that is 60′ by 30′ (20m by 10m). Circle formation signal is revised and reinforced.

EQUIPMENT REQUIRED:

"Pink Panther" music; cassette/CD Player
Tag belts, flags, or tagging objects
Whiteboard or flip chart, marking pens
15 cone markers

WARMING-UP/FITNESS SIGNALS

1. Lead class through an Aerobic Snake (see the previous lesson). Add other locomotor movements as the snake winds its way in different movement patterns.

2. Use the following break signals to give children a change of pace, as well as develop overall body balance and coordination. (Refer to Break Signals on page 13.)

   ➤ "Thread the Needle"
   ➤ "Spinning Top"
   ➤ "Bucking Bronco"
   ➤ "Pogo Springs"

3. *Circle Formation Break.* "Sticky Popcorn!" Children start "popping" (light bouncing) as they move into a popcorn ball. Challenge the children to see how long it will take them to form their popcorn ball (tight circle facing middle).

4. In circle formation, divide the class into two groups and number each group as shown. On signal "Circle Run," each child in turn runs clockwise around the circle and back to his/her place. Which group will finish in cross-leg sitting quicker?

   ➤ Repeat circle run in counterclockwise direction.

186

MOTOR MEMORY

1. *Right and Left.*

- ➤ Touch an object with your left foot.

- ➤ Place beanbag on the right side of you.

- ➤ Touch a cone marker on a sideline with your left elbow.

- ➤ Touch a cone on an endline with your right knee.

- ➤ Run to the other sideline and touch the cone with your right shoulder.

- ➤ Run to the opposite endline and touch a cone with your right foot.

- ➤ Shake hands (right hands) with 5 different team members who are not on your team.

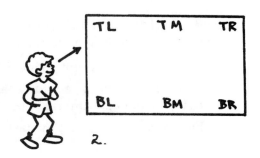

- ➤ Give low fives using only your left hand with 5 different team members.

2. *The Eye Box.* On a whiteboard or flip chart draw a large rectangular box as shown. Tell the class that this is an "Eye Box." Use a different colored marking pen to indicate the following locations in the box: top right, top middle, top left, bottom right, bottom middle, bottom left. Ask children to stand tall in a Home space. Make sure that they can all see the Eye Box. Call out different locations and have each child move only the eyes to those places. Remind them to keep the head still. Observe their actions and comment.

SPATIAL AWARENESS

1. *Partner Challenges.* ("Homes," side-by-side starting position.) Partners try to complete the task before the other partner, then returning to Home position. Partner who finishes "second" must do "3 of something" as instructed by first partner; for example, 3 push-ups or 3 sit-ups.

- ➤ Touch an endline with your right hand and the other endline with left hand. Signal "Endline!"

- ➤ Touch one corner with your right foot; touch the diagonally opposite corner with your left foot. Signal "Corners."

- ➤ Hop to one sideline, touching it with a knee. Hop to the other sideline, touching it with the opposite knee. Signal "Sideline."

2. ***Pirates Are Coming!*** Stand at one end of the ship. Choose three players to be the Pirates who stand in the middle of the ship. Pirates call out, "You may cross our ship if you are wearing (name a color or wearing apparel)." On signal "Pirates Are Coming!" all other players must try to cross the ship without being tagged. All those tagged become Pirates. Continue until everyone is caught. Have children wear "tag belts" that are pulled to be caught, or have Pirates tag with an object in their hand (beanbag, deck ring).

Body Awareness

Body Balances. Find your Home space. Show me how you make a:

➤ 3-point shape; 4-point shape; 5-point shape.

➤ Make a long shape; a wide shape, a twisted shape; a round shape.

➤ Find a partner. Repeat the tasks above.

Closing Activities

1. ***Pink Panther.*** Use the theme music, if possible. Sleepers find a Home space in the play area and get into back lying position, arms folded across the chest, and eyes closed, except for two players who are the Pink Panthers. When the music starts, the Pink Panthers, keeping hands behind the backs, prowl around the area and bend down to talk to a sleeping player. Panthers, be clever and humorous as you try to get a sleeping player to wake up. If the sleeping player moves in any way, he or she is automatically awakened and becomes a Pink Panther helper trying to wake up other sleepers. The challenge is to see which sleeping player(s) can last the length of the song and become the best concentrator(s) of the day!

2. ***Legend(s) of the Day!***

MOVEMENT STATIONS
Lesson 16, Level 2

MOVEMENT AREA: Body Management
MOVEMENT: Static Balance

EQUIPMENT REQUIRED:

Carpeted or even surface

Individual and partner balancing cards

Wooden blocks or dome markers

Beanbags

Large rope

6 hoops

Several mats

2 balance benches

Assessment Recording Sheet

MOVEMENT STATIONS

1. *Balance Object Play.* Explore and practice balancing tasks:

   ➤ Balance on different body parts using wooden blocks or soft dome markers.

   ➤ Balance a beanbag on different body parts.

   ➤ Use a hoop to create different balanced positions.

2. *Balancing Challenges.* Perform individual balancing challenges. (See page 191.) Enlarge these onto cards and have children perform on mats.

3. *Static Balance—Assessment.* Observe and record performance in doing a static balance. (See Book 1, *Ready-to-Use Fundamental Motor Skills & Movement Activities for Young Children*, for a Recording Sheet.)

4. ***Balance Bench Challenges.*** Explore different ways of balancing on the bench on 1, 2, 3, 4, etc., body parts. (Mats should be placed around the apparatus for safety.)

5. ***Large Rope Balancing.*** Together use a large rope to explore different ways of balancing as a whole group.

6. ***Partner Balances.*** (See page 191.) Enlarge these onto cards and have children work in pairs to perform the balancing positions.

4.

5.

#2 INDIVIDUAL BALANCING CHALLENGES

#6 PARTNER BALANCING CHALLENGES

ORGANIZATION: Identify the play area by setting up cone markers around the perimeter. As a general rule, space cone markers every 10 feet (3 meters) apart, using about 15 markers for a play area that is 60´ by 30´ (20m by 10m). Signals are reinforced. Team concept of "Islands" is developed.

EQUIPMENT REQUIRED:

Cone markers placed in a large circle or oval
Suitable music; cassette/CD player
1 large sheet of drawing paper for each team
2 different colored marking pens per team
Whiteboard or flip chart
1 set of bibs per team
15 hoops

WARMING-UP/FITNESS SIGNALS

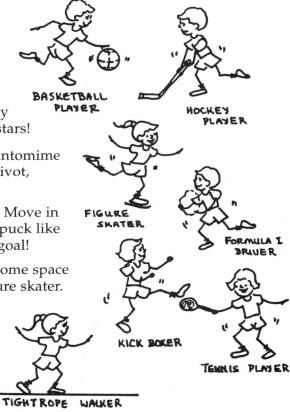

BASKETBALL PLAYER

HOCKEY PLAYER

FIGURE SKATER

FORMULA I DRIVER

KICK BOXER

TENNIS PLAYER

TIGHTROPE WALKER

Superstar Warm-up. Listen carefully for my signal as I turn you into Superstars!

➤ "Blue Lines—Basketball Player!" Pantomime dribbling a basketball, jump-stop, pivot, shoot!

➤ "Scrambled Eggs—Hockey Player!" Move in and out of each other dribbling the puck like a hockey player. "Iceberg!" Score a goal!

➤ "Homes—Figure Skater." In your Home space create different movements as a figure skater.

➤ "Activity Circle Clockwise— Formula I Driver!" Show me how you move in and out of each other as a racing car driver. "Iceberg!"

➤ "Black Line—Kick Boxer!" Run to a corner of the play area and perform karate kicks and boxing arm actions.

➤ "Corners—Tennis Player!" Find a corner and show me how you can move as a tennis player.

➤ "Home/Line—Tightrope Walker." Find a Home space on a line, and show me how you would walk across a suspended wire. Careful!

➤ Make up your own Superstar move!

192

MOTOR MEMORY

The Eye Box. (Refer to Lesson 8 on page 168 for description.) Stand tall in a Home space. Make sure that you can all see the Eye Box. Now march in place, touching your hands lightly to your knees and listen to what I say: top middle, bottom left, top right, bottom middle, top left; bottom right. Move only your eyes to those places. Remember that your head must stay still! Observe actions and comment.

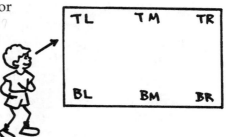

SPATIAL AWARENESS

1. ***Colors Team Tag.*** Give each team a set of colored pinnies to wear (red, green, blue, yellow). Select the Red team to be the tagging team and give each team member a tagging object. On signal "Red Tag," Red team members try to tag as many of the other players as they can in 20 seconds. A tagged player must jog on the spot. At the end of 20 seconds, count the number of tagged players. This is the Red team's score. Each team has a turn at being the IT team, and is given the tagging objects. Which team will make the most number of tags?

2. ***Islands.*** Create several "islands" using hoops scattered throughout the play area. On signal "Scrambled Eggs—Jogging" (each time vary locomotor movements used), move in and out of the islands without touching them. On signal "Islands!" quickly find an island and jump into it. You will need to share your island with others. Each time we "Scramble Eggs," I will take away one or two islands. Eventually the islands will become more and more crowded. You will have to cooperate in order to all fit into your island. Do so carefully!

BODY AWARENESS

Create a Being. Mark out several team "Islands" as shown. Assign each team to an island. Let the team choose a name for the island. Each team is given marking pens and a large sheet of drawing paper.

➤ One team member gets into back lying position on the large piece of paper. Using a marking pen, the team traces an outline of this member onto the paper. Then, taking turns, fill in the body parts: head, eyes, mouth, ears, nose, neck, body, arms, hands, fingers, and so on.

➤ Now have each island come up with 2 words that are positives (attributes) that you would like your being to have.

➤ Ask the captain and co-captain of each team to give you their positive words. Write them *inside* the being on the whiteboard.

➤ Now ask each team to think of 2 negative words. These words—the "emotional hurts"—will go on the *outside* of the body.

Ask children to think about how they can be a positive being for the whole day.

HAPPY BEING

CLOSING ACTIVITIES

1. On signal "Robots," move around the play area like a robot. Slowly let your batteries run down until you come to a complete stop.

2. Now curl up into a tight ball. On signal "Sunrise," slowly open to make yourself as wide and "bright" as possible. On signal "Sunset," slowly curl up into a ball, sinking, sinking until you disappear.

3. In cross-leg sit position, take 4 counts to breathe in slowly; 4 counts to breathe out slowly. Repeat.

4. *Legend(s) of the Day!*

• SUNRISE•   2.   "SUNSET"

3.

MOVEMENT AREA: Body Management
MOVEMENT: Dynamic Balance

TEACHABLE POINTS:

1. Feet are flat on the floor with toes extended.
2. Keep the knees slightly flexed
3. All body parts are kept straight and still.
4. Arms can be used to assist in balancing.
5. Head is up and the eyes are focused straight ahead on a fixed point.

HEEL-TOE

EQUIPMENT REQUIRED:

Firm flat surface preferably marked with lines
Cone markers
Hoops
Balancing equipment; mats

3.

TEACHING GOALS:

☛ Promote correct posture.
☛ Promote correct arm action to assist balance.

4.

TEACHING PROGRESSIONS

1. Demonstrate various forms of dynamic balance emphasizing the teaching goals.
2. Have children walk forward heel to toe, then backward with arms out to sides. Use a line, if possible, to walk along.
3. Have child walk forward heel to toe with hands on hips. Repeat walking backward.
4. Set up a balance circuit using some of the objects such as: lengths of timber, rope, marked lines, marker domes. Children walk along these objects forward and backward, as well as heel to toe walks; jump off low benches; walk up and down an incline; use balancing feathers to explore balance boards.

   ➤ Variations: Eyes closed, hands on hips, carrying or catching objects while moving.

ACTIVITIES

1. ***Crocodile Relay.*** Divide the children into teams of 6. The children link with their teammates by holding the hips of the person in front of them and must move as a team, walking heel to toe *at all times* to complete the course.

2. ***Balancing Tugs.*** With a partner about the same size, each take up a balance on your right foot with left hand holding left foot behind. Now using a wrist grip, try to pull your partner off balance.

   ➤ Repeat balancing on the left foot.

   ➤ Repeat using a left hand wrist hold.

FOUNDATION MOVEMENT REVISION
Lesson 19, Level 2

ORGANIZATION: Identify the play area by setting up cone markers around the perimeter. As a general rule, space cone markers every 10 feet (3 meters) apart, using about 15 markers for a play area that is 60′ by 30′ (20m by 10m). The shuttle formation signal is revised, practiced, and then reinforced through relays.

EQUIPMENT REQUIRED:

Cone markers

Cassette/CD player

Carpet squares or floor tape

1 jump-hoop per team

1 ball per team

WARMING-UP/FITNESS SIGNALS

1. *Grand Prix.* Mark out a large oval area using cone markers. Ideally have one cone marker for each child in your class.

   ➤ You are racing car drivers, moving around a track. Everyone stand on the outside of a cone marker, rev up your engine, and wait for your start signal!

   ➤ When you hear the signal "Circle Up—Clockwise" (clockwise hand signal), race around the oval in a clockwise direction, like the hands of a clock.

   ➤ The rule at this race track is that you pass on the *outside* only!

   ➤ On signal "Circle Up—Counterclockwise" (counter clockwise hand signal), travel in the opposite direction.

   ➤ On signal "Pitstop," stop where you are and do the task: "Bridge"; "Periscope!"; "Bucking Bronco."

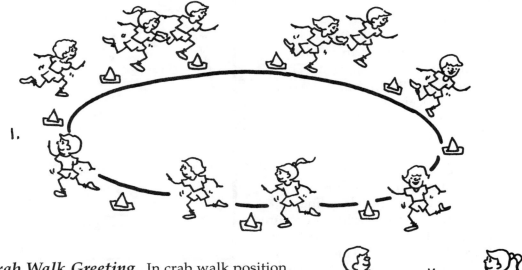

2. *Crab Walk Greeting.* In crab walk position, greet everyone on your team by "shaking feet" (touching bottom of foot to partner's).

197

MOTOR MEMORY

Grid Patterns. Mark out a grid pattern for each team as shown using floor tape. Have each team member in turn start in Square One. Give signals to move: make 2 jumps straight ahead; 3 jumps to the right; take 1 step backward; place your left foot in the square on your left side; put your right foot in the square behind you; make 3 jumps diagonally upward, etc.

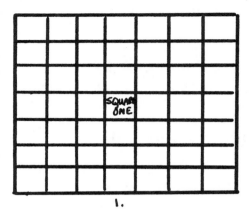

1.

SPATIAL AWARENESS

1. ***Partner Chase.*** 2's, side-by-side. One partner is a "1"; the other, a "2." On signal "One," #1 becomes the IT and gives chase to partner #2 On "Two," roles are reversed. Remind pairs to watch where they are going!

   ➤ Set up new partners and continue the game.

   ➤ Use beanbags or flag pulls to make the tag.

"ICEBERG!" 1. "CHASE!"

2. ***The Black Hole.*** Give each team a "Star Wars" name such as Han Solo; Luke Skywalker; Chewbacca; C3PO; or R2D2. Select one team to be the IT team (Darth Vader and Storm Troopers) that stands in the middle of a circular area ("the black hole"). (See diagram.) The other teams "fly" around the outside of this circular area, saying "Whose spaceship are you?" Darth Vader can give several answers, but when he/she says "Yours!" the chase is on. Outside spaceships must fly to the safe zones (outside boundary lines of play area). If a spaceship is captured (tagged), that spaceship must join Darth Vader and his/her team.

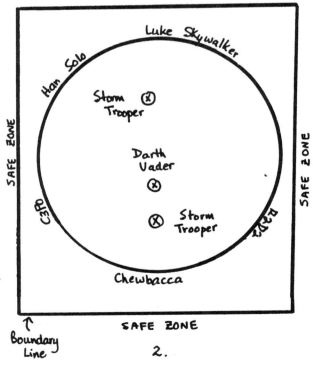

2.

BODY AWARENESS

Human Shapes.

Partners:

➤ Make the letter C, T, L, O . . .

➤ Make the following numbers: 3, 6, 7, 11 . . .

➤ Make two-letter words.

Three's

➤ Make different single-digit numbers; double-digit; triple-digit.

➤ Make triangles, circles, squares, diamonds.

➤ Make different letters.

➤ Make simple words.

TRIANGLE

CLOSING ACTIVITIES

1. **Shuttle Relays.**

   Shuttle formation. (See Formation Signals, page 9.)

   ➤ Run to opposite side giving high fives for the next player to go.

   ➤ Run to the opposite side passing a ball to the next player in line.

   ➤ Zigzag through the markers to the opposite line.

SHUTTLE RELAY - BALL PASSING

1.

   ➤ Do different locomotor movements: skip, slide-step, hop, jump.

   ➤ Do different Animal Walks.

   ➤ Use a jump-hoop to travel to the other side.

2. **Legend(s) of the Day!**

2.

MOVEMENT STATIONS
Lesson 20, Level 2

MOVEMENT AREA: Body Control
MOVEMENT: Dynamic Balance

TEACHING GOALS:

☛ Keep head up, feet flat on the ground.

☛ Keep upper body quiet (relatively still).

EQUIPMENT REQUIRED:

Long ropes	6 cone markers
Wooden blocks or cone markers	1 beanbag
Balance boards	Low box horse
Foam stilts or bucket steppers	Low hurdles
2-3 balance benches	Suspended ball
Assessment Recording Sheet	

MOVEMENT STATIONS

1. *Snake Walk.* Place several long ropes scattered on the ground in snaking patterns, then have children:

   ➤ walk forward; walk backward along the rope, then sideways, finally heel-to-toe

   ➤ stretch the rope and jump back and forth over the rope.

2. *Balance Board Challenges.*

   ➤ Explore using balance boards such as a Duck Walker. Rock from side-to-side; spin 360 degrees on a smooth surface; walk like a "duck" using balance board.

   DUCK WALKER   BUCKET STEPPER   FOAM STILTS

   2.

   ➤ Explore using foam stilts or foam bucket steppers.

3. *Zigzag Shuttle Run.* Set up a zigzag shuttle course as shown using cone markers. Group is in shuttle formation. Each runner dodges through the zigzag course carrying a beanbag that is handed over to the next runner. Continue in this way.

6 4 2   3.   1   3 5

4. ***Dynamic Balance—Assessment.*** Observe and record performance of dynamic balance. (See Book 1, *Ready-to-Use Fundamental Motor Skills & Movement Activities for Young Children*, for a Recording Sheet.)

5. ***Balance Bench Challenges.*** Put the following tasks on large posterboard:

   ➤ Walk forward along the bench to the other end.

   ➤ Walk backward along the bench to the start.

   ➤ Walk heel–toe along the bench.

   ➤ Run forward along the bench, jump off the end, landing gently.

   ➤ Carefully jump your way along a bench.

   ➤ Try moving along the bench with one foot on bench, other foot on floor.

   ➤ Explore other ways of moving along the bench.

6. ***Jumping and Landing Circuit.*** Create jumping and landing challenges such as:

   ➤ Jump from low box horse onto a mat as far as possible.

   ➤ Walk along a bench, jump off to land in a hoop.

   ➤ Jump over low hurdles.

   ➤ Jump upward to hit an object suspended from a support or tree.

MOVEMENT AREA: Object Control
MOVEMENT: Receiving a Rolled Small Ball

TEACHABLE POINTS:

1. Keep a balanced position with the feet spread comfortably apart.
2. Preferred leg is in front and knees bend to get down to the ball.
3. Get the bottom close to the ground.
4. Body must be positioned behind the ball.
5. Arms slightly bent, fingers must be spread and face downward.
6. Eyes are focused initially on the thrower and then track the ball at all times.

EQUIPMENT REQUIRED:

Firm flat surface
Cone markers
Floor tape or ropes to
    mark out squares
1 small ball per person

TEACHING GOALS:
- ☞ Keep eyes focused on ball.
- ☞ Promote correct hand and finger position.
- ☞ Use correct body positioning.

TEACHING PROGRESSIONS

1. Demonstrate how to roll a small ball using the cue words: "swing back-step forward and swing through." Ready position is square on to the target, ball held in front in both hands. Eyes on target. Step forward with the opposite foot to throwing hand.

   ➤ Have children practice rolling technique, sending ball toward a wall.

2. Demonstrate receiving a rolled ball, emphasizing the teaching goals. In pairs using a large ball, the children practice rolling and receiving the ball. Emphasize correct bending of the knees and the correct hand and finger position. Gradually increase the rolling distance.

3. As #2 but have the children roll the ball slightly away from their partner who must now move across to receive the ball. Emphasize getting the body and hands behind the ball. Gradually increase the distance.

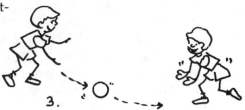

4. *Rolling Stunts.* Find a Home space in which to start. Always roll your ball into open space for these stunts.

> ➤ Roll ball ahead of you, run after it to get in front, and field the ball in the receiving position.

> ➤ Roll ball ahead of you and try to jump back and forth over the moving ball.

> ➤ Keep the ball rolling—don't let it bump into any other balls.

> ➤ Roll the ball in a figure-8 between your legs.

> ➤ Roll the ball along a line on the floor. Follow its path to see how long it will roll along the line.

> ➤ Roll the ball between two cone markers spaced 1 yard (meter) apart. Gradually reduce the distance between markers.

> ➤ Create a rolling stunt of your own! Teach it to a partner.

ACTIVITIES

1. *Square Spry.* Children are placed into 4 teams. Each player stands on a corner or side of a large marked square; the leader from each team stands in the middle of the square. On signal "Roll!" the leader rolls the ball to each team member in turn. When the last child returns the ball, he/she runs in and replaces the leader, who runs to the head of the line.

2. ***Beat the Ball.*** Divide the class into 4 teams. Mark out two fields of play opposite each other so that the teacher can control both games. Game consists of a roll-and-run team and a fielding team. The first runner must roll the ball as far as possible into the field of play. The fielding team must collect the ball and quickly position at one of the bases, with the ball starting at base 1; then roll it around the bases until base 6 is reached. Meanwhile, the runner tries to complete as many circuits of the running area as possible before the ball has been rolled around all the bases. The running team counts out loud the number of circuits each player completes.

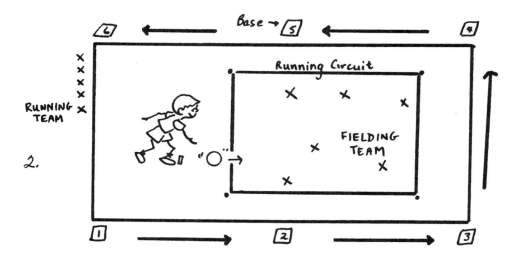

3. ***Rolling Soccer.*** Using cone markers, make goals 3 yards (meters) a part and just in front of a wall. Have partners take turns being the roller who stands 4 yards (meters) away and tries to roll the ball between the goals. Goalie uses hands to protect the goals. Repeat the above activities using a small ball.

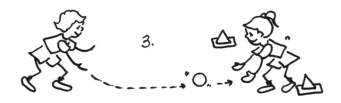

MOVEMENT STATIONS
Lesson 22, Level 2

MOVEMENT AREA: Object Control
MOVEMENT: Receiving a Rolled Small Ball

TEACHING GOALS:

☛ Keep eyes focused on ball.

☛ Promote correct hand and finger position.

☛ Use correct body positioning.

EQUIPMENT REQUIRED:

> Large balls and small balls
> 12 pins or skittles, small cones or plastic jugs
> 2 long ropes
> 1 large bin
> 1 large ball attached to a rope
> Assessment Recording Sheet

MOVEMENT STATIONS

1. *Guard the Bin.* The children form a circle with 1 child in the middle of the circle whose job is to protect the bin from being touched by the rolling ball sent by circle players. When the middle child stops the ball, he/she rolls it to the next person in the circle. Each child has a turn in the middle.

2. *Circle Pattern Roll.* Group knee-sits in a circle, one player with a ball. Ball is rolled across the circle to a player not on either side of roller. Each player in turn does the same. Finally the ball will be returned to the first player. Remember the pattern and begin again. How many times can group repeat pattern before moving on to next station?

3. *Six-Pin Bowl.* Set up 6 skittles, small cones, or plastic jugs as shown. Two identical stations are ideal to create more participation. In turn, children take 2 tries to knock over as many of the skittles as possible. Organize station so that there is a Bowler, a Setter-Up, and a Ball Returner.

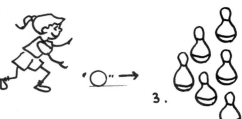

4. ***Receiving a Rolled Small Ball—Assessment.*** Observe and record performance. (See Book 1, *Ready-to-Use Fundamental Motor Skills & Movement Activities for Young Children*, for a Recording Sheet.)

5. ***Jump the Stream.*** Place two long ropes as shown in the diagram. Children take turns jumping across the "stream" from its narrowest point to its widest.

6. ***Jump the Ball.*** One child swings a large ball attached to a rope in a large circle along the ground. Children try to jump the ball each time it passes under their feet. Children take turns being the rope swinger, changing places after each minute.

| MOVEMENT AREA: Object Control |
| MOVEMENT: Underhand Throwing |

TEACHABLE POINTS:

1. Stand square on to the target.
2. Keep a balanced position with the feet comfortably spread.
3. Transfer weight from back to front foot during the throw by stepping forward with the foot opposite to the throwing arm.
4. Ball held in the fingers.
5. Good arm extension in the wind-up; then in the throw and follow-through.
6. Release the ball in front of the body.
7. Follow-through toward the target.
8. Eyes focused on the target.

EQUIPMENT REQUIRED:

1 beanbag per child
1 hoop per pair
Wall to throw at, if possible

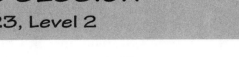

TEACHING GOALS:

☛ Use good extension in wind-up and follow-through.
☛ Be accurate through correct release and direction of follow-through.

TEACHING PROGRESSIONS

1. Demonstrate the correct technique for underhand throwing, emphasizing the teaching goals for the lesson.

2. Have the children take a beanbag with a correct grip and stand square on to a wall in front of them. For arm action, use the cue words: "Down as far as you can; back as far as you can; swing through and throw." Repeat a number of times. Reduce the cues to "Down, back, swing through, throw."

DOWN-BACK 2. SWING-THROUGH

3. Have the children stand with feet shoulder-width apart facing the wall and step forward with opposite foot as hand swings through to release a beanbag "up and out" toward wall. Emphasize good follow-through, holding beanbag in fingers. Have children practice stepping forward with opposite foot as throwing hand swings up and out first without beanbag, then with beanbag.

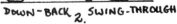

4. Have children pair up, collect 2 beanbags and hoop and find a Home space. One partner underhand throws the ball through a hoop held by the other partner who stands near a wall. Switch roles after every 4 throws.

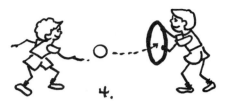

5. Partners stand back to back, walk 2 giant steps away, jump-turn, and face each other. At this distance begin underhand throwing back and forth to each other. After every 4 throws take a walking step away from each other. Continue in this way. Emphasize throwing "up and out" to partner and catching with hands in the correct position.

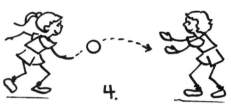

ACTIVITIES

1. **Wasps.** Children pair off, find a Home space to start in. One partner is the "wasp" and holds a "stinger" (beanbag). On signal "Wasps!" each Wasp counts to 5, then gives chase, trying to "sting" partner with an underhand throw below the knees. If successful, the "stung" partner becomes IT and gives chase. Tag game continues in this way.

2. **Stuck in the Middle.** Divide the class into teams of 6. Each team forms a circle made of 3 giant steps with captain of team in the middle. Circle players throw the beanbag around and across the circle, trying to keep it away from the captain. If the middle player intercepts the beanbag, the circle player making the throw comes to the middle. If captain cannot intercept the beanbag after a certain time, then choose another player to be "stuck" in the middle!

MOVEMENT STATIONS
Lesson 24, Level 2

MOVEMENT AREA: Object Control
MOVEMENT: Underhand Throwing

TEACHING GOALS:

☞ Use good extension in wind-up and follow-through.

☞ Be accurate through correct release and direction of follow-through.

EQUIPMENT REQUIRED:

3 Buckets
Cone markers
3 Beanbags
Assessment Recording Sheet

3 deckrings
Wall targets
2 balance benches
2 balance boards

MOVEMENT STATIONS

1. **Bucket Toss.** Working in pairs, partners underhand throw beanbags into a bucket from marked distances as shown: 3 markers, each 1 yard (meter) apart with the first marker 2 yards (meters) from the bucket. Each partner gets 2 tries at each marker. Score 1 point for hitting the bucket and 2 points for landing the beanbag in the bucket.

2. **Deckring/Beanbag Play.** Pair off children, each with a beanbag and a deckring between the partners.

   ➤ *Beanbag Basketball.* One partner throws beanbag through partner's deckring held horizontally with both hands. Partner with deckring tracks beanbag so that it will go through. Change roles after 3 throws. Find a new partner and repeat.

   ➤ *Beanbag Horseshoes.* Deckring is placed on the floor or ground at a certain distance away from throwers. Partners take turns tossing their beanbag at the ring to see whose beanbag can get the closer. Play best 2 out of 3 and challenge a new partner.

3. **Underhand Throwing—Assessment.** Observe and record performance. (See Book 1, *Ready-to-Use Fundamental Motor Skills & Movement Activities for Young Children*, for a Recording Sheet.)

4. **Walk-and-Jog Circuit.** Set up a walk-and-jog circuit as shown. Children complete a circuit, then take a stretch break for 30 seconds, then do the circuit again.

5. **Wall Target Tossing.** Create 3 different targets using wall tape as shown. Children, in pairs, take turns to underhand throw a beanbag at the target. Each thrower has 3 beanbag attempts. Switch to different targets after a certain time.

6. **Toss and Balancing Tasks.**

   ➤ Walk in general space tossing and catching a beanbag.

   ➤ Walk along a bench tossing and catching a beanbag.

   ➤ One partner tosses beanbag back and forth to a partner who is standing on the bench.

   ➤ Balance on a Duck Walker while tossing and catching beanbag.

   ➤ Create your own toss-and-balance stunt!

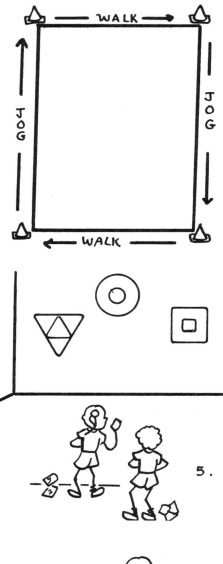

TEACHING SESSION
Lesson 25, Level 2

| MOVEMENT AREA: Object Control |
| MOVEMENT: Catching a Large Ball |

TEACHABLE POINTS:

1. Keep in a balanced position with the feet comfortably spread.

2. Arms with elbows bent and fingers spread must be ready to receive the oncoming ball (ready position).

3. Ball is caught with the hands, *not* the arms.

4. Hands (with fingers spread) and the arms move to meet the ball.

5. When ball meets the hands, arms bend at the elbows and cushion the impact of the ball.

6. Fingers face upward for a high ball; downward for a low ball.

7. Eyes are focused on the ball.

EQUIPMENT REQUIRED:

Firm even surface   Cone markers
4 low nets   1 large soft ball per pair

TEACHING PROGRESSIONS

1. Demonstrate and explain the teaching goals for this lesson.

2. Children in pairs underhand throw a large ball to each other. Stress moving the hands early to meet the ball, keeping eyes on the ball, and watching it land right in the hands.

3. Throw ball to a partner, letting it bounce once before making the catch. Then throw ball through the air for partner to make the catch. Emphasize "targeting" with hands to receive ball. Use the cue: "Reach and give."

4. Children in groups of 6 stand in a semi-circle with a leader holding a large ball and standing in front of the group. The leader throws the ball in turn to each person, who returns it. Then leader joins the end of the semi-circle and a new leader takes over.

3.

211

ACTIVITIES

1. *Newcombe.* Divide the class into 4 teams and play 2 games. Use a volleyball court or similar, but with a low net to play game. Teams underhand throw the ball over the net and the other team must catch it on the full or first bounce and return it. When a player catches the ball, he/she must throw it from where the ball is caught.

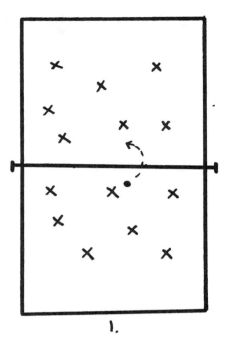

1.

2. *Sky Ball.* Divide the class into teams of 6 and have each team form a circle. One child stands in the middle of the circle and calls out a classmate's name. Middle player then throws ball up into the air in the circle and the player whose name was called must attempt to catch the ball on the first bounce or on the full. If successful, that player becomes the middle thrower. Assist the child having difficulties.

Variation: Form one large circle. Stand in the center and toss the ball upward calling out one of the circle player's names. If he/she makes an unsuccessful catch, he/she must run around the circle back to place.

2.

MOVEMENT STATIONS
Lesson 26, Level 2

MOVEMENT AREA: Object Control

MOVEMENT: Catching a Large Ball

TEACHING GOALS:

☞ Use correct hand and body position.

☞ Cushion the ball on impact.

EQUIPMENT REQUIRED:

3 playground balls, 3 footballs, 3 mini-basketballs, 3 large balls
9 deck rings
6 beanbags
Music; cassette/CD player, prepared tape
Cone markers
Assessment Recording Sheet

MOVEMENT STATIONS

1. *Newcombe.* See Lesson 25. Use a smaller court and 3 on 3.

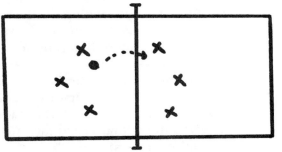

2. *Ring Toss and Catch.* Explore tossing and catching throwing rings. Tasks are put on posterboard:

   ➤ Toss with one hand, catch with two hands.

   ➤ Toss with right hand, catch with right hand; repeat with left hand.

   ➤ Toss from one hand to the other hand.

   ➤ Toss and catch with a partner.

3. *Catching a Large Ball—Assessment.* Observe and record performance. (See Book 1, *Ready-to-Use Fundamental Motor Skills & Movement Activities for Young Children*, for a Recording Sheet.)

2.

4. ***Deckring/Beanbag Play.*** Pair off children, each with a beanbag and a deckring between the two.

HORSESHOES

4.

ROLL AND HIT

➤ *Beanbag Basketball.* One partner throws beanbag through partner's deckring held horizontally with both hands. Partner with deckring tracks beanbag so that it will go through. Change roles after 3 throws. Find a new partner and repeat.

➤ *Beanbag Horseshoes.* Deckring is placed on the floor or ground at a certain distance away from throwers. Partners take turns tossing their beanbag at the ring to see whose beanbag can get closer. Play best 2 out of 3 and challenge a new partner.

➤ *Roll and Hit.* Child rolls deckring and partner attempts to hit it.

5. ***Music Run.*** (Create a tape using popular music with varying tempos. Change the tempo every 20 seconds; provide rest breaks such as stretch breaks of "reaching for the sky" or "breathing breaks," before picking up the tempo again. Suggest 3 minutes of activity; 3 minutes of passive movement.) Keep in time to the music as it changes tempo from quick, to jogging tempo, to walking or marching tempo. Move on the spot or in general space, watching where you are going. When the music stops, you stop by jump-stopping!

5.

6. ***Egg Toss.*** Children explore throwing and catching a variety of balls such as playground ball, football, mini-basketball. Rules are simple: Start two giant steps away facing a partner. If you both succeed in making a catch, then take one walking step away from each other. Continue in this way. Do the task using each of the different balls.

6.

TEACHING SESSION
Lesson 27, Level 2

MOVEMENT AREA: Locomotion
MOVEMENT: Catching a Small Ball

TEACHABLE POINTS:

1. Keep in a balanced position.
2. Body is positioned behind the ball.
3. Arms reach for ball; fingers spread and curved ready to receive the oncoming ball.
4. Hands adjust for the size of the ball.
5. Arms bend at the elbows and give when the ball meets the hands.
6. Fingers face upward for a high ball; downward for a low ball.
7. Fingers wrap around the ball, not "clap it."
8. Eyes focused on the ball.

EQUIPMENT REQUIRED:

1 Beanbag per child   Cone markers
1 small ball per child   4 Hoops

TEACHING GOALS:
- ☞ Keep eyes focused on the ball.
- ☞ Use correct body position.
- ☞ Use correct hand position.

TEACHING PROGRESSIONS

1. Demonstrate the "catching" action yourself. Emphasize having hands the right distance apart, fingers relaxed and spread, feet apart and balanced; eyes watching the ball.

2. Have the children throw a beanbag up in the air and catch it. Observe for correct hand, fingers, and arm positioning. *Variations:* Catch beanbag high; catch beanbag low. Catch beanbag softly. Clap and catch beanbag. Touch a body part before catching beanbag.

3. Repeat #2 using small balls. At first allow the children to let the ball bounce. Those successful at this can attempt to catch it on the full.

4. Then have children in pairs underhand throw to each other.

5. In pairs have the children stand approximately 2 yards (meters) apart. When both children catch the ball, they take a step backward; if unsuccessful, a step forward.

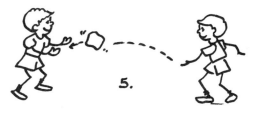

5.

ACTIVITIES

1. ***Triangle Pass and Catch.*** Divide class into groups of 3. Each group finds a Home space and stands in a triangle formation about 3 giant steps apart from each other as shown. Children underhand pass the beanbag in this order: Player 1 passes to player 2 who passes back to 1; then player 1 passes ball to player 3 who returns pass to player 1. Then player 2 becomes the lead passer. Continue in this way.

   ➤ How many catches can be made in a certain time?

2. ***Catch and Capture.*** Divide the class into 4 teams and set up two playing areas. Playing area is a large rectangle with a neutral area in the middle about 5 yards (meters) wide. On the outside of the court at either end is a hoop. The game is started by a member of the throwing team calling the name of a child on the opposite team. The ball is then thrown over to any team member on this team, who must catch the ball. If not caught, the child whose name was called must stand in the hoop at the opposition team's end. A team may free a "prisoner" by calling out his/her name. If the ball is dropped by the opposition, the "prisoner" is freed.

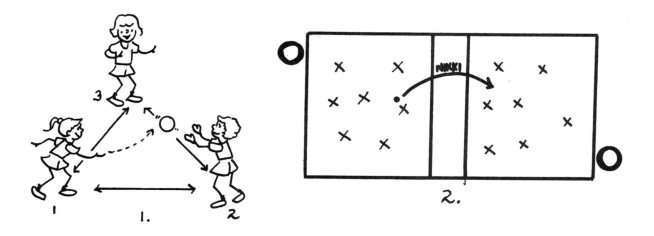

MOVEMENT STATIONS
Lesson 28, Level 2

MOVEMENT AREA: **Object Control**
MOVEMENT: **Catching a Small Ball**

TEACHING GOALS:
- ☞ Keep eyes focused on the ball.
- ☞ Use correct body position.
- ☞ Use correct hand position.

EQUIPMENT REQUIRED:

Cone markers
Variety of small balls
3–4 foxtails or balls in long socks
Floor tape
9–12 beanbags
Boxes, large cones, or bowling pins
Assessment Recording Sheet

MOVEMENT STATIONS

1. *Foxtail Catch.* Children pair off and underhand throw or "windmill throw" a foxtail (or ball in a long sock) to each other. A windmill throw is performed by grabbing the tail midway and swinging the tail outward (clockwise) in a large circle, then letting go. Catch is made by grabbing the tail.

2. *Make the Catch.* Children pair off and explore throwing and catching a variety of small objects such as: mini-footballs, tennis balls, whiffle balls (plastic balls with holes in them), squellet balls (soft balls filled with beads), spider balls, etc.

3. *Catching a Large Ball—Assessment.* Observe and record performance. (See Book 1, *Ready-to-Use Fundamental Motor Skills & Movement Activities for Young Children*, for a Recording Sheet.)

4. *Shuffle Grid.* Mark out a large square divided into 9 areas using floor tape, large sheet of plastic, or colored chalk on tarmac. Each square is marked with a 1, 2, or 3 as shown. Have children stand with a partner two giant steps away (cone markers) on either side of square. Each partner takes 3 throws of the beanbag into the grid and keeps score. Each pair should have a different colored set of beanbags to toss.

1	2	3
2	3	1
1	2	3

4.

5. *Fit-kid Circuit.* Children complete a fitness circuit of stretches, runs, and strength activities. (See Fitness Strategies on page 15.) Place these on cards.

6. *Rolling Targets.* Set up different targets: open boxes on the side; large cone markers; bowling pins. Children pair off and take turns rolling their ball into the target or knocking it over.

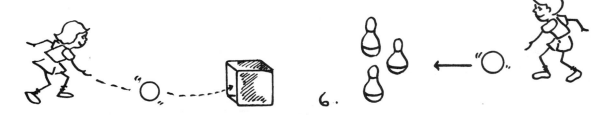

6.

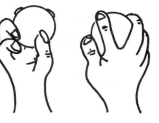

MOVEMENT AREA: Object Control
MOVEMENT: Overhand Throwing

TEACHABLE POINTS:

1. Stand side on to target with head and eyes facing target.
2. Keep in a balanced position with the feet comfortably apart.
3. Ball held in the fingers, wrist cocked, nonthrowing arm points at the target.
4. Throwing arm moves in a downward and backward arc.
5. Transfer weight onto back foot.
6. Elbow bends as throwing hand moves behind head.
7. Front foot steps forward as weight transfers from back foot.
8. Hips, then shoulders, rotate forward.
9. Forearm and hand lag behind upper arm.
10. Follow-through down and across the body.

EQUIPMENT REQUIRED:

20 cone markers
1 beanbag per person
2 sets of 6 bases

TEACHING GOALS:

☛ **Stand side on while throwing.**
☛ **Use good extension in the wind-up.**
☛ **Use correct follow-through.**

TEACHING PROGRESSIONS

1. Demonstrate the overhand throw emphasizing the teaching goals.

2. Children stand side on to a wall, feet close together, and practice stepping to front foot. Use cue words: "one" is the lift (weight is shifted to the back foot); "and" is the pause; and "two" is the step with non-throwing foot toward the target.

"ONE"   and   "TWO"
2.

219

3. Children hold a beanbag with the correct grip (with their fingers) and stand side on to the target. Nonthrowing arm points at the target. Use the cues: "Down as far as you can; back as far as you can; bend and throw."

3.

➤ Practice the action first without a beanbag in the hand.

➤ Then practice overhand throwing the beanbag at the wall.

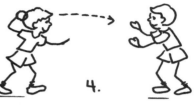

4.

4. In pairs have the children overhand throw back and forth. Start close and gradually move farther away as the children begin to master the task. Be aware of catching ability. (If a child is experiencing difficulty in catching the ball, have the partner roll it back or hand it to him or her.).

1.

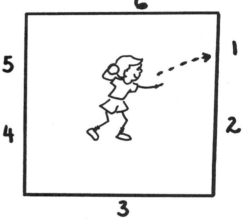

ACTIVITIES

1. *Square Spry.* Children are placed into 4 teams. For each team, players stand along the sides of a large marked square, with a leader from each team standing in the middle as shown. Team members number off 1, 2, 3, . . . On signal "Spry!" the leader overhand throws the beanbag to each team member in turn. When the last player returns the beanbag, that player goes in the middle to replace the leader, who then becomes the first player.

2. *Beat the Ball.* Divide the class into 4 teams. Mark out two fields of play opposite each other so that the teacher can control both games. Game consists of a running team and a throwing team. The first runner must overhand throw the beanbag as far as possible into the field of play. The throwing team must collect the beanbag, quickly position at a base, and throw it around to all the other bases. In this time the runner earns a point for every circuit of the running area he/she completes before the beanbag has been thrown around all the bases.

2.

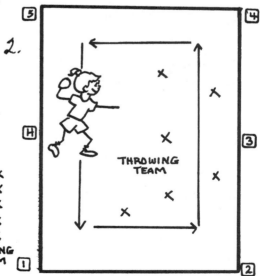

MOVEMENT STATIONS
Lesson 30, Level 2

| MOVEMENT AREA: Object Control |
| MOVEMENT: Overhand Throwing |

TEACHING GOALS:

- ☞ Stand side on while throwing.
- ☞ Use good extension in the wind-up.
- ☞ Be accurate. Use correct follow-through.

EQUIPMENT REQUIRED:

2 hoops with ropes and weights
3 wall targets
9 beanbags
Floor tape
3 mini-footballs or vortex footballs

6 large mats
3 hoops
3 large cone markers
6 beanbags
Assessment Recording Sheet

MOVEMENT STATIONS

1. **Overhand Target Throw.** Set up 3 different wall targets as shown and mark off 3 different throwing distances using floor tape. Children pair off with each pair facing a target. Taking turns, partners overhand throw beanbags at targets. Each partner has 3 turns. Keep score.

2. **Hoop Target Throw.** Suspend a hoop from a basketball framework or other suitable fixture. Secure it with a rope and weight to the floor as shown. Children work in three's and take turns to overhand throw a football or junior vortex throwing football into the hoop. If possible, set up two identical hoop targets. Use cone markers to set distances. *Variation:* Suspend a hoop between two chairs or in a grooved cone marker.

3. **Overhand Throwing—Assessment.** Observe and record performance. (See Book 1, *Ready-to-Use Fundamental Motor Skills & Movement Activities for Young Children*, for a Recording Sheet.)

221

4. **Triangle Run.** Set up 3 markers in a triangular pattern, spaced 15 feet (5 meters) apart. Mark them 1, 2, and 3 as shown. Set up 2 identical patterns. Each child, in turn, starts at the first marker, runs around the second, back around the first, then around the third, and back around the first marker. This circuit must be completed twice.

5. **Mini Golf.** Set up a number of "fairways" using hoops as holes and marker cones as tees as shown. Children pair off and take turns overhand throwing beanbags around the course. Each pair keeps track of its score. *Variation:* Use spider balls.

6. **Relaxation Station.** Children lie quietly on mat, relaxing body parts starting with the feet and working up to the head: first tense body part for 5 seconds; relax for 5 seconds.

➤ Finally do an overall body stretch: Pencil Stretch—curl up into a ball—Pencil Stretch.

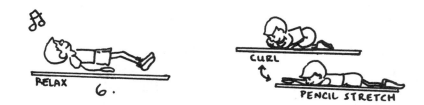

TEACHING SESSION
Lesson 31, Level 2

MOVEMENT AREA: Object Control
MOVEMENT: Overhand Throwing

TEACHABLE POINTS:

1. Stand side-on to target, head and eyes facing target.
2. Keep in a balanced position with the feet comfortably apart.
3. Ball held in the fingers, wrist cocked, nonthrowing arm points at the target.
4. Throwing arm moves in a downward and backward arc.
5. Transfer weight onto back foot.
6. Elbow bends as throwing hand moves behind head.
7. Front foot steps forward as weight transfers from back foot.
8. Hips, then shoulders, rotate forward.
9. Forearm and hand lag behind upper arm.
10. Follow-through down and across the body.

EQUIPMENT REQUIRED:

1 small ball and beanbag per thrower	4 hoops
Cone markers	Deckrings

TEACHING GOALS:

☞ **Use good weight transference.**
☞ **Extend in wind-up and follow through.**
☞ **Go for distance.**

TEACHING PROGRESSIONS

1. Revise and demonstrate the overhand throw, emphasizing the goals.

2. In pairs, children overhand throw to each other. Explore using different objects to overhand throw, such as tennis balls, beanbags, small playground balls.

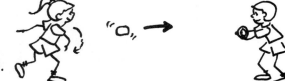

3. Use the "listening line" signal and have children stand on one of the sidelines of the play area, with one partner in front and the other partner behind. Check for ample spacing between each pair. First partner runs forward with a deckring, which will be used to mark second partner's throw. Second partner has two attempts to overhand throw beanbag as far as possible. Change roles and continue.

ACTIVITIES

1. *Catch and Capture.* Divide the class into 4 teams and set up two playing areas. Playing area is a large rectangle with a neutral area in the middle about 5 yards (meters) wide. On the outside of the court at either end is a hoop. The game is started by a member of the throwing team calling the name of a child on the opposite team. The ball is then thrown over to this team who must catch the ball. If they fail, the child whose name was called must stand in the hoop at the opposition team's end. A team may free a prisoner by calling out his/her name. If the ball is dropped by the opposition, prisoner is freed.

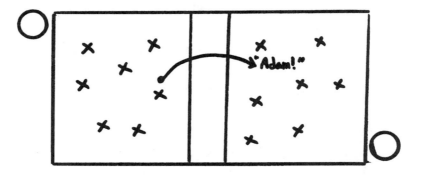

2. *Wall Throw & Catch.* Children pair off and find a free wall space to throw and catch a small playground ball. Use the overhand throw and catch ball on one bounce, then no bounces, if possible.

MOVEMENT STATIONS
Lesson 32, Level 2

MOVEMENT AREA: Object Control
MOVEMENT: Overhand Throwing

TEACHING GOALS:
- ☞ Use good weight transference.
- ☞ Extend in wind-up and follow through.
- ☞ Go for distance.

EQUIPMENT REQUIRED:

Music; cassette/CD player
Cone markers
Small balls
3 plastic bottles, 3 small cones, 3 skittles

2 balance benches
Fling-It™ Nets or small sheets
Foxtail™ or balls in socks
Assessment Recording Sheet

MOVEMENT STATIONS

1. *Music Run.* (Create a tape using popular music, with varying tempos. Change the tempo every 20 seconds; provide rest breaks such as stretch breaks of "reaching for the sky" or "breathing breaks" before picking up the tempo again. Suggest 3 minutes of activity; 3 minutes of passive movement.) Keep in time to the music as it changes tempo from quick, to jogging tempo, to walking or marching tempo. Move on the spot or in general space, watching where you are going. When the music stops, you stop by jump-stopping!

2. *Knock 'em Over Target Throw.* Set up several targets on benches using small cones, plastic bottles, or plastic skittles. Children pair off and take turns to overhand throw 2 small balls at targets and knock them over. Keep score. Change to a different target and continue. Vary the throwing distances using cone markers.

3. ***Foxtail Throw.*** Children pair off and overhand throw a foxtail (or ball in sock) back and forth to each other. Emphasize good follow-through. Receiver tracks ball all the way into the hands.

4. ***Continue Overhand Throwing— Assessment.*** Observe and record performance. (See Book 1, *Ready-to-Use Fundamental Motor Skills & Movement Activities for Young Children*, for a Recording Sheet.)

5. ***Derby Ball.*** Children form a large circle with one player in the middle. Middle player attempts to roll a small ball out of the circle. Circle players use hands, feet, or body to stop the ball from going out. Middle player is given 5 attempts, then the next circle player goes. Continue in this way.

6. ***Fling-it Play.*** Children pair off. Using Fling-It™ Nets or lightweight sheets (about the size of a towel), they send a ball up into the air and catch it in the net.

TEACHING SESSION
Lesson 33, Level 2

> **MOVEMENT AREA:** Object Control
>
> **MOVEMENT:** Single-Handed Striking

TEACHABLE POINTS:

1. Start in "Ready Position," keeping in balance with feet comfortably apart.
2. Keep the knees bent through the movement.
3. Side-on body position is achieved when hitting.
4. Transfer the weight forward by stepping into the swing.
5. Take a big backswing.
6. Keep the head of the racquet slightly above the wrist; keep the wrist firm.
7. Follow-through in the intended direction.
8. Eyes are focused and head is kept steady throughout the movement.

EQUIPMENT REQUIRED:

Paddle raquet per group of 4   4 bases
Medium-sized soft balls or plastic whiffle balls   1 hoop
Cone markers   Large traffic cone or tee stand
Tall witch's hats or T-ball stands

> **TEACHING GOALS:**
> - Use big backswing.
> - Use correct weight transference.
> - Use correct follow-through.
> - Keep wrist firm.

TEACHING PROGRESSIONS

1. Demonstrate the forehand strike, emphasizing the teaching goals.
2. Have children stand in waves and get into a sideways stance. Move weight from the front foot to the back foot and back again on the signal "Front," "Back."
3. Now add the arm swing, making the action rhythmical by counting "one and two." "One" is the back swing; "and" is the pause at the top; and "two" is the downswing and follow-through.

"ONE"   "AND"   "TWO"

227

4. Divide children in groups of 4; a Hitter, a Catcher, and two Fielders, with 2 balls per group. The Hitter strikes the ball with a small racket from a tall witch's hat or tee ball stand. The fielders return the ball to the Catcher who places the ball on the stand. Rotate positions after 10 hits each. Have the children alter their hits between preferred hand, nonpreferred hand, and two hands.

4.

ACTIVITIES

Modified T-ball. Class is split into 6 teams of 5–6 players. To start, three teams are selected to be the batting teams and three teams to be the fielding teams. Designate an area for each game, set up 4 bases and a hoop in the area as shown, and have Batting Team 1 play against Fielding Team 1. *Rules:*

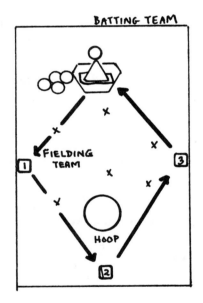

➤ Each batter hits 5 balls with a racquet from a large traffic cone or a T-ball stand into the field of play.

➤ The fielding team must collect the balls and return them to a hoop near the catcher's base before the runner makes it around the bases.

➤ If the runner makes it before the balls are returned, a homerun is scored. If the fielders beat the runner, then it is no score.

➤ All hitters bat and then change roles with the fielding team. Keep reminding children of the correct technique when striking the ball.

MOVEMENT STATIONS
Lesson 34, Level 2

MOVEMENT AREA: Object Control
MOVEMENT: Single-Handed Striking

TEACHING GOALS:
- ☛ Use big backswing.
- ☛ Transfer correct weight.
- ☛ Use correct follow-through.

EQUIPMENT REQUIRED:

6 balloons
Wooden bats
2 totem tennis set-ups
3 large cones or T-ball stands
3 medium-sized lightweight balls
2 long jumping ropes
1 shuffle grid
3 sets of colored beanbags
Assessment Recording Sheet

MOVEMENT STATIONS

1. **Balloon Bat.** Children, in pairs, bat a balloon back and forth using wooden bats.

2. **Totem Tennis.** Children take turns striking a suspended ball in a stocking with an open hand. If possible, set up two totem tennis areas.

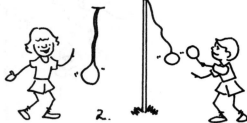

3. **T-Ball Strike.** Children, in pairs, take turns striking a ball with a small paddle. The ball is positioned on a large cone marker as shown. Suggest that ball be hit toward a wall so that it can be easily retrieved. Encourage use of either hand.

4. ***Single-handed Striking—Assessment.*** Observe and record performance.(See Book 1, *Ready-to-Use Fundamental Motor Skills & Movement Activities for Young Children,* for a Recording Sheet.)

5. ***Long Rope Jumping.*** Children split up into three's. Each group has two turners and one jumper. Jumpers perform the following tasks:

➤ Start in the center and try to jump the turning rope as long as you can.

➤ Run in front door (at the top of the rope turn as the rope turns toward you); jump 5 times; run out.

➤ Run in front door and straight out.

➤ Run in front door and do jump-turns.

➤ Create your own jumping stunt!

5.

6. ***Shuffle Grid.*** Mark out a large square divided into 9 areas using floor tape, or large sheet of plastic, or colored chalk on tarmac. Each square is marked with a 1, 2, or 3 as shown. Have children stand with a partner two giant steps away (cone markers) on either side of square. Each partner takes 3 throws of the beanbag into the grid and keeps score. Each pair should have a different colored set of beanbags to toss.

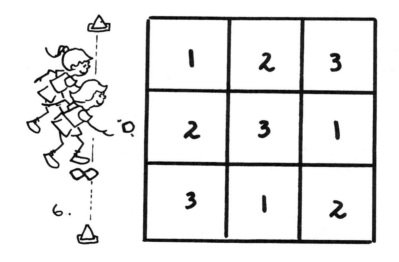

TEACHING SESSION
Lesson 35, Level 2

MOVEMENT AREA: Object Control
MOVEMENT: Single-Handed Striking

TEACHABLE POINTS:

1. Start in "Ready Position," keeping in balance with feet comfortably apart.
2. Keep the knees bent through the movement.
3. Side-on body position is achieved when hitting.
4. Transfer the weight forward by stepping into the swing.
5. Take a big backswing.
6. Keep the head of the racquet slightly above the wrist; keep the wrist firm.
7. Follow-through in the intended direction.
8. Eyes are focused and head is kept steady throughout the movement.

EQUIPMENT REQUIRED:

Small racquets   Light large balls
Witch's hats   T-ball stands
Small balls   Cone markers
Medium-size balls

> ### TEACHING GOALS:
> - Use side-on body position.
> - Use big backswing.
> - Follow-through in the direction of the target.
> - Use firm wrist.

TEACHING PROGRESSIONS

1. Structure free play with small bats and different sized balls.
2. Children use a small racket to see how many times they can bounce the ball with their racquet. Hit the ball up and down on the racquet.
3. Demonstrate and emphasize the goals for today's lesson. Have children show you the difference between "floppy" wrists and firm wrists. Which is better when hitting the ball with the hand or racquet?

231

4. Have children stand in a "ready position" or square position facing a wall, then step to the side-on position. (For a right-hander, the left foot will step forward.) Use signal "Ready position, lift, and step." Practice.

5. Now add the arm swing as for rhythmical count in #3 on page 231. Emphasize keeping wrist firm.

6. In pairs, one partner is the striker; the other, the Tosser. Striker lets the ball bounce once, then hits it with the open hand. Use a medium-sized ball. Remind Striker to step to the side-on position, keep eyes on ball, swing, and follow through! After 5 attempts to strike the ball, switch roles.

7. Have children collect a paddle racquet and find a Home space. Put racquet down and shake hands with a partner. Then "shake hands" with the racquet. This is the proper grip for holding a racquet.

8. Practice the swinging action with the racquet as for #3. Move from "ready position" to side-on position, then swing racquet.

9. Repeat #6, using a racquet to hit a light plastic ball to a wall. Emphasize keeping wrist firm.

ACTIVITY

1. *T-Ball Play.* Children, in pairs, take turns striking a medium-sized ball off a large cone or T-ball stand. Remind striker to be side on to ball, and keep eyes on ball as hand swings through; then follow-through. *Variation:* Strike the ball with the paddle racquet.

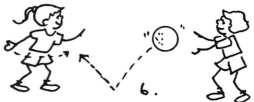

MOVEMENT STATIONS
Lesson 36, Level 2

MOVEMENT AREA: Object Control
MOVEMENT: Single-Handed Striking

TEACHING GOALS:
- ☛ Use side-on body position.
- ☛ Use big backswing.
- ☛ Follow-through in the direction of the target.
- ☛ Use firm wrist.

EQUIPMENT REQUIRED:

T-ball stand	3 balloon balls
Medium-sized playground ball	Tether ball stand
Large base	2 balance boards
Cone markers	2 balance benches
Assessment Recording Sheet	Fitness Cards (1 set)

MOVEMENT STATIONS

1. *Long Base.* For each group of 3, have 1 Hitter, 1 Catcher, and 1 Fielder. Set up as shown in diagram with a base located about 10 yards (meters) from the T-ball stand. Hitter gets 2 attempts to strike the ball off the tee with a paddle, run and touch a long base, then return home. Racquet is carried with the Runner and used to touch inside a hoop when she/he reaches home. This scores a run. Everyone keeps own score; players rotate positions after every 2 hits. Continue in this way.

2. *Balloon Ball Play.* Children, in pairs, keep the balloon afloat using hands, then small racquets. (Balloon balls are cloth spherical covers with a large inflated balloon inside.)

3. *Tether Ball Play.* Suspend a ball on a rope from a pole and have children stand in a circle around the pole. As ball swings toward each player, he/she strikes it with the open hand. If possible, set up two totem pole areas.

1. LONG BASE

2.

3.

4. ***Continue Single-Handed Striking—Assessment.*** Observe and record performance. (See Book 1, *Ready-to-Use Fundamental Motor Skills & Movement Activities for Young Children*, for a Recording Sheet.)

5. ***Balancing Circuit.*** Children work in pairs, partners assisting if necessary.

   ➤ *Balance on a balancing board:* feet apart, feet together, one foot in front of other; rock back and forth.

   ➤ *Moving balances on the bench:* Move across a balance bench in different ways: slide across on front; walk across on hands and feet; hop across; move across with feet on bench and hands on floor. Create other moving stunts.

6. ***Fit-Kid Circuit.*** Children complete a fitness circuit of stretches, runs, and strength activities. (See Fitness Strategies on page 15.) Place these on cards.

6.

| MOVEMENT AREA: Object Control |
| MOVEMENT: Slide-Stepping |

TEACHABLE POINTS:

1. Body is side on to the intended direction of travel.
2. Head is held up and still. Eyes look in the direction of travel.
3. Slide step is on the forefoot.
4. Leading leg side-steps, followed by a sliding action of the trailing leg, back to the leading leg.
5. Width of the slide step is not too wide or too narrow, about shoulder-width apart.
6. Knees are slightly bent throughout the movement.
7. Arms remain relaxed but may assist the movement.
8. Child can slide both ways.
9. Movement should be smooth and rhythmical.

EQUIPMENT REQUIRED:

Firm even surface
Cone markers, hoops, or deckrings
Music with a steady 4/4 beat; cassette/CD player

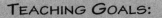

TEACHING GOALS:
- Look for a step, then a slide.
- Be sure body is side on to direction of travel.
- Push off the trailing leg as leading leg side steps.

TEACHING PROGRESSIONS

1. Demonstrate the slide-stepping action, emphasizing the goals.
2. Slowly, at first, guide children through the sequence using the cue words: "Step to side, feet together."
3. Reverse direction, going through the same steps. Now the other foot leads the action.
4. Have child slide-step to the right; slide-step to the left. On signal have them "jump stop."

5. Scatter hoops, cones, or deckrings on the floor and have children slide-step around the objects.

6. Have children slide-step in a big circle; slide-step in a zigzag pattern; slide-step in a square pathway.

7. Side-by-side, holding hands, children slide-step together to music.

ACTIVITIES

1. *This Way and That Way.* Have children stand facing you in "wave" formation. Point with your right hand to slide-step to the right; left hand to slide-step to the left; both hands pointing to floor to bounce lightly in place; both hands in air to have children stretch up high. *Variation:* Add other hand signals, such as extend hands out in front with fingers pointing upward as if to gently push children backward. They respond by carefully jogging backward. Motion them with hands to move forward.

2. *Slide-Step Tag.* Play simple tag using the slide-step movement. Establish a "safe" position by freezing for a 3-second count in a static balance such as a "Stork Stand." Have 3 taggers each with a tagging object. Change taggers frequently. *Variation:* Use other locomotor movements.

TAGGER

STORK STAND 'SAFE'

MOVEMENT STATIONS
Lesson 38, Level 2

MOVEMENT AREA: Object Control
MOVEMENT: Slide-Stepping

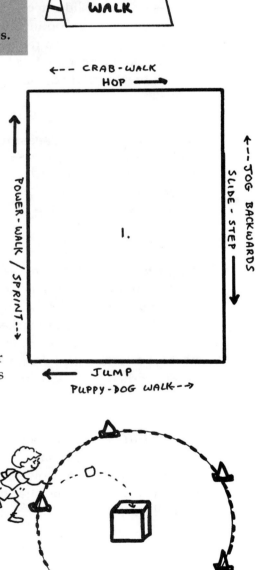

EQUIPMENT REQUIRED:

4 locomotion signs
Cone markers
12 beanbags
1 laundry basket or box
6 dome markers
10 numbered large cone markers
6 balls in socks or 6 tennis balls
1 tether ball set
6 racquets
Assessment Recording Sheet

MOVEMENT STATIONS

1. *Locomotion Circuit.* Mark out a rectangular area. At each corner set up a sign that indicates the movement to be done along this line as shown: Power Walk a length; Hop a width; Slide-Step a length; Jump a Width.

   ➤ After completing two circuits, children stop to stretch; then travel in the reverse direction: Sprint a length; Puppy Walk a width; Jog backwards a length; Crab Walk a width.

2. *Beanbag Circle Toss.* Underhand toss beanbags into a laundry basket or box from markers set up in a circle formation as shown. Increase the throwing distance by moving marker with every successful 2 throws.

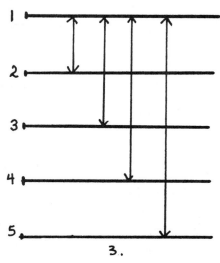

3. *Slide-Step Shuttle Lines.* Mark off a series of lines using cone markers as shown. Number the lines 1, 2, 3, 4, and 5, with line 1 being the start line. Children slide step from starting line across to touch line 2 with two hands, then return to line 1 facing the opposite direction as the slide-step. Then slide-step to line 3 returning to line 1; continue to slide-step to each line, touch, and return to starting line. When they complete set of lines, take a stretch break and do the lines again.

3.

4. *Slide-Stepping—Assessment.* Observe and record performance. (See Book 1, *Ready-to-Use Fundamental Motor Skills & Movement Activities for Young Children,* for a Recording Sheet.)

5. *Egg Toss Play.* Challenge each other to see who in the group can catch a tennis ball (or ball in a sock) over the greatest distance. Start at the first step of marked cones and, with each successful catch, move to the next set of cones. (See diagram.) Emphasize good overhand throwing to partner.

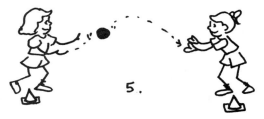

5.

6. *Tether Ball Play.* Suspend a ball on a rope from a pole and have children stand in a circle around the pole. As ball swings toward each player, he/she strikes it with a small racquet.

6.

TEACHING SESSION
Lesson 39, Level 2

MOVEMENT AREA: Locomotion
MOVEMENT: Hopping and Leaping

TEACHABLE POINTS: HOPPING

1. Hop starts on one foot and lands on the same foot (both on the forefoot).
2. Swinging leg remains bent and moves back and forth during the hop, in opposition to the support leg, assisting in the forward movement.
3. Hopping leg bends to absorb the landing force.
4. Arms move in opposition. Nonsupport leg assists in the forward movement.
5. Head remains stable with the eyes looking forward.
6. Keep movement smooth and in balance.

TEACHABLE POINTS: LEAPING

1. Leaping action is on the balls of the feet during take-off and landing, springing from one foot to the other.
2. Knees flex at landing to absorb the force of the landing.
3. Arms assist in the propulsion by extending forward and upward vigorously as the legs extend forcefully.
4. Head remains up with eyes focused forward during the action.
5. Movement is continuous and rhythmical.

EQUIPMENT REQUIRED:

Firm flat surface
Cone markers
4–6 long ropes
Music; cassette/CD player
2 low hurdles per team
6–8 large hoops
Chalk or carpet squares

TEACHING GOALS:

Hopping
☛ **Promote knee drive from nonsupporting leg.**
☛ **Promote correct landing.**
☛ **Promote balance.**

Leaping:
☛ **Promote correct take-off.**
☛ **Promote correct landing.**

TEACHING PROGRESSIONS

Hopping and leaping are extremely fatiguing movements and should be used in conjunction with other movements. When hopping, the duration should be short, with adequate rest between efforts. Encourage hopping and leaping on both legs.

HOPPING:

1. Demonstrate the correct hopping action to the children, emphasizing the teaching goals.

2. Have children practice single-leg balance activities. Use both arms to balance.

3. In pairs, taking turns, children hop in place, with support from their partner. Concentrate on knee action and support leg position.

4. Children hop in general space, using arms to help them. Change hopping foot every 4 hops. Hop to music.

5. In teams of 5, shuttle formation, have a hopping relay.

LEAPING:

1. Demonstrate the correct leaping action to the children, emphasizing the teaching goals.

2. Have children run forward and leap off one foot into the air, landing softly on 2 feet. Repeat, leaping off the other foot. Try to convey the feeling of "flying" through the air.

2. "FLYING"

3. Have children leap over a line or stretched rope, landing on both feet. Explore leaping over the line with one foot, then the other.

4. Set up 4–6 long ropes, spaced about 1 yard (meter) apart. Have child leap over the ropes, changing leading foot. Observe that opposite arm to opposite leg occurs. Increase the distance between ropes.

5. In pairs, have children leapfrog over the back of their partner as they move from one sideline to the other.

ACTIVITIES

1. ***Hopscotch.*** Using chalk or carpet squares mark out a hopscotch court (see diagram). Children start outside square 1 and throw their beanbag into square 1. Using a hop or leap to land in single squares and a jump to land in double squares, they progress up the court and back again. Generally they must pick up their beanbag on the return journey and they may not land in an area that contains a marker. If successful, they throw to square 2 and repeat the process.

2. ***Hurdle Leap Relay.*** Divide the class into 4 teams and have each team set up in shuttle formation 30 feet (10 meters) apart from each other. Set up 2 low hurdles in the middle between each team as shown. On signal "Leap away!" each team member, in turn, travels across to the opposite group, leaping over the hurdles.

3. ***"Hooping" Mad.*** Hoops are placed randomly in a marked area. The teacher calls "Scrambled Eggs...!" and a movement (running, walking, bouncing, leaping, etc). On the call of a number, the children must hop to a hoop and form a group of that size. Last group to form must walk around the outside of the area for the next turn. The use of music adds to this activity.

MOVEMENT STATIONS
Lesson 40, Level 2

> **MOVEMENT AREA:** Locomotion
>
> **MOVEMENT:** Hopping and Leaping

TEACHING GOALS:

Hopping:

- ☛ Promote knee drive from nonsupporting leg.
- ☛ Promote correct landing.
- ☛ Promote balance.

Leaping:

- ☛ Promote correct take-off.
- ☛ Promote correct landing.

EQUIPMENT REQUIRED:

2 long ropes
1 long rope with ball attached
6 short skipping ropes
Variety of different types of medium and large balls
Cone markers
Assessment Recording Sheet

MOVEMENT STATIONS

1. ***Alligator Leap.*** Place 2 long ropes at an angle to each other as shown, about 1 yard (meter) at the narrow end and about 3 yards (meters) at the wide end. Children, in turn, attempt to leap across the "river" which is full of alligators. With each successful leap, child attempts to leap across a wider part.

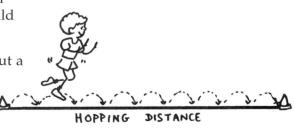

2. ***Hopping Sprint.*** Use markers to set out a certain traveling distance and have children in turn hop through this distance. Emphasize using arms to assist in hopping action.

   ➤ Use preferred foot to hop; then hop using the other foot.

242

3. ***Jump the Ball.*** One child in group swings a ball attached to a rope in a circle along the ground. Other children try to hop, leap, or jump over the ball each time it passes under their feet. Switch rope swinger after every 5 complete swings. If rope catches someone's feet, that player must run around the circle, then back in place to continue.

4. ***Hopping and Leaping—Assessment.*** Observe and record performance. (See Book 1, *Ready-to-Use Fundamental Motor Skills & Movement Activities for Young Children,* for a Recording Sheet.)

5. ***Ball Throw & Catch.*** Children in pairs practice overhand throwing and catching. Use a variety of different types of balls at this station.

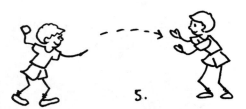

6. ***Short Rope Jumping.*** Children practice short rope jumping skills.

TEACHING SESSION
Lesson 41, Level 2

> **MOVEMENT AREA:** Locomotion
>
> **MOVEMENT:** Skipping

TEACHABLE POINTS:

1. Skipping action is done on the balls of the feet.
2. Use the command "step, hop."
3. Arms and legs move in opposite direction to each other.
4. Head remains up with eyes focused forward during the action.
5. Keep in balance.

EQUIPMENT REQUIRED:

Small balls/beanbags
Cone markers
Music; cassette/CD player
6–8 large hoops

TEACHING GOALS:

☛ Be sure action is on the balls of the feet.
☛ Use correct arm swing.
☛ Use rhythmical action.

TEACHING PROGRESSIONS

2. "STEP" – "HOP"

Using music with a strong 4/4 beat will help establish the skipping rhythm. Choose a moderate tempo that the child can easily follow.

1. Demonstrate the correct technique, emphasizing the teaching goals.

2. Place a series of markers on the ground. Have the children step to one marker and then hop to the next. Talk children through the movement slowly: "Step right, hop; step left, hop." Allow them to initially look at their feet; then repeat the activity without looking at their feet.

4.

3. Repeat without markers.

4. Have children skip forward to music (slowly at first).

5. Ask children to skip forward, making slight changes of direction.

6. Ask children to show you skipping in a happy way—swinging arms and lifting knees high.

7. Have children hold hands with a partner and skip forward together.

ACTIVITIES

1. ***Skipping Dance.*** Make up or use a dance that has different movements in it, including skipping. Country music lends itself to this.

2. ***Skipping Attack!*** Scatter several hoops throughout a defined play area. Choose 3 players to be the "Sharks" who each hold a beanbag. Players ("Fish") move ("swim") around the play area by skipping. Sharks try to catch (tag) free players with their beanbags. Players can jump into any hoop to be safe—Only one player per hoop. After a 3-second count— "one shark, two sharks, three sharks"—player must leave hoop. Fish that are caught must skip in place. After a certain time, count all the Fish that the Sharks caught. Choose new Sharks and play again.

MOVEMENT STATIONS
Lesson 42, Level 2

MOVEMENT AREA: Locomotion
MOVEMENT: Skipping

TEACHING GOALS:

- ☞ Be sure action is on the balls of the feet.
- ☞ Use correct arm swing.
- ☞ Use rhythmical action.

EQUIPMENT REQUIRED:

CD/cassette player; music
12 juggling scarves
6 short jump ropes or skipping hoops
2 Foxtail™ or balls in socks
3 foam stilts and 3 foam steppers
Assessment Recording Sheet

MOVEMENT STATIONS

1. *Skipping Dance.* Children create a skipping dance to music provided. Encourage them to use other locomotor movements as well in their dance.

2. *Short Rope Skipping or Hoop Skipping Play.* Children use short ropes or skipping hoops in free play.

3. *Juggling Scarves Play.* Children explore sending and receiving one juggling scarf on different body parts; then using two scarves.

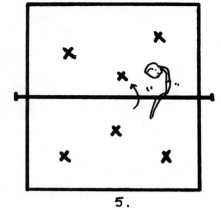

5.

4. ***Continue Single-Handed Striking—Assessment.*** Observe and record performance. (See Book 1, *Ready-to-Use Fundamental Motor Skills & Movement Activities for Young Children,* for a Recording Sheet.)

5. ***Foxtail Newcombe.*** Set up a court with a net or rope at a height just above children's head. Group splits into 3 on each side. Each side has a foxtail and sends it over to the opposite side using an overhand, underhand, or windmill throw. A side scores a point if the opposition fails to catch the foxtail. Ball in a long sock can be used if foxtails are not available.

6. ***Balance Walkers.*** Children use foam stilts or foam steppers to practice walking and keeping their balance. Set up a course for them to walk through.

6.

TEACHING SESSION
Lesson 43, Level 2

MOVEMENT AREA: Object Control
MOVEMENT: One-Handed Bouncing with Large Ball

TEACHABLE POINTS:

1. Keep in a balanced position with the feet comfortably spread.
2. Eyes are focused on the ball. When skill increases, eyes can look away from the ball.
3. Ball is pushed down with hand by extending arm downward.
4. Fingers are relaxed and spread.
5. Be in ready position to receive the bouncing ball, with elbow slightly bent.
6. Let arms give or move slightly upward as ball contacts the hands.
7. Bounce ball in front of and to side of the body.

EQUIPMENT REQUIRED:

Firm even surface
Cone markers
Variety of large balls, 1 per child
1 hoop or carpet square per child

TEACHING GOALS:

☛ **Keep head up and eyes focused.**
☛ **Use pumping action, not slapping at ball.**

TEACHING PROGRESSIONS

1. Hold the ball in both hands and feel the ball by gently turning the ball in your hands. Roll the ball through your legs in a figure-8 pattern.

2. Get into kneeling position. Bounce ball in your Home space. Remember to relax fingers and not slap at the ball. Let the fingers meet the ball and push it downward.

248

3. Now play the "piano" on your ball. Start with your pointer finger first and use it to bounce the ball. Then let each of the other fingers have a turn: middle, ring, pinky, and thumb. Now use all your fingers working together to bounce the ball.

4. Stand so that your knees are bent and feet shoulder-width apart. Put your foot opposite the bouncing hand slightly ahead. Now bounce the ball in your preferred hand in the "pocket" formed by your body and feet. Bounce at waist height; bounce low; bounce high. Can you bounce your ball while looking slightly ahead of the ball? Listen to the rhythm of your ball bouncing: "bounce–bounce–bounce."

5. Bounce your ball from one sideline to the other. Jump stop on that sideline when you get there. Jump turn to face opposite way. Bounce your ball back to the starting sideline. Continue in this way.

6. Hold your ball as you jog forward. On signal "Freeze!" jump stop and hold the ball in both hands near your hip. On signal "Jog," travel forward again.

7. Repeat #5, but bounce the ball as you move forward.

ACTIVITIES

1. *Musical Hoop Bounce.* Randomly spread hoops or carpet squares, one for each child, around the play area. Have children move as instructed to music, while holding their ball. When the music stops, call out a number. The children must move to a hoop and bounce their ball the instructed number of times in the hoop.

2. *Bounce Relay.* Divide the class into groups of 4 and have each group stand in file formation behind a start line, facing a cone marker 10 yards (meters) away, as shown. Each member, in turn, bounces ball to cone marker with preferred hand, and returns using other hand to bounce ball back to start line.

MOVEMENT STATIONS
Lesson 44, Level 2

MOVEMENT AREA: Object Control
MOVEMENT: Bouncing with One Hand (large ball)

TEACHING GOALS:

- Keep eyes on ball.
- Move arms in pumping action, as fingers push ball downward (not slapping ball).

EQUIPMENT REQUIRED:

15 hoops
Cone markers
Variety of balls per station

Variety of low, medium, and high targets
Poster on stretching
Several objects for obstacle course

MOVEMENT STATIONS

1. *Obstacle Course.* Scatter several objects, such as chairs, mats, hoops, ropes, cones, boxes, or bins, around the station area. Children bounce their ball in and out of objects. Every time they come to a hoop, they must bounce their ball 5 times inside the hoop before traveling onward.

2. *Figure-8 Bounce.* Set up 2 identical figure-8 courses using cone markers as shown. Children take turns bouncing ball through the figure-8 course. Use the preferred hand to bounce ball toward cone marker, then switch to other hand to bounce the ball on the return to Home. Continue in this way until the course is completed.

3. ***Target Tossing.*** Set up a variety of high, medium, and low targets. Have children underhand toss different objects into the targets. Vary the throwing distances. *Variation:* Use the overhand throw for one of the accuracy throwing tasks.

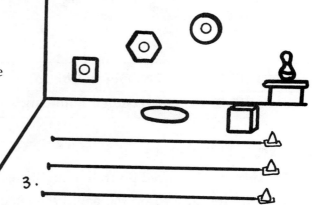

4. ***Bouncing Ball with One Hand—Assessment.*** Observe and record performance. (See Book 1, *Ready-to-Use Fundamental Motor Skills & Movement Activities for Young Children*, for a Recording Sheet.)

5. ***Line Shuttle Bounce.*** Mark off a set of lines that are 10 yards (meters) apart as shown. Place a numbered cone marker by each line. Children bounce to Line 1 with preferred hand; back to start line with other hand. Continue to bounce ball to Line 2, then back to start line; bounce ball to Line 3, back to start line; and so on to endline and back to start. After completing a set, do a ball stretch for 30 seconds, then complete another set of line shuttle bouncing.

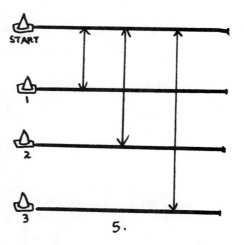

6. ***Stretch & Relax Station.*** Select stretches from Fitness Strategies and Stretching Signals on pages 15–29. Enlarge and put on a large poster. Emphasize that the stretch is held for 10 seconds.

TEACHING SESSION
Lesson 45, Level 2

MOVEMENT AREA: Object Control
MOVEMENT: One-Handed Bouncing

TEACHABLE POINTS:

1. Keep in a balanced position with the feet comfortably spread.

2. Eyes are focused on the ball. When skill increases, eyes can look away from the ball.

3. Ball is pushed down with hand by extending arm downward.

4. Fingers are relaxed and spread.

5. Be in ready position to receive the bouncing ball, with elbow slightly bent.

6. Let arms give or move slightly upward as ball contacts the hands.

7. Bounce ball in front of and to side of the body.

EQUIPMENT REQUIRED:

Firm even surface
Cone markers
Variety of large balls,1 per child

TEACHING GOALS:
☞ **Control ball-handling.**
☞ **Bounce ball with either hand.**

TEACHING PROGRESSIONS

1. In standing position, toss the ball from hand to hand by gently pushing it off the fingers.

1.

2. Get into a position so that the knee opposite your bouncing hand is up and the other knee is down. This forms a "bouncing pocket." Bounce the ball in your "pocket." Switch hands and knee position, and bounce the ball.

2.

3. Revise playing the "piano" on your ball. Start with your pointer finger first and use it to bounce the ball. Then let each of the other fingers have a turn: middle, ring, pinky, and thumb. Use all your fingers working together to bounce the ball. Emphasize that children relax fingers and not slap at the ball. Let the fingers meet the ball and push it downward.

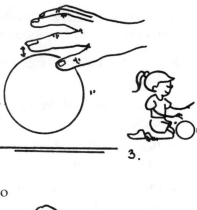

➤ Who can play the "piano ball" with your eyes closed?

➤ Repeat with the other hand.

4. Revise the stance for the "pocket bounce." Stand so that your knees are bent and feet shoulder-width apart. Put your foot opposite the bouncing hand slightly ahead. Now bounce the ball in your preferred hand in the "pocket" formed by your body and feet.

➤ Bounce ball at knee height; bounce ball at waist height.

➤ Bounce ball low; bounce ball high; fast; slow.

➤ Bounce ball while looking slightly ahead of the ball.

➤ How many bounces can you do in a row?

➤ Pocket bounce using your other hand.

5. Start on one sideline. Bounce ball in a forward direction with preferred hand to opposite sideline; bounce ball back to place with other hand.

6. Now stand facing square on and bend your knees. Bounce the ball from one hand to the other. The ball travels in a "V" pathway on the crossover. Remember to stay low, knees bent!

7. *Ball Stunts.*

➤ Pass the ball around your waist; around your knees. Go the opposite direction.

➤ Bounce the ball from standing position to kneeling position to sitting position, and back up again. Repeat.

➤ Bounce the ball in place while you walk around it.

➤ Bounce the ball around you while you stand in place.

➤ Try to get the ball bouncing from its stationary place on the floor.

➤ Think up a stunt of your own!

ACTIVITIES

1. ***Mirror Bouncing.*** Children mirror your movements and ball-bouncing positions:

   ➤ Pass the ball in a figure-8 between your legs.

   ➤ Bounce the ball in a figure-8 between the legs.

   ➤ Bounce ball while marching in place; jogging in place; jumping in place.

   ➤ On signal "Freeze," children jump-stop and hold the ball in both hands near hip (opposite to leading foot).

   ➤ On signal "Pivot," keep the toe of one foot in touch with the floor while you use the other foot to push off and turn yourself in different directions.

   ➤ On signal "Bounce," bounce your ball with your preferred hand as you travel forward.

   ➤ On signal "Crossover," crossover bounce in place.

2. ***Bouncing Relay.*** Form groups of 4, with one ball per group, and have each group stand in file formation behind a starting line, facing 4 cone markers that are spaced 2 yards (meters) apart. On signal "Bounce," take turns as you bounce the ball between the cone markers with your preferred hand. Return straight back, bouncing ball with other hand. As soon as a bouncer has gone around the last cone, the next bouncer can go. How many crossings can your team make in a certain time limit (such as 2 minutes)?

MOVEMENT STATIONS
Lesson 46, Level 2

MOVEMENT AREA: Object Control
MOVEMENT: Bouncing and Catching with One Hand (large ball)

TEACHING GOALS:

- ☛ **Keep eyes on ball.**
- ☛ **Move arms in pumping action, as fingers push ball downward (not slapping ball).**

EQUIPMENT REQUIRED:

Wall and floor targets
Cone markers
6–7 Balance feathers
6 Tennis balls
Music; cassette/CD player
Assessment Recording Sheet

MOVEMENT STATIONS

1. ***Musical Bouncing.*** Use music with a steady 4/4 beat. Bounce the ball in time to the beat; first with the preferred hand, then with the other hand, then crossover "V" bouncing.

   ➤ Now try an 8-count pattern: 8 bounces with preferred hand, 8 counts with other hand; 8 "V" bounces. Continue this pattern.

   ➤ Make up a bouncing pattern of your own.

2. ***Shuttle Bounce.*** Group sets up in shuttle formation as shown. Each member bounces ball across to opposite line and hands ball to next member. Continue in this way.

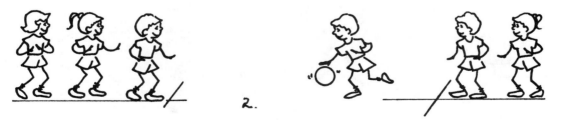

3. **Balance Feathers.** Explore balancing a feather on different parts of your hand: palm of hand, back of hand, fingers, wrist; right hand; left hand.

➤ Balance feathers on other body parts: elbow, knee, shoulder, forehead, etc.

➤ Balance your feather from one body part to another; for example, palm of hand to back of hand.

➤ Create a feather balance of your own.

4. **Bouncing Ball with One Hand— Assessment.** Observe and record performance. (See Book 1, *Ready-to-Use Fundamental Motor Skills & Movement Activities for Young Children*, for a Recording Sheet.)

5. **Target Bounce.** Each person has an empty tennis tin and a tennis ball. Perform the following tasks:

➤ Bounce tennis ball and catch it in the tennis tin.

➤ Bounce tennis ball off a wall and catch it in tennis tin.

➤ Bounce ball to a partner who tries to receive ball in tennis tin.

➤ Create a stunt of your own!

6. **Hit the Target.** Use wall targets such as shown. Have 2–3 different targets set up and children in turn overhand throw at targets. Emphasize good follow-through. Vary the throwing distances.

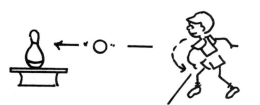

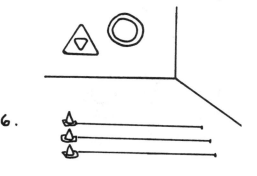

TEACHING SESSION
Lesson 47, Level 2

MOVEMENT AREA: Object Control

MOVEMENT: Kicking for Distance

TEACHABLE POINTS:

1. Keep in balance.

2. Nonkicking foot placed near and to side of the ball.

3. Knee is bent on backswing (at least 90 degrees).

4. Kick with the instep (shoelaces) and contact at bottom of ball.

5. Arm opposite the kicking leg is away from the body assisting balance.

6. Follow-through toward the target.

7. Eyes focused on the ball.

EQUIPMENT REQUIRED:

Firm even surface
Cone markers
1 Large ball per person
2 Beanbag markers per pair

TEACHING GOALS:

☛ **Keep head up and eyes focused.**

☛ **Use correct placement of kicking foot.**

☛ **Use correct contact with instep.**

TEACHING PROGRESSIONS

1. Demonstrate the kicking action using a ball. Emphasize the goals.

2. Children demonstrate the kicking action in slow motion. Note the children who fall off balance while doing this. These children may find the kick difficult.

3. In pairs have the children stand 10 yards (meters) apart. Children kick to each other, stopping the ball with their hands.

1.

3.

257

4. Children, in pairs, have 1 ball between each pair and 2 markers. From a kicking line and on the signal "Kick," one of the pair kicks the ball as far as he/she can. The partner marks the ball where it stops. Children take alternate turns to kick for distance. Ensure that you keep emphasizing the main points and provide feedback to individual children.

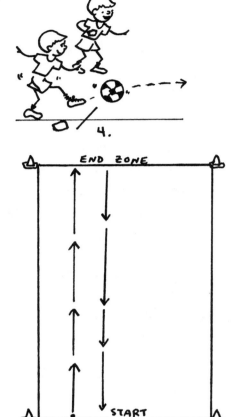

ACTIVITIES

1. *Cumulative Kicking.* Use the end zones of a large marked field, or use cones to mark two end zones up to 50 yards (meters) apart. Place children into groups of 2–3. Each group has one ball and a marker. The aim of this game is for each member of the group to have turns at kicking the ball from where the previous kick stopped. The team counts how many kicks it takes to cross the field and return to the start.

2. *Kicking Relay.* Divide the children into 4 teams. Children kick to a set of goals 10 yards (meters) in front of the team. If the goal is not scored, the kicker moves to the 5-yard (-meter) marker and kicks again. The ball is returned to the team by a player standing behind the goals. When this player returns the ball, he/she runs to the back of the line and the kicker moves to the position behind the goals.

GOAL

MOVEMENT STATIONS
Lesson 48, Level 2

MOVEMENT AREA: Object Control

MOVEMENT: Kicking for Distance

EQUIPMENT REQUIRED:

    3 large playground balls or soccer balls
    9 large cone markers
    3 soccer balls
    1 medium-sized ball
    Tee stand
    Long base
    6 basketballs
    12 juggling scarves
    Lightweight mats

MOVEMENT STATIONS

1. *Wall Kick and Trap.* Children pair off and face a wall. One partner kicks a playground ball at wall. Other partner tries to trap the ball with the sole of the foot as the ball rebounds off the wall. Then partner kicks ball to wall. Gradually increase the distance of the kick.

2. *T-Ball Strike.* Have two Strikers, one Catcher, and three Fielders for a group of 6. Strikers take two turns each to strike a medium-sized ball off a tee stand. Fielders must field the ball and return it to Catcher before Striker can run to touch a base and return to touch tee circle.

3. *Kicking Golf.* Set up 3 fairways with a "tee-off" and a "green" for each as shown. Have children pair off with each partner kicking in turn and counting the number of kicks taken to kick the ball through the hole.

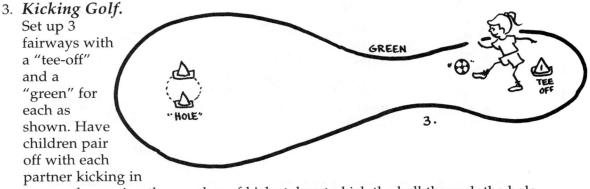

4. *Scrambled Eggs—Bounce.* Bounce your ball with one hand as you move in and out of each other. Listen for my "Touch" signal. Use your free hand to touch the objects called out: red line, wall, cone marker, someone's elbow, shake hands. On "Scramble Eggs—Bounce," continue to bounce your ball while moving in and out of each other.

5. *Individual Stunts.* Enlarge these (see diagram) onto cards and have the children perform the balancing/ weight-bearing stunts on lightweight mats.

6. *Juggling Scarf Play.* Children explore keeping the scarf afloat using two juggling scarves.

4.

6.

➤ Start first with one, toss it upward, and catch it on different body parts.

➤ Then toss it upward, and wait until it nearly touches the floor before grabbing it with a downward swing.

➤ Toss one scarf from one hand to the other, grabbing it downward.

➤ Toss two scarves at the same time and grab them.

➤ Hold a scarf in each hand. Toss the first one across to the other side, just above head, then toss the second scarf to the opposite side. Grab scarves with the hand on that side as they float downward.

➤ Create a scarf juggling move of your own!

5·INDIVIDUAL STUNTS

INCHWORM   SPINNING TOP   SEAL WALK

BUCKING BRONCO   KANGAROO   PUPPY DOG WALK   CRAB WALK

BUNNY HOP

TEACHING SESSION
Lesson 49, Level 2

MOVEMENT AREA: Object Control
MOVEMENT: Kicking for Distance

TEACHABLE POINTS:

1. Keep in balance.
2. Nonkicking foot placed near and to side of the ball.
3. Knee is bent on backswing (at least 90 degrees).
4. Kick with the instep (shoelaces) and contact at bottom of ball.
5. Arm opposite the kicking leg is away from the body assisting balance.
6. Follow-through toward the target.
7. Eyes focused on the ball.

EQUIPMENT REQUIRED:

Firm even surface
Cone or dome markers
Large playground balls or soccer balls

2 Beanbag markers per pair
3 Carpet squares per group of 6
   or flat markers

TEACHING GOALS:
- Use good leg backswing.
- Follow-through in direction of the target.
- Use correct contact with instep.
- Control ball with sole-of-foot trap.

TEACHING PROGRESSIONS

1. Revise and demonstrate the kicking action using a ball, emphasizing point of contact on the ball (instep) or shoelaces of the shoe.

   ➤ Revise and demonstrate how to stop the ball with the sole of the foot. This is called "trapping" the ball.

   ➤ Have children stand near ball and place foot on top of ball, with heel closer to the ground. Do this with the other foot.

   ➤ Then, in pairs, have one partner roll the ball toward the other partner, who traps the ball with the sole of the foot.

2. Children, in pairs, kick to each other. Start close together and move farther apart. Practice trapping the ball.

ACTIVITIES

1. *Goal Kicking.* Divide class into groups of 6. Each group has 3 balls, 3 carpet squares or flat markers, and 2 cone markers. The group sets up goals 4 paces wide using the cones and randomly place the squares at least 5 yards (meters) from the goals. One child is the goalkeeper, 2 back up the goalkeeper, and the other 3 take turns at kicking from the markers. Have kicking group then switch places with goalkeepers.

2. *Distance Kicking.* Children, in pairs, have 2 balls and 2 markers for each pair. From a kicking line and on the signal "Kick," one of the pair kicks the ball as far as he/she can. The other partner marks the ball where it stops. First partner makes a second kick, trying to further the distance. Fielding partner marks the better kick, then returns with balls to kicking line to now take a turn. Ensure that you keep emphasizing the goals and provide feedback to individual children.

2.

MOVEMENT STATIONS
Lesson 50, Level 2

MOVEMENT AREA: Object Control
MOVEMENT: Kicking for Distance

TEACHING GOALS:
- ☞ Use good leg backswing.
- ☞ Follow-through in direction of the target.
- ☞ Use correct contact with instep.
- ☞ Control ball with sole-of-foot trap.

EQUIPMENT REQUIRED:

3 large kicking balls
Cone markers
3 soccer balls
6 large bouncing and catching balls
6 partner stunt cards
2 soccer balls
6 balance feathers
Music; cassette/CD player
Assessment Recording Sheet

MOVEMENT STATIONS

1. *Target Kick.* Children pair off; one partner places two cones 3 paces apart, which the kicker has to attempt to kick through. Gradually the distance is increased with each successful attempt. Have preset distances marked at the side of the playing area so the children have an indication of where to place their markers.

2. *Kicking Golf.* Continue Kicking Golf as set up in Lesson 48.

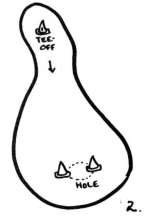

3. *Ball Stunts.*
   - ➤ Roll the ball through your legs in a figure-8 pattern.
   - ➤ Pass the ball around your waist. Go the opposite direction.
   - ➤ Bounce the ball from standing position to kneeling position and back up again. Repeat.
   - ➤ Bounce ball 5 times with one hand, then 5 times with the other. Repeat this pattern.
   - ➤ Bounce the ball from one hand to the other in a "V" pattern.
   - ➤ Bounce your ball while touching different body parts or objects.
   - ➤ Think up a stunt of your own!

4. *Kicking for Distance—Assessment.* Have children kick to a wall. Observe and record performance in kicking a stationary ball. (See Book 1, *Ready-to-Use Fundamental Motor Skills & Movement Activities for Young Children*, for a Recording Sheet.) Also observe ability to trap and control the ball.

5. *Partner Stunts.* Enlarge these onto cards (see diagram) and have the children work in pairs on lightweight mats to perform the balancing/weight-bearing stunts.

6. *Balance Feathers.* Children explore balancing feathers on different body parts and transferring the feather from one body part to another. If possible, play relaxing background music.

`5. PARTNER STUNTS`

TEACHING SESSION
Lesson 51, Level 2

MOVEMENT AREA: Object Control
MOVEMENT: Kicking for Accuracy and Trapping

TEACHABLE POINTS:

Kicking

1. Nonkicking foot is placed near and to side of the ball.
2. Kicking foot is turned so that the inside of the foot faces the ball.
3. Kicking leg is bent on the backswing.
4. Kicking foot remains firm at the ankle while kicking.
5. To assist balance, the opposite arm moves forward as kicking leg moves back.
6. Ball is contacted on the inside of the kicking foot.
7. Arm on same side as kicking leg swings away from the body to assist balance, as kicking leg swings through.
8. Follow-through toward the target.
9. Eyes stay focused on the ball during the movement.

INSIDE OF
FOOT CONTACT

Trapping

1. Keep in balance.
2. Nontrapping foot is placed near and to side of the ball.
3. Knee is bent on contact
4. Trap with the inside of the foot.
5. Arm opposite the kicking leg is away from the body assisting balance.
6. Give with the ball to cushion on contact.
7. Eyes focused on the ball.

EQUIPMENT REQUIRED:

Firm even surface
Cone markers
Large playground balls or soccer balls
Markers for Kicking Croquet course

TEACHING GOALS:

Kicking
☛ Keep head up and eyes focused.
☛ Place nonkicking foot near and to side of the ball.
☛ Bend knee on backswing (at least 90 degrees).
☛ Kick with the inside of the foot.

Trapping
☛ Keep in balance.
☛ Place nontrapping foot near and to side of the ball.
☛ Trap with the inside of the foot.

TEACHING PROGRESSIONS

1. Have children hold a one-leg balance with left arm forward and the right arm to the side. Extend the other foot back, then swing through.

1-2.

2. Repeat but have children step to an imaginary ball and swing kicking leg through, turning the kicking foot out to the side. Emphasize that the kicking leg finishes by pointing toward the target on the follow-through.

3. In pairs, 1 child rolls a ball slowly to a partner, who stops the ball with the sole of the foot. As the rolling speed increases, have the child stop the ball with the side of foot.

3.

4. In pairs, have 1 child kick a stationary ball toward a wall. Contact with ball is made on the inside of the foot by turning the kicking foot out to the side. As the ball rebounds off the wall, have partner stop (trap) the ball by using the inside of the foot. Gradually increase the distance away from the wall.

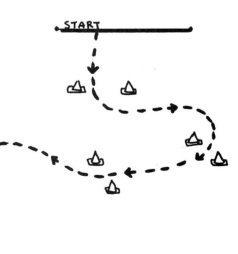

5. As #4 except place 2 markers near the wall that are 3 yards (meters) apart. Have child kick a stationary ball between these 2 markers. Gradually increase the kicking distance.

6. Free kick back and forth to a partner. Gradually increase the distance. Remind child to trap ball each time before kicking.

5-7.

7. Repeat activities 3–5, with child approaching ball from a 3-step run-up and kicking the ball to a wall; into a wall target; to a partner.

8. In pairs, 1 child rolls the ball slowly toward and slightly to the side of a partner. Children move toward the ball and trap it with the inside the foot, then kick it back to the partner.

ACTIVITY

Kicking Croquet. Divide the class into groups of 4. Explain to them how to set up a course as shown in the diagram. Ensure good spacing to allow for successful accuracy when kicking. Establish a start and a finish to the course. Each successful kick must go between the markers. As skill level improves, increase the distance and reduce the space between the 2 markers.

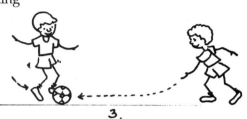

START

FINISH

MOVEMENT STATIONS
Lesson 52, Level 2

MOVEMENT AREA: Object Control
MOVEMENT: Dribbling and Trapping

TEACHING GOALS:

Kicking

☞ Keep head up and eyes focused.
☞ Place nonkicking foot near and to side of the ball.
☞ Bend knee on backswing (at least 90 degrees).
☞ Kick with the inside of the foot.

Trapping

☞ Keep in balance.
☞ Place nontrapping foot near and to side of the ball.
☞ Trap with the inside of the foot.

EQUIPMENT REQUIRED:

Numbered cone markers
Soccer balls
3 wall goals marked off with floor tape
5 plastic bottles or skittles (pins)
2 kicking balls
Dome markers
3 Catchballs
3 hoops
Cone markers
3 beanbags or spider balls
Assessment Recording Sheet

MOVEMENT STATIONS

1. *Spot Kicking.* Use cones or rope circles to designate 6 kicking spots around a goal area as shown. Each spot is worth so many points according to difficulty (as indicated on cone marker). Children pair off, with one partner being the Kicker; the other, the Retriever. Kicker kicks from each spot to send the ball through goal area. Then the players change roles.

2. ***Goal Kicking.*** Use floor tape to mark out 7–8-foot (2.5 meters) square on a wall as shown. Ideally, there is one goal for every 2 kickers. Children are paired off and take turns trying to kick the ball into goal at 3 set distances as marked off by dome markers. Each kicker has 2 attempts at each distance.

2.

3. ***Five-Pin Kick.*** For each group of 3, set up 5 plastic bottles or skittles near a wall in a triangular pattern as shown. Vary the kicking distance using cone markers. Children take turns using the inside-of-the-foot kick to try to knock over the pins. Each player gets 2 attempts. Keep score.

4. ***Kicking for Accuracy and Trapping—Assessment.*** Observe and record performance in kicking of a stationary ball. (See Book 1, *Ready-to-Use Fundamental Motor Skills & Movement Activities for Young Children*, for a Recording Sheet.)

5. ***Catchball™ Play.*** Children pair off and practice throwing and catching with a catchball, which has 6 handles, 4 of which have a score on the end. Children can keep score for each successful catch.

3.

6. ***Mini-Throw Golf.*** Set up 3 "fairways" using hoops as holes, cone markers as the tee-off area, and Spider Balls™ or beanbags as the throwing object. Children use the overhand throw and keep track of the number of throws made to land in "the hole."

5.

TEE-OFF

"HOLE"

6.

MOVEMENT AREA: Object Control
MOVEMENT: Kicking for Accuracy and Trapping

TEACHABLE POINTS:

Kicking

1. Nonkicking foot is placed near and to side of the ball.
2. Kicking foot is turned so that the inside of the foot faces the ball.
3. Kicking leg is bent on the backswing.
4. Kicking foot remains firm at the ankle while kicking.
5. To assist balance, the opposite arm moves forward as kicking leg moves back.
6. Ball is contacted on the inside of the kicking foot.
7. Arm on same side as kicking leg swings away from the body to assist balance, as kicking leg swings through.
8. Follow-through toward the target.
9. Eyes stay focused on the ball during the movement.

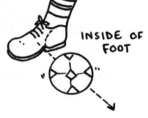

Trapping

1. Keep in balance.
2. Nontrapping foot is placed near and to side of the ball.
3. Knee is bent on contact.
4. Trap with the inside of the foot.
5. Arm opposite the kicking leg is away from the body to assist balance.
6. Give with the ball to cushion on contact.
7. Eyes focused on the ball.

EQUIPMENT REQUIRED:

Firm even surface
Large balls
Cone markers

TEACHING GOALS:

Kicking
☛ Keep in balance.
☛ Kick with the inside of the foot.
☛ Follow-through in the direction of the target.

Trapping
☛ Keep in balance.
☛ Trap with the inside of the foot.
☛ Cushion the ball on impact.

TEACHING PROGRESSIONS

1. Demonstrate the kicking action first without and then with a ball. Ask the children questions about:

   ➤ Where should the toes of the kicking foot be pointed? (to the right for a right footer)

   ➤ Where does the foot strike the ball? (on the inside of the foot)

   ➤ How is the ball stopped as it comes toward you? Have children demonstrate using preferred foot; then ask them to use the other foot.

2. In pairs at a distance of 5 yards (meters), have the children practice this kicking position. Stress kicking just enough to reach their partner, not too hard.

3. Place the children into groups of 3. Each group forms a triangle with each kicker spaced 5 giant steps away. Children pass around the triangle using an instep kick and trapping with inside-of-the-foot. Then have them reverse the passing direction and use the other foot.

2.

3.

ACTIVITY

Shuttle Kicking Relay. Form teams of 6 and have each team get into shuttle formation, with a distance of 7 yards (meters) between the two sides as shown. Kick the ball to the player on the opposite side; then run to join the end of the opposite side. Continue in this way.

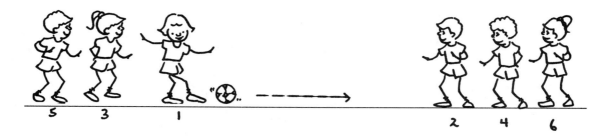

MOVEMENT STATIONS
Lesson 54, Level 2

MOVEMENT AREA: Object Control
MOVEMENT: Kicking for Accuracy; Trapping

TEACHING GOALS:

Kicking
- ☞ Keep in balance.
- ☞ Kick with the inside of the foot.
- ☞ Follow-through in the direction of the target.

Trapping
- ☞ Keep in balance.
- ☞ Trap with the inside of the foot.
- ☞ Cushion the ball on impact.

EQUIPMENT REQUIRED:

Kicking balls
Plastic bottles or skittles
Cone markers
Short ropes and measuring sticks
Running circuit cards
3 chairs
9 deckrings
Assessment Recording Sheet

MOVEMENT STATIONS

1. *Three- or Six-Pin Kick.* Set up 3 plastic bottles or skittles near a wall in a triangular fashion. Set up another area with 6 plastic bottles (or skittles) in a triangle. Children in 3's take turns to kick the ball and knock over the bottles (skittles). Gradually increase the distance with markers.

2. *Goal Kicking.* Use witch's hats to mark out 3-yard (-meter) goals near a wall. One partner tries to kick goals in 5 attempts; the other partner is the goalie who traps ball with his or her feet. Then change roles. Keep score.

271

3. ***Deckring Toss.*** Turn a chair upside down near a wall. Set up 3 mini-stations and have partners take turns trying to toss a ring on the chair leg in 3 attempts. Keep score.

4. ***Kicking for Accuracy and Trapping—Assessment.*** Observe and record performance in kicking and trapping a ball. (See Book 1, *Ready-to-Use Fundamental Motor Skills & Movement Activities for Young Children*, for a Recording Sheet.)

5. ***Standing Jump.*** Children pair off and find a Home space. Each pair has two pieces of rope that are placed on the ground parallel to each other and approximately 18 inches (45 cm) apart. Partners, taking turns, must stand behind the first rope and jump over the second rope. When each partner has completed this jump twice, place the second rope 1 measuring stick further apart. (Each pair has a measuring stick that is 5 inches (12 cm) long.) They can use the stick to measure how far they jumped.

6. ***Running Task Circuit.*** Children complete a running circuit. Each leg of the circuit is placed on a separate card that the children have to read. (This also prevents children from following each other.) Children who find it difficult to read may follow the diagram or ask another child or helper. Example: Run to the large tree at the end of the oval and collect a counter; next to the basketball courts collect a counter; next to the flag pole collect a counter, etc.

Run to the large tree and collect a counter.

TEACHING SESSION
Lesson 55, Level 2

MOVEMENT AREA: Object Control
MOVEMENT: Dribbling a Large Ball (with feet)

TEACHABLE POINTS:

1. Ball is kept close to the body.
2. Ball is controlled with the inside and outside of the feet.
3. Control is attained before speed.
4. Arms used for balance.
5. Head up and eyes focused.

EQUIPMENT REQUIRED:

Firm even surface
Large playground balls or soccer balls
Cone markers

TEACHING GOALS:
☞ **Keep the ball close.**
☞ **Control before speed.**

TEACHING PROGRESSIONS

1. Demonstrate the dribbling action, emphasizing the goals.
   - ➤ Have children start in a Home space, then dribble the ball with the insides of either foot in general space.
   - ➤ Dribble the ball with the outside of the feet.
   - ➤ Dribble the ball with inside or outside of either foot.

2. On signal "Scrambled Eggs—Dribble!" children dribble the ball in and out of each other. On signal "Iceberg!" ball is immediately stopped with a sole-of-the-foot trap.

3. Now children pair off and dribble pass to each other. Emphasize stopping the ball with the inside-of-the-foot trap first to control it, then passing to a partner. Partners start close to each other, gradually increasing passing distance.

4. Each partner has a turn at dribbling up and around a marker and back to the start line.

ACTIVITY

Shuttle Dribble Relay. Divide class into teams of 4 players with each team set up in shuttle formation across a distance of 10 yards (meters). Space two large cone markers 3 yards (meters) apart between two sides. (See diagram.) Each member dribbles ball in and out of markers to the opposite side. Ball is passed with the inside of the foot to next dribbler who controls it with a sole-of-the-foot trap, then dribbles across to the other side. First dribbler goes to the end of this side. Continue in this way.

MOVEMENT STATIONS
Lesson 56, Level 2

MOVEMENT AREA: Object Control
MOVEMENT: Dribbling a Large Ball (with feet)

EQUIPMENT REQUIRED:

Large cone markers
Soccer balls
1 large playground ball
    per pair
Assessment Recording Sheet

14–16 small cone markers
3–4 balloons
5 numbered cones

MOVEMENT STATIONS

1. ***Zigzag Dribble.*** Set up 2 identical courses. Children take turns dribbling in and out of markers. Once they reach the end marker, they dribble straight back.

2. ***Partner Dribble.*** Children, in pairs, dribble a soccer ball back and forth to each other.

3. ***Kicking Croquet.*** Explain to children how to set up a course as shown in the diagram. Ensure good spacing to allow for successful accuracy when kicking. Establish a start and a finish to the course. Each successful kick must go between the markers. As skill level improves, increase the distance and reduce the space between the 2 markers.

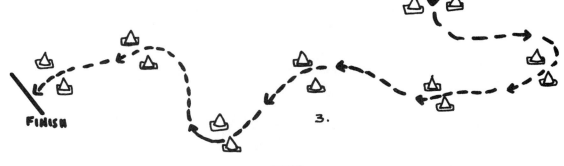

275

4. ***Dribbling and Trapping—Assessment.***
Observe and record performance in dribbling a
ball with the feet. (See Book 1, *Ready-to-Use
Fundamental Motor Skills & Movement Activities
for Young Children,* for a Recording Sheet.)

5. ***Balloon Ball Play.*** Keep the ball afloat by
striking with either hand. Count the number of
times group strikes the ball before it touches the
ground. Continue in this way.

6. ***Star Bounce.*** Use numbered markers to set up
2 identical Star Courses as shown. Dribblers
take turns dribbling ball through the course:
start at number 1 cone and dribble to number 2,
to number 3, to 4, to 5 and back again to number
1. While waiting for their turn, children can
bounce pass the ball back and forth to each
other.

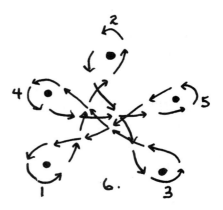

MOVEMENT AREA: Object Control
MOVEMENT: Two-Handed Striking

TEACHABLE POINTS:

1. Eyes are focused on the ball, head steady throughout movement.
2. Knees are bent through the movement.
3. Body is moved to the side-on position.
4. Weight is transferred forward by stepping into the swing.
5. Good shoulder turn occurs in backswing.
6. Nonpreferred arm remains relatively straight in back swing.
7. Hit starts with the hips rotating toward the target.
8. Good extension in the follow-through is evident.

EQUIPMENT REQUIRED:

Firm even surface
Rolled-up newspapers
Soft medium-sized balls
Paper or socks in stockings
1 T-ball stand
1 home base per team

Cone markers
2 sets of baseball bases
1 small bat per group
1 hoop

TEACHING GOALS:
➤ Keep head up and eyes focused.
➤ Use side-on stance.
➤ Transfer weight.

TEACHING PROGRESSIONS

A two-handed strike is used in a number of sports. This lesson will focus on a strike with a T-ball bat.

1. Demonstrate the stance, hand positioning, and swinging action of a two-handed strike. Emphasize the goals.

2. Have children stand side on to a wall or sideline and shift weight back and forth from front foot to back foot on your call.

3. As #2, but have children practice swinging their arms in time with the weight transference. Arm swing starts with a small action backward, then slowly increases as the arms swing through and around the body. Make the action rhythmical by calling out a "one and two" count: "one" is the backswing; "and" is the pause at the top; and "two" is the swing through.

4. Give the children a taped rolled-up newspaper. (They can make these for homework.) Have them repeat #3.

5. In pairs have 1 child gently lob a soft medium-sized ball or a stocking filled with paper or old socks and the partner strike it with the newspaper. Stress that the *action*, rather than contact, is important.

6. Children are in groups of 4: a Hitter, a Catcher, and two Fielders, with 3 balls per group. The Hitter strikes the ball with a small bat from a witch's hat or T-ball stand. The Fielders return the ball to the Catcher, who places the ball on the stand. Rotate positions after 3 hits each.

ACTIVITIES

1. *Rounders.* The field is a large rectangle. Children are placed in teams. Hitting team strikes a medium-sized soft ball from a tee. When ball is struck, the hitter must run to the far end of the marked court. The fielding team must attempt to throw the ball and hit the runner below the knees with the ball. The runner must return on the next player's hit. Going up and back scores 1 run. Once the children have the concept of the game, run 2 games simultaneously, if possible.

2. *Modified T-ball.* Class is split into 4 teams and 2 fields of play are set up. Batting team hits 5 balls from a tee into the field of play. The fielding team must collect the balls and return them to a hoop near the home base before the runner makes it around the bases. If the runner makes it before the balls are returned, a homerun is scored. If the fielders beat the runner, then it is no score. All hitters bat and then change roles with the fielding team. Keep reminding children of the correct technique when batting.

MOVEMENT STATIONS
Lesson 58, Level 2

MOVEMENT AREA: Object Control

MOVEMENT: Two-Handed Strike

TEACHING GOALS:
- ☛ Keep head up and eyes focused.
- ☛ Use side-on stance.
- ☛ Transfer weight.

EQUIPMENT REQUIRED:

    1 T-ball stand or large cone marker
    Medium-sized balls
    Cricket bats
    Foam ball
    Cone markers
    1 racquet per player
    1 light plastic ball per pair
    Large mats
    1 small bat per team
    Assessment Recording Sheet

MOVEMENT STATIONS

1. ***T-Ball Play.*** For each group, set up a medium-sized ball on a large cone marker or proper T-ball equipment. One player bats; others field the ball. Children take turns striking the ball with a bat toward an open field. After every 3 hits, a new batter takes a turn.

2. ***Cricket Ball Play.*** Children in three's find a free space. Each threesome has a medium-sized ball and a modified cricket bat (smaller, lighter). One player is the Striker; second player, the Roller; and a third, the Fielder. (See diagram.) Players change roles after Striker has hit a rolled ball 3 times.

3. **Stuck in the Middle.** Group forms a circle with one player "stuck" in the middle. Group underhand throws or rolls ball toward middle player, trying to hit him/her below the waist. Middle player tries to last for 5 attempts; then another player comes in the middle.

3.

4. **Two-Handed Striking—Assessment.** Observe and record performance in doing a two-handed strike. (See Book 1, *Ready-to-Use Fundamental Motor Skills & Movement Activities for Young Children,* for a Recording Sheet.)

5. **Racquet Ball Play.** In pairs, using small racquets, children practice hitting a light plastic ball back and forth to each other.

5.

6. **Partner-Stretch Like Me.** In pairs, partners stretch together, mirroring each other's actions. Emphasize slow, gentle stretching, holding each stretch for 10 seconds.

6.

MOVEMENT AREA: Object Control
MOVEMENT: Two-Handed Strike

TEACHABLE POINTS:

1. Eyes focused on the ball and the head is steady.
2. Child stands in a sideways position.
3. Weight transference occurs back and then forward with the arm swing.
4. Good shoulder turn on the backswing.
5. Hit starts with the hips rotating toward the target.
6. Knees remain flexed during the hit.
7. Good extension in the follow-through.

EQUIPMENT REQUIRED:

Firm even surface
1 soft medium-sized ball per pair
1 small ball per pair
1 plastic bat per pair
1 T-ball stand or large cone per pair
Cone markers
2 sets of baseball bases

TEACHING GOALS:

- ☛ Use side-on stance.
- ☛ Use large backswing.
- ☛ Transfer weight.

TEACHING PROGRESSIONS

1. Revise the two-handed strike, emphasizing the goals.

2. Children face back to back with their partner and, without moving their feet, turn and pass a ball to each other. Arms must be relatively straight when passing the ball. Stress to the children that this is the shoulder turn they should try to feel in their backswing.

3. In pairs have children further practice this by hitting a large light ball positioned on a tee or high cone.

4. Repeat #3 using a smaller ball.

5. One partner rolls a large ball to other partner, who strikes it with a bat. Change roles after 3 hits.

6. Repeat #5 using a smaller ball.

7. One partner underhand throws a large soft ball toward the batter. Batter keeps eye on ball and tries to strike it.

ACTIVITY

T-Ball. Introduce the basics of T-ball. You will need to modify the rules; for example, the runner is out if the ball is thrown and caught by any baseman. No tagging is required; no base sneaking. Keep it simple.

➤ This introduction to this popular game will allow the teacher to view many aspects of a child's motor development, such as throwing, catching, hitting, and running, as well as social skills, enthusiasm, etc. When the children are playing the game, keep up the feedback on their movement skills and promote enthusiasm.

MOVEMENT STATIONS
Lesson 60, Level 2

MOVEMENT AREA: Object Control
MOVEMENT: Two-Handed Strike

TEACHING GOALS:
- ☛ Use side-on stance.
- ☛ Use large backswing.
- ☛ Transfer weight.

EQUIPMENT REQUIRED:

Cone markers

T-ball stand or large cone marker

2–3 Medium-sized balls

2 Medium lightweight bats

Assessment Recording Sheet

1 Soccer ball per group

1 plastic whiffle ball per pair

6–7 scoops

Relaxation music; CD/ cassette player

Large mats

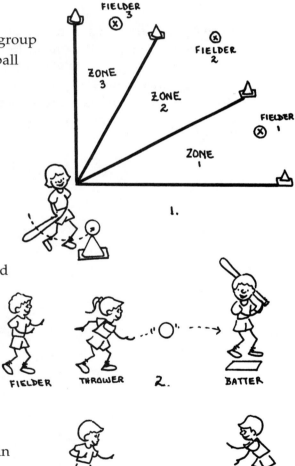

Movement Stations

1. **Batter's Box.** Mark out a right angle and use 4 cone markers to divide this angle equally into 3 zones as shown. The batter hits off the batting tee or high cone, but now must select into which zone he or she will hit the ball. Batter must try to hit beyond the markers. Fielders position beyond the markers. Have players rotate one position after every 3 hits.

2. **Strike the Moving Ball.** Children are in 3's: one Batter, one Thrower, one Fielder. Practice striking an underhand tossed ball. Rotate one position after every 3 attempts.

3. **Kick the Moving Ball.** As for #2, but ball is rolled. Kicker attempts to kick the ball.

283

4. ***Two-Handed Striking—Assessment.*** Observe and record performance in doing a two-handed strike. (See Book 1, *Ready-to-Use Fundamental Motor Skills & Movement Activities for Young Children*, for a Recording Sheet.)

5. ***Scoop Ball™ Play.*** Children are in pairs, with a scoop each and a plastic whiffle ball between the two. Explore sending and receiving the ball using the scoops. "Flick" the ball from the scoop, track it, and gently reach and give with the ball as it comes into the scoop.

6. ***Relaxation Tape.*** Children lie quietly on mats and listen to the music. Relax. Close your eyes. Think of something very pleasant. Now gently tense and stretch your body parts, starting with your feet and working your way up to the head.

FOUNDATION MOVEMENT REVISION
Lesson 1, Level 3

ORGANIZATION: Identify the play area by setting up cone markers around the perimeter. As a general rule, space cone markers every 10 feet (3 meters) apart, using about 15 markers for a play area that is 60′ by 30′ (20m by 10m). Try to use different polygonal figures such as square, rectangle, pentagon, hexagon, octagon.

EQUIPMENT REQUIRED:

15 cone markers	Cardboard
1 throwing ring (beanbag) per child	Marking pens

WARMING-UP/FITNESS SIGNALS

"HOME" "STAND TALL"

1. Find your Home space inside the play area. Check that you cannot touch anyone or anything. This is your first signal, "Home!" (Show hand signal.) Whenever you hear this signal, find your Home and "Stand Tall" in it. Leave your home to shake hands with 5 different children, then return to stand tall in your Home space.

1.

SHAKE HANDS

2. Now leave your Home and touch 6 different markers with 6 different body parts. Alternate right and left body parts. Then return Home and Stand Tall, crossing left arms/legs over right. Go!

3. This position is called the "Corkscrew." Show me how you can sink your corkscrew to the floor to "Cross-leg Sit" position. Return to standing tall without undoing your corkscrew.

" "

3.

4. Let's play the game "Touch!":

   ➤ Touch a cone marker on a sideline with your right knee.

   ➤ Touch a cone on an endline with your left foot and right hand.

   ➤ Run to the other sideline and touch a cone with your head.

   ➤ Run to the opposite endline and touch a cone with your right elbow and left knee.

   ➤ Go Home and corkscrew with left arms and legs crossed!

   ➤ Sink your corkscrew to cross-leg sit. Now try to stand tall.

4.

5. I am going to give you 3 important rules to remember:

   ➤ Don't hurt yourself!

   ➤ Don't hurt anyone else!

   ➤ Don't hurt the equipment!

6. *Scrambled Eggs—Power Walking!* (Hand signal.) Remember to move in and out of each other without "touching" anyone. Walk vigorously, pumping your arms and making quick changes of direction.

7. *Iceberg!* (Hand signal.) This is your stopping signal. When you hear this word, stop immediately by "jump stopping." Land on your feet at the same time, knees bent, hands out for balance. Let's practice this.

8. *"Scrambled Eggs—Marching!"* *"Iceberg!"* "One!" Stand on one foot, close your eyes, and hold your balance for 5 seconds.

   ➤ "Scrambled Eggs—High Fives!" "Iceberg!" "Five." Touch the floor with any five body parts.

   ➤ "Scrambled Eggs—Jogging!" "Iceberg!"Stay in a frozen shape without moving for 5 seconds!

HIGH FIVES!

FIVE!

MOTOR MEMORY

1. Copy touching movements to different body parts. Examples: Touch your right elbow to your left knee. Have right hand on hip, and left hand holding left ankle behind.

2. Play *Animal Charades.* Ask children to pick a favorite animal. Point to different children, asking them in turn to act out their animal. Guess the name of it, then everyone mimics.

SPATIAL AWARENESS

1. In standing tall position, feet shoulder-width apart, face this wall of the room (or boundary line of play area). You are now *square on* to the wall. Turn so that you are *side on* to the wall. Show me another way to be side on to the wall. Position so that your back is to the wall. Square up again. Turn to face a corner. You are now in *diagonal* stance. Face the other corner in diagonal stance.

SQUARE ON

SIDE ON

DIAGONAL

2. ***Stop and Stand.*** On stiff 20″ by 8″ (51cm by 20cm) cardboard use marking pen to print the following stance words: *Square On*; *Side On*; *Diagonal*; *Back-to-Back*; *Face-to-Face*. Move around to music. When the music stops, come to a jump-stop, observe the sign, and move into that stance. For example: "Square on to the chair"; "Side on" to this wall; "Diagonal to this corner"; sit "Back-to-Back with another player; stand "Face-to-Face" with someone your size.

BODY AWARENESS

Listen Carefully. I will ask you to move just a certain body part at a time:

➤ Gently turn your head from side to side.

➤ Gently lift right knee up and touch it with the opposite hand. Lift the other knee up and touch it with the opposite hand.

➤ Snap your fingers out wide; in close.

➤ Blink slowly with one eye, then the other.

➤ In sitting position, touch right elbow to left foot.

CLOSING ACTIVITIES

1. ***Good Morning Stretch!*** Pretend you are still in your bed and just beginning to wake up. Lying on your tummy, stretch as wide as possible. Do this slowly. Now stretch like a pencil. Yawn! Smile a "good morning" smile!

2. ***Shrugs!*** Stand tall. Raise and lower your shoulders as if you are saying "I don't know!"

3. ***Rolls!*** Now gently roll your shoulders backward, then forward.

4. ***Heads Nods.*** Stand tall. Gently and slowly nod your head as if you are saying "Yes!" Now gently nod your head as if you are saying "No!"

5. ***Legend(s) of the Day!***

| MOVEMENT AREA: Locomotion |
| MOVEMENT: Running |

TEACHABLE POINTS:

1. When sprinting, land on the forefoot.
2. Foot plant is along a narrow pathway.
3. Knees are up high at the front; feet are close to the buttocks at the back of the action.
4. Arms are bent at 90 degrees and work in opposition to legs.
5. Arms move back and forth in a straight line.
6. Hands held in a relaxed position (as if holding an egg in each hand).
7. Head and upper body are stable and eyes look straight ahead.

EQUIPMENT REQUIRED:

Marked courts are useful, as the lines provide visual guidelines for the children
Music helps establish a sense of rhythm
Hoops
Tagging objects, beanbags or flags

TEACHING GOALS:

☛ Increase stride length.
☛ Encourage correct body alignment.

TEACHING PROGRESSIONS

1. Revise and demonstrate running technique. Emphasize the teaching goals.

2. To increase stride length, place 10 markers at even intervals and have the children place a foot at each marker while running. Gradually increase the distance between the markers. (Do not increase the distance to the point where the action looks uncomfortable.)

3. Use running lanes marked off with cones. Have children run in these lanes over a distance of 30 yards (meters) up to 50 yards (meters).

288

4. Using hoops, have the children bound (spring) from one hoop to the next. Look for and emphasize high knee action.

5. *Running Signals.*

➤ Run forward.

➤ Run backward.

➤ "Scrambled Eggs—Running!"

➤ Run slowly, run quickly . . . slowly . . . quickly.

➤ Run in place, drop to the ground, stand up, and run.

➤ Run in slow motion

6. *Friendly Races.* Mark off a 50-yard (-meter) distance. Have children pair off and race each other to the finish line. Challenge someone else for the next race.

ACTIVITIES

1. *Line Run and Return.* This is best completed on a basketball court, but markers can also be used. The most motivating way for this to be completed is in relay format, but it can also be done individually. The children must start at the baseline, run out to the first line and back again, out to the next line and back, continuing until all lines have been run to.

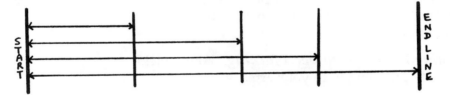

2. *Bird Tag.* Split the class into 4–5 groups and let each group choose a name of a bird. The "Birdcatcher" stands inside the marked field and calls the name of a bird. Children in that group must run across the field to the other side, try-

ing to avoid being tagged. If caught, they must stand in the "Birdcage" (a hoop) in the middle of the field. They may be released if one of their team members tags their hand when next called across. Change the Birdcatcher frequently to avoid exhaustion. Make it more difficult by having more than 1 Birdcatcher. Use an object, such as a beanbag, to make the tag or pull a flag tucked in back of shorts.

3. *Relay.* Relays always remain a favorite of children and are a low organizational activity. Relays may be completed in a line, shuttle, circle, rectangle (like base running). Or they can involve running and returning.

FOUNDATION MOVEMENT REVISION
Lesson 3, Level 3

ORGANIZATION: Identify the play area by setting up cone markers around the perimeter. As a general rule, space cone markers every 10 feet (3 meters) apart, using about 15 markers for a play area that is 60′ by 30′ (20m by 10m). Organizational signals are further revised.

EQUIPMENT REQUIRED:

    15 cone markers
    Equipment or objects in teaching environment

WARMING-UP/FITNESS SIGNALS

1. Run to touch one corner of the play area with your right hand and left foot; then run to touch the diagonal corner with your left hand and right foot. Find your Home. Check for good spacing. "Sky Reaches!" Stretch high into the sky; then slowly curl down into a ball. Take 5 counts to curl into a ball. Take 5 counts to stretch tall again.

2. Now on signal give high tens (two-handed gentle slap in the air) to 5 different people. "Quiet!" (Stop–Look–Listen.) Remember to give me your full attention.

3. *Scrambled Eggs!—Power Walking.* Walk quickly, vigorously pumping with your arms.

   – "Iceberg!" "Dead Bug!" Quickly lie on your back and wiggle your hands and feet in the air!

   – Walk happily; walk angrily; walk frightened; walk sadly.

   – "Iceberg!" "Stork Stand!" Balance on one foot with eyes closed.

   – Walk backward in a straight line; walk forward in a zigzag pattern; walk in a figure-8. "Iceberg!" Touch 3 body parts to ground.

   – Walk in a triangle. "Iceberg!" Touch 5 body parts to the ground.

4. *Clear the Deck!* (Hand signal.) Travel quickly to stand *outside* on one side of the marked play area. Clear the deck again by traveling in a different way! (Continue in this way.)

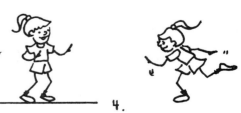

OUTSIDE ENDLINE

5. *Scrambled Eggs—Marching!* Be a happy marcher, lifting your knees high and swinging your arms. Change directions every 4 counts. "Hit the Deck!" (Hand signal.) (Drop to the floor, quickly getting into front lying position.) "Scrambled Eggs—Marching!" "Hit the Deck!" (Repeat.)

MOTOR MEMORY

1. Copy my body movements:

   ➤ Kick-kick, punch-punch, slash-slash.

   ➤ Start low and gradually get wider; stretch to a pencil shape.

   ➤ Turn around, jump in place, corkscrew down, stand tall.

2. Locomotion/rhythm sequencing:

   ➤ Walk forward 4 steps and clap (1-2-3-4 and clap).

   ➤ Walk backward 4 steps and clap (1-2-3-4 and clap).

   ➤ "Cool" walk in a circle for 8 counts snapping fingers (1-2-3-4 . . . 8).

   ➤ Side-step, side-step, stamp-stamp-stamp.

   ➤ Repeat pattern.

   ➤ Add onto pattern.

   ➤ Create other movement patterns.

SPATIAL AWARENESS

Let's Pretend you are . . . (Remember to watch where you are going!)

➤ a 747 jet taking off down the runway, lifting off, flying; now land

➤ a jet-ski slicing through the water

➤ a lion pouncing on its prey

➤ a kangaroo bounding across the field

➤ a hockey player scoring a goal

v a figure skater spinning through the air

➤ a boxer punching into the air and "dancing" with the feet

➤ a karate-kid kicking with the feet and slashing with the hands

➤ a bucking bronco

➤ a snake wriggling along the ground

➤ a dolphin jumping out of the water

BODY AWARENESS

Find a partner and take turns imitating each other's body part movements: "turning head from side to side"; "snapping fingers"; "opening and closing hands"; "winking eyes"; "clapping hands"; "stamping feet"; "lifting one knee, then the other"; "shaking different body parts."

CLAPPING

SNAPPING

CLOSING ACTIVITIES

1. *Finger Stretcher.* In stand tall position, interlock your fingers of both hands, then gently straighten your arms, pushing the palms of your fingers outward. Hold this stretch for 5–10 seconds; relax.

   ➤ Stretch in this position with arms overhead.

   ➤ Stretch one arm out with fingers upward. Use your other hand to push gently against these fingers. Reverse and repeat.

1.

2. *Flagpole.* Lean back and onto one side, then grab the top leg with the same hand on that side. Stretch leg into the air and hold for 5–10 seconds. Then repeat with other leg.

2.

3. *Foot Artist.* In sitting position, lean back on hands for support. Lift one leg and draw circles in the air with your pointed toes. Now draw circles in the opposite direction. Repeat using the other foot.

   ➤ Draw waves, figure-8's.

   ➤ Bring your foot in and out; up and down.

   ➤ Trace your favorite number; the word "FIT"; your initials.

CIRCLES

3.

UP - DOWN

4. *Legend(s) of the Day!*

4.

MOVEMENT STATION

Lesson 4, Level 3 Extension

MOVEMENT AREA: Locomotion
MOVEMENT: Running

TEACHING GOALS:

- **Increase stride length.**
- **Encourage correct body alignment.**

EQUIPMENT REQUIRED:

Hoops, cones, chairs, low hurdles, ropes, box horse
8 bases
Large numbered cone markers
Running Circuit cards, counters, counter box
Stretch Cards
Assessment Recording Sheet

MOVEMENT STATIONS

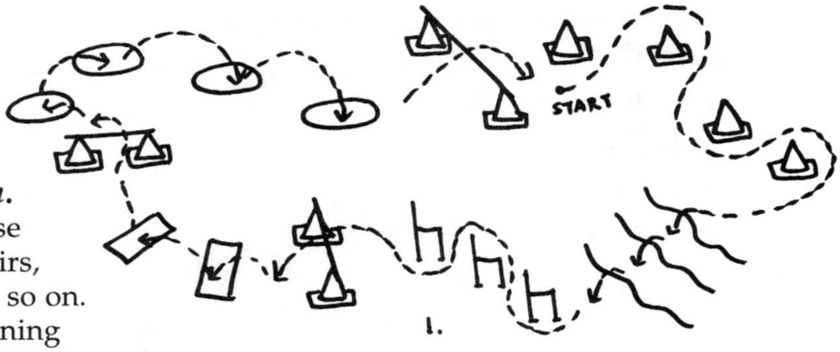

1. ***Obstacle Course Run.*** Create an obstacle course using hoops, cones, chairs, low hurdles, ropes, and so on. Children take turns running through the course. Emphasize safety.

2. ***Diamond Run.*** Set up 4 bases in the shape of a diamond as shown. Start with bases spaced 6 yards (meters) apart. Set up two identical courses and use arrows to indicate direction of travel (one course, run clockwise; other course, counterclockwise). Children take turns running the bases with a foot tag at each base.

   ➤ Children could time each other to see how quickly they can complete the diamond run.

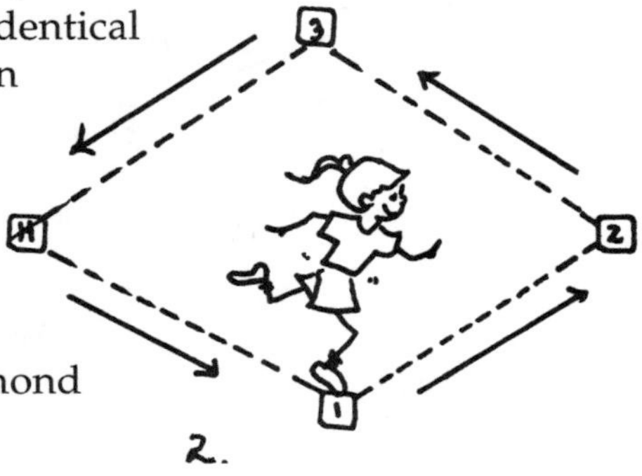

3. *Four-Leaf Clover Agility Run.* Set up an agility course using large numbered cone markers as shown in the diagram. Each runner starts in the middle and must complete the run as shown. Runners can record each other's time taken to do the agility run.

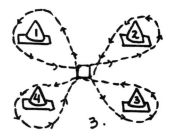

3.

4. *Running—Assessment.* Observe and record running performance. (See Book 1, *Ready-to-Use Fundamental Motor Skills & Movement Activities for Young Children*, for a Recording Sheet.)

5. *Running Circuit.* Each group member is given a map of a running circuit. Each map is slightly different in terms of *order* from the next map. Children must run to each of the different locations and collect a counter (colored card, chip, etc.). For example, directions on the map could be: Run to the large tree at the end of the oval and collect a counter; next run to the basketball/tennis courts and collect a counter in a box in keyway; next run to flag pole and collect a counter; next power walk to the play-ground slide and collect a counter.

COUNTER BOX
5.

6. *Stretching Station.* Hold each stretch for 10 seconds.

➤ Calf Stretch
➤ Sprinter Stretch
➤ Quad Stretch
➤ Butterfly Stretch

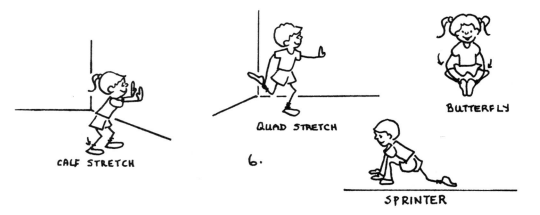

CALF STRETCH

QUAD STRETCH

6.

BUTTERFLY

SPRINTER

FOUNDATION MOVEMENT REVISION
Lesson 5, Level 3

ORGANIZATION: Identify the play area by setting up cone markers around the perimeter. As a general rule, space cone markers every 10 feet (3 meters) apart, using about 15 markers for a play area that is 60´ by 30´ (20m by 10m). Formation signals and starting positions are revised. Be patient, but insist that children immediately respond to these signals. Practice!

EQUIPMENT REQUIRED:

    15 cone markers
    1 hoop per child
    3 beanbags

WARMING-UP/FITNESS SIGNALS

"HERE!"

1. *Here, Where, There.* Listen carefully to the word I will say. If you hear the word "Here," hop quickly toward me; "Where," jump on the spot; "There," run quickly away from me. Repeat this activity, having children move in other ways, such as: skipping, slide-stepping, power walking. In between these signals, call out "Hook Sit," then lean back and pretend to climb a rope (tummy strengthener). "All Fours," face-up, and crab walk "dance" in your personal space (arm/leg strengthener).

I.

Hook Sit

2. *Listening Line.* (*Hand signal:* Arms outstretched sideways as you stand near and face line. Use the boundaries of the play area.) Immediately run and stand in a long line where I am pointing. Face me and space yourself arm's length apart. Now take *giant steps* across to the opposite side and stand on a listening line once there. How many giant steps did you take? Return to your listening line, again counting the number of steps.

2.

> ➤ Repeat, this time *leaping* across in as few giant steps as you can possibly do!

3. *Listening Circle.* (*Hand signal:* Point with index finger to the floor near you while circling the other index finger overhead.) Run quickly and safely to cross-leg sit in the circle that I am pointing to and face me. Give me your full attention.

3.

MOTOR MEMORY

· WINGERS·

1. *Airplane Signals.* You are an airplane. Show me how you can . . . "Clear the Deck!" "Propellers!" (Gently circle arms forward.)

   ➤ "Clear the Deck!" "Squeeze!" (Gently close and open your hands.)

   ➤ "Clear the Deck again!" "Wingers!" Start with arms bent and parallel to ground, hands at chest level and closed. Gently pull arms backward, squeezing shoulder blades together, and continue to open sideways holding the stretch. Repeat from beginning.

FLYING

1.

HIT THE DECK

   ➤ "Scrambled Eggs—Flying!" (Run only on the lines of the court.) "Hit the Deck!" "Clear the Deck!" and land gently on your boundary line (runway).

2. *Movement Sequencing.*

2.

   ➤ Walk on all fours—roll—jump up.

   ➤ Walk, changing direction every 8 steps; every 4 steps.

   ➤ Walk a pattern such as straight, zigzag, circle.

3. *Hoop Pattern Jumping.* Start from inside your hoop, jump out to the front, jump out to the back; jump to the right side and jump to the left. Jump in and out all around your hoop. Create a jumping pattern of your own!

3.

SPATIAL AWARENESS

1. *Traffic Cop Tag.* Spread 5 hoops throughout the play area. These hoops are the "safe zones." A player can stay in one of these Homes without getting tagged as long as she/he keeps her/his balance on one foot (without switching to the other foot). Select 3 Traffic Cops to be IT and give each a beanbag to hold. The Traffic Cops give chase to the other players, trying to tag them with their beanbag. A tagged player becomes "glued to a spot" and must jog in place. Use the "Iceberg!" signal to stop the play; select new Traffic Cops and continue the tagging game.

SAFE ZONE

BODY AWARENESS

Simon Says. When you say "Simon Says," child responds by doing the task; when you ask child to do a task without first saying "Simon Says," child does not respond. How good a listener can each child be? "Simon says . . . wiggle your left fingers." "Stamp your feet!" "Simon says . . . click your right fingers." "Blink your left eye."

WIGGLE FINGERS

STAMP FEET

BLINK EYE

CLOSING ACTIVITIES

1. ***Side Stretcher.*** Standing tall, slowly reach down one side of your body, "walking" your fingers as far down as you can go. Walk your fingers back up to starting position, and then walk your fingers down the other side.

1.

2. ***Butterfly Stretch.*** In sitting position, place the bottoms of your feet together. Holding at the ankles with your hands, let your arms gently push along the inside of the knees. Hold for 10 seconds.

3. ***Pencil Stretch.*** In back lying position, stretch as long as you can make yourself. Hold for 10 seconds. Roll over to front lying position and hold pencil stretch.

1.

4. ***Legend(s) of the Day!***

2.

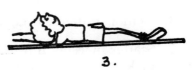

3.

4.

| MOVEMENT AREA: Locomotion |
| MOVEMENT: Dodging |

TEACHABLE POINTS:

1. When dodging, push off with the outside of the foot.
2. Keep eyes focused in which direction you want to move.
3. Keep your head up and move into open spaces.
4. Bend at the knees to keep the body lowered in order to change direction quickly.
5. Use your arms to help propel yourself into a new direction.
6. Move only as quickly as you can control, without falling over.

EQUIPMENT REQUIRED:

Markers such as cones, domes, or small hoops
Gym floors with marked lines are ideal for setting up dodging courses
Music; cassette/CD player

TEACHING GOALS:
☛ Promote quick change of direction.
☛ Promote correct foot action.

TEACHING PROGRESSIONS

1. Demonstrate the dodging action to the children, going over the teaching goals.

2. Scatter markers throughout the play area. Ask children to walk to a marker and make a quick dodging movement to one side. Emphasize the push off the outside of the foot. They will need to watch where they are going. Slowly increase the speed of execution.

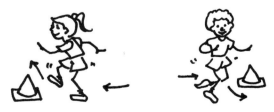

3. Split the class into teams of 6. Have each team stand in file formation behind a starting line and face a series of 5 markers, each spaced about 3 yards (meters) apart as shown. On signal "Dodge!" each runner in turn runs in and out of the markers until he/she reaches the end marker, then runs straight back to join end of file. As soon as runner crosses the start line, the next runner can go.

4. Repeat #3 with teams in shuttle formation.

ACTIVITIES

1. *Artful Dodger.* Children pair off and stand one behind the other. Music is used to start and stop the action. Front partner is the "Dodger" who moves in general space making quick changes of direction. The other partner is the "Shadow" who tries to follow as closely as possible to the Dodger without touching him or her. When music stops, everyone jump-stops ("Iceberg!"). If Shadow can take one pivot step forward to touch the Dodger, then the two partners change roles. Activity continues in this way.

   ➤ Use different locomotor movements such as power walking, jogging, slide-stepping, skipping, moving backward, hopping.

2. *Transformation Tag.* Have children get into groups of 3. In each group designate one person to be a "Head" who places preferred hand on head; a "Tail" who places preferred hand on bottom; and a "Pocket" who places preferred hand in pocket. On signal "Tag!" Heads, Tails, and Pockets try to tag each other, transforming the tagged player to look like the tagger. In the beginning there is one-third of each tagging group. On signal "Iceberg!" game stops. Now count the numbers in each group and make a comparison. Play game again!

ORGANIZATION: Identify the play area by setting up cone markers around the perimeter. As a general rule, space cone markers every 10 feet (3 meters) apart, using about 15 markers for a play area that is 60′ by 30′ (20m by 10m). More organization and formations signals are revised.

EQUIPMENT REQUIRED:

15 cone markers
Large throwing die
"Alphabet Arms" chart
Gym with line markings

WARMING-UP/FITNESS SIGNALS

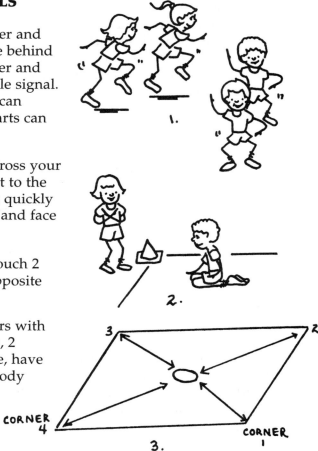

1. *Follow-the-Leader.* Find a partner and stand together in a Home space one behind the other. Take turns being the leader and the follower, changing on my whistle signal. Think of lots of different ways you can move. How many different body parts can you warm up?

2. *Listening Corner.* (*Hand signal:* Cross your arms making the letter X, then point to the corner with your index finger.) Run quickly and safely to knee-sit in this corner and face me.

3. *Corners!* On signal "2 Corners!" touch 2 opposite corners with elbow and opposite knee.

   ➤ On "4 Corners" touch all 4 corners with two body parts (2 hands, 2 knees, 2 feet . . .). If there is a center circle, have children touch the circle with a body part before running to a corner.

4. *Lines.*

> ➤ Run to the *Red* line, Jump stop on it, then drop to All-Fours and Puppy Walk along the line.

RED LINE

> ➤ Run to the *Blue* line. In front support position, Seal Walk along the line by moving on your forearms and dragging your feet.

BLUE LINE

> ➤ Jump your way to a *Black* line. In back support position, Crab Walk along the black line.

> v Jog along the boundary lines of the play area in a counterclockwise direction. On my whistle travel in the opposite direction (clockwise). "Iceberg!"

BOUNDARY LINE

> ➤ "Half Hook Sit." Lift your straight leg off the ground, alternately pointing and flexing foot 8 times. Repeat with the other leg.

5. *End Line.* (*Hand signal:* Arms outstretched to sides, with fingers of hand facing upward.) Run safely and quickly to jump-stop/jump-turn on the endline to which I am pointing. Check for good spacing (arm's length apart if possible). On signal "Endline" quickly run to the opposite endline, jump-stop on the line, and jump-turn to face me!

ENDLINE

MOTOR MEMORY

Alphabet Arms. On a large piece of paper write the letters of the alphabet using upper-case letters. Underneath each letter write a C, or F, or S. Choose one color for the letters of the alphabet and another color for the movement letters. For "C," have child clap hands together; for "F," click fingers in the air; for S," slap knees with hands. Have child say the letter and do the associated movement with that letter. Encourage child to progress at own rate. Practice part by part, slowly, until children have mastered each part. Observe coordination of actions with saying the letters.

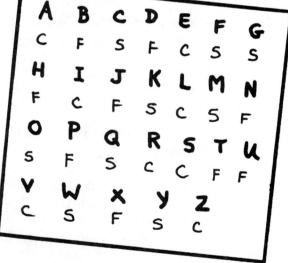

> ➤ *Challenge:* Repeat by saying the alphabet backward. Do activity reading letters from right to left.

VARIATIONS:

➤ Randomly mix letters and movements.

➤ Use geometric shapes, health words, or action pictures instead of letters.

➤ Vary the movements used: jump in the air; turn around, stamp feet.

SPATIAL AWARENESS

Six Corners. Use markers positioned at 6 locations in a rectangular area or hexagonal shape. With a marking pen, number the markers 1 through 6 as shown in the diagram. On signal "Corner!" players run to a corner of their choice and stay there jogging on the spot. Throw a large die and see which number comes up. Players caught in the corner with that number must come to the center of the play area and do stretches; the other players continue the game. When only 6 players remain, each player must run to a different corner! Who will be the last player left?

1.

BODY AWARENESS

1. *Busy Body Parts.* Call out the name of 2 body parts such as "knee and elbow." Children find a partner and touch each other's elbow and knee. Continue in this way, but each time find a new partner.

1.

   ➤ Touch right hand and left foot, etc.

   ➤ Touch 3 different body parts.

2. *Busy Muscles.* Call out name of a muscle; for example, "hamstrings." Child uses beanbag to touch partner's hamstring. Call out another muscle; for example, "biceps." Now child must find a new partner, and use a beanbag to touch this muscle.

2.

3. *Busy Bones.* Call out the name of a bone; for example, "patella" (knee cap). Partners then touch knee caps.

3.

" PATELLA"

CLOSING ACTIVITIES

1. *Angels in the Snow.* Begin in wide sit position, then slowly sink to back lying position.

    ➤ Spread your arms/legs apart; bring together. Repeat.

    ➤ Spread your legs apart, hold for 3 seconds, then bring legs together. Repeat.

    ➤ Spread your arms out to the side and bring slowly together.

    ➤ Let just your right side spread away from your body. Bring in. Now repeat with the other side.

2. *Heavy Head.* Roll over into front lying position. Pretend your head weighs 1,000 pounds! Slowly move to stand tall with your head being the last to come up.

3. *Rhythm Breathing.* Slowly breathe in (inhaling) while circling your arms outward to cross in front. Slowly breathe out (exhaling) while circling your arms in the opposite direction.

4. *Legend(s) of the Day!*

MOVEMENT STATIONS
Lesson 8, Level 3

> **MOVEMENT AREA:** Locomotion
>
> **MOVEMENT:** Dodging

TEACHING GOALS:

☞ Promote quick change of direction.

☞ Promote correct foot action.

EQUIPMENT REQUIRED:

4 large cone markers

Cones, chairs, and other obstacles

6–7 flags

Rectangle Circuit movement cards

Stretching/Strengthening poster

6–7 mats

Assessment Recording Sheet

MOVEMENT STATIONS

1. *Figure-8 Agility Run.* Set up two agility run courses in a figure-8 pattern as shown. Children take turns running the course in as quick a time as they can.

   ➤ Children could race each other through the course.

   ➤ Children could time each other to get through the course.

2. *Zigzag Dodge Course.* Set up an obstacle zigzag course as shown. Children take turns moving through the course.

3. *Tail Tag.* Each player has a tail tucked in at the back of the shorts, except for one player who is IT. If IT successfully snatches a tail, then that player becomes the new IT. Continue to play in this way.

4. ***Dodging—Assessment.*** Observe and record dodging performance. (See Book 1, *Ready-to-Use Fundamental Motor Skills & Movement Activities for Young Children,* for a Recording Sheet.)

5. ***Rectangle Circuit.*** Set up the rectangular circuit as shown in the diagram. Moving clockwise, run the length; Puppy Walk the width; backward jog the length; Crab Walk the width. Take turns to do circuit. When everyone has completed this circuit, reverse direction and do new movements: skip the length; jump the width from side-to-side; slide-step the length; hop the width.

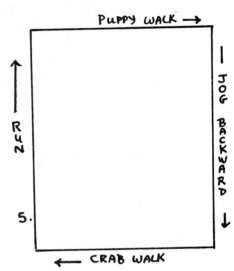

6. ***Stretching/Strengthening Station.*** Do the following stretches, holding them for a 10-second count:

Stretching	Strengtheners
Foot Artist	Hand Walkers
Periscope Stretch	Ankle Taps
Side Stretcher	Thigh Lifters

DISPLAY STRETCHES AND STRENGTHENERS ON A WALL CHART.

FOUNDATION MOVEMENT REVISION
Lesson 9, Level 3

ORGANIZATION: Identify the play area by setting up cone markers around the perimeter. As a general rule, space cone markers every 10 feet (3 meters) apart, using about 15 markers for a play area that is 60′ by 30′ (20m by 10m). The signals taught in previous lessons are further revised and extended. The organizational signal of "grouping" is extended.

EQUIPMENT REQUIRED:

15 cone markers
"Alphabet Arms" charts
CD/Cassette player and quiet "mood" music
Objects in the play area

BRONCO

WARMING-UP/FITNESS SIGNALS

Refer to Strengthening Signals, page 21.

1. Try **combinations of signals** and watch the action!

   ➤ "Scrambled Eggs!—Slide-stepping!" "Clear the Deck!" "Dead Bug!"

   ➤ Hop to a "Corner." Hop to "Home!" Be a "Bucking Bronco!"

   ➤ "Scrambled Eggs!—Duck Walking" "Iceberg!" "Hit the Deck!"

   ➤ "Home!" "Puppy Walk" from one sideline to other.

   ➤ "Scrambled Eggs!—Leaping" "Hit the Deck!" "Roll . . . !"

   ➤ "Scrambled Eggs!—Skipping" "Iceberg!" "Shake–Shake–Shake!" all over.

   ➤ "Home!" "4 Inchworms!"

DOG WALK

INCHWORM

2. *Group Signals—"2!"; "3!"; . . .*

   ➤ **"2's"** (*Hand signal:* Show 2 fingers in the air.) Find a partner and stand face-to-face. Give each other low tens, high tens, in between tens.

   ➤ **"3's"** (*Hand signal:* Show 3 fingers in the air.) Form groups of 3 and stand back to back, link elbows, and sink to the floor. Now try to stand up without breaking your hold.

   ➤ **"4's"** (*Hand signal:* Show 4 fingers in the air.) Form a circle, joining hands and | facing inward. Circle skip clockwise for 8 counts; the circle skip counterclockwise for another 8 counts. Stamp-stamp-stamp. Rest. Repeat.

"2's"
LOW TENS

"3's"

"4's"

MOTOR MEMORY

1. *Alphabet Arms.* Group children in "3's" and have each group create a new Alphabet Arms. Select some of the charts and have the whole class do the activity.

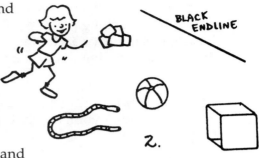

2. *Memory Order Game.* Have children form groups of 5–6. In each group, children take turns being IT in playing the game. The group selects 5 objects and decides what IT should touch and in what order. The objects and order could be different for each game played. Use playground objects or scatter several objects in the play area.

SPATIAL AWARENESS

1. *Knee Box.* Quickly find a partner and stand face-to-face in your Home space. On signal "Knee Box," try to touch partner's knee without your partner touching yours. Remember to stay in your Home space. When you hear "Knee Box" again, find a new partner to challenge!

   ➤ Repeat this activity trying to grab each other's tag belts or flags.

2. *Shadow Play.* With your new partner, stand one behind the other. Front partner leads, back partner follows like a "shadow." Listen for your moving signal (walk, jog, skip, hop, slide-step). Start on the music (whistle); stop when the music (whistle) stops. If the Shadow can take a step forward and touch Partner, then change roles. Change partners on signal "New Partners!"

3. *Tick-Tock.* Stand back-to-back with new partner. Stand half a step away from each other and interlock fingers with your partner. Together lean to one side to touch hands to floor ("Tick"); stand tall; then lean to other side and touch ("Tock"). Remember to bend your knees! Can you do 3 "Tick-Tocks" in this way?

BODY AWARENESS

1. *Mirrors.* Find a partner and stand facing each other, touching palm to palm. Show me how you can mirror each other's movements. Take turns changing roles on my signal "Mirrors!"

MIRRORS

2. *Statues.* Work in pairs to create different statues by taking your weight on different body parts.

2. STATUES

3. *Tripods.* Work in groups of 3 to create different tripods (balances).

3. TRIPODS

CLOSING ACTIVITIES

1. *Belly-Button Circles.* Pretend your belly button is the center of the circle. Trace 3 circles in one direction, then 3 circles in the opposite direction. Repeat.

   ➤ Push your tummy out, then in. Then turn from side to side.

1.

2. *Side Stretcher.* Standing tall, slowly reach down one side of your body, "walking" your fingers as far down as you can go. Now stretch one arm overhead, hold for 3 seconds, grab the wrist of that arm with the other hand, and hold for another 8 seconds. Repeat with the other arm.

3. *Partner Stretch.* "2's—Home space" "Mirrors." One partner leads the other to stretch through the body in different ways. Switch roles on signal. Mirror each other's movements.

2.

4. *Legend(s) of the Day!*

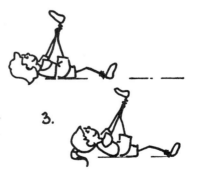

3.

TEACHING SESSION
Lesson 10, Level 3

MOVEMENT AREA: Locomotion
MOVEMENT: Jumps and Landings for Distance (Horizontal) and for Height (Vertical) **Revision**

TEACHABLE POINTS:

Jumping for Distance

1. Head up with eyes looking forward.
2. Arms extend behind the body as knees, hips, and ankles bend.
3. At same time, body leans slightly forward.
4. Legs extend vigorously and forcefully; at the same time arms extend forward and upward vigorously.
5. Body remains leaning slightly forward.

Jumping for Height

1. Head up with eyes looking forward.
2. Arms extend behind the body as knees, hips, and ankles bend.
3. At same time, boy leans slightly forward.
4. Legs and arms extend forcefully.
5. Arm action is synchronized with leg action.
6. Body extends upward.
7. Arms extend upward.

Landing

1. Land on balls of both feet, then roll back onto flat feet.
2. Ankles, knees, and hips bend to absorb force.
3. On landing, lean slightly forward at the hips.
4. Arms are held out in front or to side of body to assist balance.
5. Head should be up and eyes looking forward to stop falling forward.

EQUIPMENT REQUIRED:

1 hoop per child
Even surface or carpeted area
1 flag per child

TEACHING GOALS:

☛ Keep head up on landing.
☛ Bend knees on landing.
☛ Coordinate use of arms/legs in jump.

TEACHING PROGRESSIONS

1. Have children jump upward without using their arms. Do this again using arms. Which way is better?

2. Repeat #1, having children jump forward for distance.

3. How do knees help you to jump upward? Jump forward? Land?

4. Have children mirror your actions as you stand, swinging arms back and forth as knees bend and straighten.

5.

5. Have children stand behind a line and jump as far forward as possible. Emphasize bending knees and using arms to swing forward. Land softly, bending at the knees.

ROPE JUMPING

HALF JUMP TURN **6.**

6. *Jumping Signals.*

   ➤ Bounce gently like a ball in your Home space.

   ➤ Pantomime the action of rope jumping.

   ➤ Run in place, drop to the ground, then jump up high to run in place.

   ➤ Quarter jump-turn to the right; quarter jump-turn to the left.

   ➤ Jog in place; half jump-turn; jog in place; half jump-turn other way.

7.

7. *Hoop Jumping Challenges.*

   ➤ Jump forward in and out of hoop.

   ➤ Jump backward in and out of hoop.

   ➤ Jump sideways in and out of hoop.

   ➤ Jump out the front, back inside, out the back, inside, right side, inside, left side, inside.

   ➤ Walk 5 giant steps away from hoop, jump-turn to face hoop, then run to land with both feet in the hoop. Repeat.

RUN   **8.**   JUMP   LAND

8. Run, jump off one foot, and land softly, bending at the knees. Use your arms to help you keep balance.

ACTIVITIES

1. ***Clown in the Box.*** On signal "Clown in the Box!" children jump upward from their "box" (hoop), run to touch an object, then run Home to jump and land in their box. Repeat.

2. ***Wall Spring and Touch.*** Stand near a wall and spring upward to reach for a mark. Repeat, using other hand to reach for mark. Remind children to land softly, bending at the knees, arms helping to keep balance.

3. ***Frog in the Pond.*** Each "Frog" has a lily pad (hoop) and leaps from its lily pad into the pond, zapping flies in the air. Select two players to be the "Hawks." All frogs have a flag tucked into the back of their shorts. On signal "Ribbet!" Frogs must quickly but safely return to their pond before Hawks can swoop down and pull their tails. If caught, the players change places. The game continues in this way.

FOUNDATION MOVEMENT REVISION
Lesson 11, Level 3

ORGANIZATION: Identify the play area by setting up cone markers around the perimeter. As a general rule, space cone markers every 10 feet (3 meters) apart, using about 15 markers for a play area that is 60´ by 30´ (20m by 10m). The teamness concept is revised in this lesson. (Refer to page 14.)

EQUIPMENT REQUIRED:

15 cone markers
Suitable music; cassette/CD player

Whiteboard on large flip chart
Marking pens

WARMING-UP/FITNESS SIGNALS

1. *Marching Signals!* March to music and clap your hands in time. "Hit the Deck!" "March in place!" "Clear the Deck!" "March backward." "Dead Bug!" Now march forward in a big circle. March in a square, changing directions every 8 counts. March together with a partner. "Iceberg!" ("Jump-stop!")

   1.

   "DEAD BUG!"

2. Find your Home spot, facing square on to this wall. "Jump-turn" to the right to face this wall. Continue quarter jump-turning until you are facing the wall you started. Reverse and do quarter jump-turns in the opposite direction.

   ➤ Do half jump-turns (jump through 180 degrees.)

   ➤ Who can do a full jump-turn (through 360 degrees?)

3. *Teams.* Divide your class into teams of 5–6 children. Revise the team signal (hand signal), then designate where each team will cross-leg sit in file formation. Captain is at the front; co-captain at the back; boy–girl or vice versa. Each team selects an appropriate Team Name in the classroom and creates a Team Cheer. Teams, in turn, give their "Team Cheer."

   ➤ Use signals such as "Corner Touch!" Everyone must touch each corner of the play area, then quickly fall into your team. Which team will be the quickest to fall back into place?

   QUARTER JUMP-TURNS

   2.

CO-CAPTAIN   3. "TEAMS"   CAPTAIN

312

4. ***Waves.*** Stand tall in your teams and turn to face me as you position to one side of the group as shown. Space yourselves arm's length apart, facing me.

> ➤ Take 4 steps forward; 4 steps back; 4 steps to the right; 4 steps to the left; turn around in place and stamp-stamp-stamp!

MOTOR MEMORY

Directions, Patterns, and Pathways. Show directions, patterns, pathways on a whiteboard or large flip chart paper. In the classroom ask children to create a movement collage as an art project.

> ➤ Move in 3 different *directions:* forward; backward; sideways; diagonally. Do this again, but change the order.

> ➤ Move in different *pathways:* straight line; zigzag; curved. Combine any 3 together.

> ➤ Move in the different *patterns:* circle, triangle, rectangle, figure-8, spiral, a letter.

Try combinations of movements:

> ➤ Move backward in a circle.

> ➤ Move sideways in a straight line.

> ➤ Move in a triangle by zigzagging.

> ➤ Create your own movement combination of directions, pathways, and patterns.

SPATIAL AWARENESS

1. *Two-way/Four-way Traffic.* Have each team position on a different side of the play area (30′ by 30′ [10m by 10m] square). Assign the teams numbers, "1, 2, 3, and 4." Signal teams to move across the square in different ways and from a variety of starting positions:

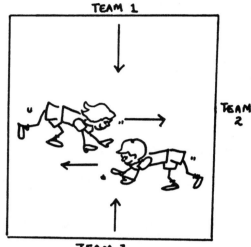

   ➤ 1 and 3's "Power Walk"; "2 and 4's" "Power Walk"

   ➤ 4 and 2's "Jog"; 3 and 1's "Jog"

   ➤ 1 and 3's "Puppy Walk"; 2 and 4's "Puppy Walk"

   ➤ 4 and 2's "Crab Walk"; 3 and 1's "Crab Walk"

   ➤ 1 . . . 2 . . . 3 . . . 4's "Skip!"

   ➤ Front lying position with head on the line, 1 and 3's "Kangaroo Jumps"; 2 and 4's "Kangaroo Jumps"

   ➤ 4 and 2's "Bunny Hops"; 3 and 1's "Frog Leaps"

2. Play *Chain Tag* with 3 players selected as the ITs. Once a player is tagged, that player must join IT. Players in chain must keep their inside hands joined and use only outside hands to make the tag. Remind players to watch where they are going at all times. Watch the action as each chain grows in size!

BODY AWARENESS

1. *Busy Body Parts.* Play this game as before (see page 293), but have players touch right or left body parts. For example, touch left elbows; touch left knee to right knee of other partner.

2. *Pockets.* In partners, move in and out of each other's shapes, filling in the empty spaces. For example, first partner forms a shape; second partner forms a shape around the first partner. First partner then moves to form a shape around second partner.

CLOSING ACTIVITIES

1. ***Imagery—R-E-L-A-X!*** Lie on a mat in back lying position and relax. Think of something that is very pleasant, that will bring a smile to your face. Listen to the quiet background music. Breathe slowly. Relax—let yourself just go.

   ➤ Now tense just your hands for a 3-second count, then relax. Tense again, relax.

   ➤ Tense your face. Relax.

   ➤ Tense your shoulders. Relax.

   ➤ Tense your stomach muscles. Relax.

   ➤ Tense your seat muscles. Relax.

   ➤ Tense your legs and feet. Relax.

   ➤ Tense all over!

   ➤ Let everything go limp. Relax!

   ➤ Tense all over again. Relax!

2. ***Legend(s) of the Day!***

MOVEMENT STATIONS
Lesson 12, Level 3

MOVEMENT AREA: Locomotion
MOVEMENT: Jumping and Landing

TEACHING GOALS:

☞ **Keep head up on landing.**

☞ **Bend knees on landing.**

☞ **Coordinate use of arms/legs in jump.**

EQUIPMENT REQUIRED:

4 long ropes

Hoops

Deckring attached to a rope

Box horse, bench, low hurdles, mats

Suspend balls in socks

Floor tape or colored chalk for hopscotch patterns

Assessment Recording Sheet

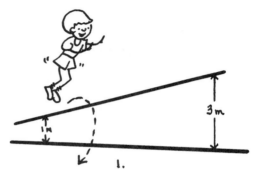

MOVEMENT STATIONS

1. **Jump the Stream.** Place two long ropes as shown in diagram. Children take turns jumping across the "stream" from its narrowest point to its widest. Set up two courses—one easy; one more difficult.

2. **Hoop Jumping Course.** Make a jumping course by placing hoops on the ground in a pattern, close enough to jump off two feet from one hoop to the other. Together create other hoop patterns and jump through it.

3. **Jump the Ring.** One child swings a deckring attached to a rope in a large circle along the ground. Children try to jump the ring each time it passes under their feet.

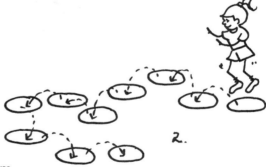

4. ***Jumping for Distance and Jumping for Height—Assessment.*** Observe and record performance. (See Book 1, *Ready-to-Use Fundamental Motor Skills & Movement Activities for Young Children*, for a Recording Sheet.)

5. ***Jumping and Landing Circuit.*** Create jumping and landing challenges such as:

   ➤ Jump from low box horse onto a mat as far as possible.

   ➤ Walk along a bench, jump off to land in a hoop.

   ➤ Jump over low hurdles.

   ➤ Jump to hit a ball suspended in a sock from a fixed structure.

   ➤ Run, jump off favorite foot from a mark, and land on a mat.

6. ***Hopscotch.*** Introduce different hopscotch patterns and let children decide on the rules for each game. Then play the game.

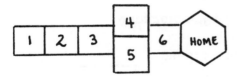

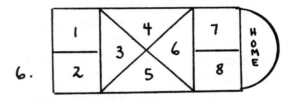

FOUNDATION MOVEMENT REVISION
Lesson 13, Level 3

ORGANIZATION: Identify the play area by setting up cone markers around the perimeter. As a general rule, space cone markers every 10 feet (3 meters) apart, using about 15 markers for a play area that is 60′ by 30′ (20m by 10m). The file formation is further revised in this lesson.

EQUIPMENT REQUIRED:

> Music with a steady 4/4 count; Cassette/CD player
> 1 light mat per child
> Several pieces of equipment such as balance bench/beam, chairs, table, low
>   hurdles, box horse, hoops
> Tagging objects or tag belts
> 15 cone markers

Warming-up/Fitness Signals

1. *Good Morning Workout.* (*Hand signal:* "Waves!")
   Do simple aerobic exercises to develop a warming-up effect and rhythm sense:

   ➤ Jog on the spot for 8 counts; pantomime rope jumping for 8 counts.

   ➤ Skip forward for 8 counts; pantomime rope jumping for 8 counts.

   ➤ Skip backward for 8 counts; 4 jump-turn bounces.

   ➤ Squat down low, and jump up high; do this again!

   ➤ Power walk with changes of direction every 8 counts. Clap on the change.

   ➤ March to music and snap fingers; jump-stop.

   ➤ Kick legs out front for 8 counts; kick legs out to side for 8 counts.

   ➤ Your "cool" dance to the music.

2. *Listening Line!* Face this wall or direction. "Snake"—remember this is your signal to get into a long file or chain. Let's move as an aerobic snake. I will be at the head of the Snake, the last child is the tail of the Snake. Everyone else in between stays in the order that you are now standing. You are the links of the Snake. Jog to the music as we snake along. Follow me. (Use different locomotor movements at an easy-to-follow pace.) Finish in an activity circle.

3. *Activity Circle.* (Refer to Fitness Signals—Warming-Up, Strengthening, and Stretching signals for activities, pages 19 through 29.)

MOTOR MEMORY

In the Jungle. Start in your Home space. Check for good spacing. Take children on a "safari" using different movements such as:

➤ stepping over tall grass (*low hurdles*)

➤ moving under the bridge (*hurdles, table, chair*)

➤ wading across the stream (*giant steps*)

➤ jumping off a rock (*box horse*)

➤ sneaking up behind a tree to watch the zebras eating grass

➤ crawling through a cave (*hoops or 4 chairs in a file*)

➤ walking across a suspended bridge (*balance beam or bench*)

➤ climbing up a tree, grabbing a vine, swinging out to splash in river

➤ sitting cross-legged in front of the fire playing African drums

➤ pantomiming a native jungle animal or bird or reptile

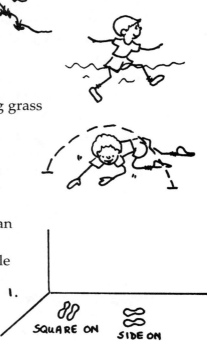

SPATIAL AWARENESS

1. *Square on, Side on, Diagonal.* Stand facing me in your Home space.

➤ You are now *square on*. Turn *side on* to me. *Square on*.

➤ Turn *side on* in a different direction.

➤ Turn your back to me. Now face me *square on*.

➤ Turn to face a corner of the play area that I point to. Now you are *diagonal on*.

➤ Stand on this listening line. Run forward *square on*. Across to the other sideline. "Iceberg!" (Jump-stop)

➤ Now move across but be *side on* to your line of direction.

2. *Ship Ahoy! signals.* Let's turn the play area into a giant ship. Face square on to this wall (or boundary line). This is the *bow* of the ship. Your back is now facing the *stern* of the ship.

➤ As you face the bow, the right side of the ship is called "starboard"; left side, "portside."

➤ Jump-turn to face each side of the ship as I call out the name: starboard; stern; port; bow.

"STARBOARD - WALK BACKWARD"

"RESCUE!"

➤ Start in your Home space and move to the front, back, or side, listening to what is called out.

Now add other Signals to this game.

➤ For example, jump to the *bow*. "Iceberg!" "Dead Bug!"

➤ Jog to the *stern*. "Periscope" (back lying position with one knee straight up into the air and hold).

➤ Walk backward to *starboard*. "Rescue"—quickly find a partner and grab each other's wrists of one hand and gently pull.

➤ Slide-step to *portside*. "Hit the Deck!" Now "Scrub the Deck."

➤ Skip to *bow*, 2's back-to-back. Do the "Sardine Walk"—lean forward and grab each other's wrists between your legs. Now walk in this way.

STARBOARD

← BOW   STERN →

PORT

BOW - JUMP!

DEAD BUG!

3. ***Pirate Tag!*** Stand at one end of the ship. Choose three players to be the Pirates who stand in the middle of the ship. On signal "Pirates Are Coming!" all other players must try to cross the ship without being tagged. If tagged, that player is "frozen" to the spot but may use arms to touch other players crossing and thus free him-/herself. After a while choose new Pirates and continue the game.

3.

BODY AWARENESS

1. In pairs, have one partner do one thing while other partner does the opposite. Example: one *in front of* something, the other *behind*; one *on* something, other *off*; move *over* something, while partner moves *under*; raise the *right hand* in the air, lower the *right hand*; squat down *low*, jump up *high*; etc.

OVER   UNDER

1.

2. Using beanbags or folded socks, have child place or throw object according to certain spatial commands:

➤ Put beanbag on top of your head.

➤ Place it behind you.

➤ Put it on the side of you; in front of you.

➤ Place beanbag on your right knee; left elbow.

➤ Toss beanbag from right hand to left hand; reverse.

➤ Toss beanbag high and catch.

➤ Toss beanbag from left foot to right hand.

➤ Toss beanbag square on to partner.

➤ Toss beanbag to right side of partner; left side.

2.

CLOSING ACTIVITIES

Pick up a mat and take it to a Home space.

1. In back lying position, do the following:

   ➤ Bring your right leg up and hold it with both hands, gently pulling it toward your chest. Hold for 10 seconds, then slowly lower.

   ➤ Bring your left leg up and gently pull it toward your chest. Hold for 10 seconds and slowly lower.

   ➤ Bring your left leg up and hold it with your right hand.

   ➤ Bring your right leg up and hold it with your left hand.

   ➤ Bring both legs up and hold each leg with the hand on that side. Spread your legs wide apart and hold.

PENCIL

2. Now roll over to front lying position:

   ➤ Gently raise your head and arms off the mat and hold.

   ➤ Now gently raise your legs off mat and hold for10 seconds. Repeat.

   ➤ Slowly raise yourself to stand tall, with your head being the last to come off the floor.

3. *Legend(s) of the Day!*

3.

MOVEMENT AREA: Body Control

MOVEMENT: Static Balance

TEACHABLE POINTS:

1. Feet are flat on the floor with toes extended.
2. Keep the knees slightly flexed.
3. All body parts are kept straight and still.
4. Use arms to assist in balancing.
5. Keep head up and eyes focused straight ahead on a fixed point.

EQUIPMENT REQUIRED:

Firm even surface
Hopscotch tiles or drawing chalk
Cone markers

TEACHING GOALS:
☞ **Keep head up and eyes focused.**
☞ **Keep feet flat on the floor.**

TEACHING PROGRESSIONS

1. Explore 3-point balances on hand and knee combinations; then hands and feet combinations.

   ➤ Explore 3-point balances using other body part combinations.

2. Explore 2-point balances. Squat with feet slightly apart and arms out to the sides. Reduce width of feet.

3. Explore 1-point balances.

   ➤ One-foot balance with hands on hips; hands on head; arms out to side. Repeat balance on other foot. Repeat balance with eyes closed.

   ➤ Lift legs off the floor while balancing on bottom.

ACTIVITIES

1. *Ship Ahoy!* The play area becomes a ship with the front being the "bow"; the back, the "stern"; right-side, "starboard"; left side, "port." Create ship signals such as:

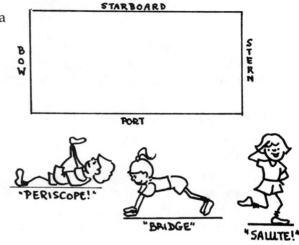

   ➤ Run to the bow. "Iceberg!" "Periscope" (back lying position with one foot in the air).

   ➤ Jump to the stern. "Bridge." Quickly find a partner and make a bridge with only 3 body parts touching the floor.

   ➤ Slide-step to port. "Salute Your Captain" by standing on one foot, opposite hand to foot on hip, and other hand saluting.

2. *De-Icer Tag.* Choose 3 players to be ITs who give chase to moving Statues. Choose another player to be the "De-Icer." If a Statue is tagged, he/she becomes "frozen" and must stay in this fixed position until the De-Icer comes along and thaws out that player. The thawed-out player must take a 3-second count to thaw out. Change taggers and De-icer after every 3 minutes. *Variation:* Create a frozen position that a tagged player must take.

3. *Hopscotch* Children in groups of 4 create their own hopscotch patterns and rules, then play the game. Use colored chalk and designate an area for each group on the tarmac.

ORGANIZATION: Identify the play area by setting up cone markers around the perimeter. As a general rule, space cone markers every 10 feet (3 meters) apart, using about 15 markers for a play area that is 60´ by 30´ (20m by 10m). Circle formation signal is revised.

EQUIPMENT REQUIRED:

> "Pink Panther" music; cassette/CD
>   player
> Tag belts, flags, or tagging objects
> Whiteboard or flip chart, marking pens
> 15 cone markers

Warming-up/Fitness Signals

1. *Aerobic Snake.* (See previous lesson plan.) Add other locomotor movements as the snake winds its way in different movement patterns.

2. Use the following break signals to give children a change of pace, as well as develop overall body balance and coordination. (Refer to Break Signals, page 13.)

    ➤ "Thread the Needle"
    ➤ "Spinning Top"
    ➤ "Bucking Bull"
    ➤ "Pogo Springs
    ➤ "Partner Snake Roll"

3. *Circle Formation Break.* "Sticky Popcorn!" Children start "popping" (light bouncing) as they move into a popcorn ball. Challenge the children to see how long it will take them to form their popcorn ball (tight circle facing middle).

4. In circle formation, number off the class "1, 2, 3, 4, 5, 6, 7" as shown in the diagram. On signal "Circle Run," each child in turn runs clockwise around the circle and back to his/her place, starting with 1's, then 2's, etc. As soon as runner gets back to his/her place, the next runner may go. Which group will finish in cross-leg sitting the quickest? Repeat circle run in counterclockwise direction.

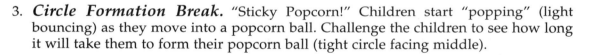

Motor Memory

The Eye Box. On a whiteboard or flip chart draw a large rectangular box as shown. Tell the class that this is an "Eye Box." Use a different colored marking pen to indicate the following locations in the box: top right, top middle, top left, bottom right, bottom middle, bottom left. Ask children to stand tall in a Home space. Make sure that they can all see the Eye Box. Call out different locations and have each child move only the eyes to those places. Remind them to keep the head still. Observe their actions and comment.

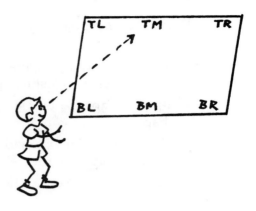

➤ Now have them imagine an Eye Box in front of them. Call out different locations.

Spatial Awareness

1. *Partner Challenges.* ("Homes," side-by-side starting position.) Partners try to complete the task before the other partner, returning to Home position. Partner who finishes "second" must do "3 of something" as instructed by first partner; for example, 3 push-ups, 3 sit-ups.

➤ Touch an endline with your right hand and left foot and the other endline with your left hand and right foot. Signal "Endline!"

➤ Touch one corner with your right elbow; the diagonally opposite corner with your left elbow. Signal "Corners."

➤ Hop to one sideline, touching it with a knee; hop to the other sideline, touching it with the opposite knee. Signal "Sideline."

2. *Pirates Are Coming!* Stand at one end of the ship. Choose three players to be the Pirates who stand in the middle of the ship. Pirates call out, "You may cross our ship if you are wearing (name a color or wearing apparel)." On signal "Pirates Are Coming!" all other players must try to cross the ship without being tagged. All those tagged become Pirates. Continue until everyone is caught. Have children wear tag belts that are pulled to be caught, or have Pirates tag with an object in their hand (beanbag, small soft ball).

BODY AWARENESS

Body Balances. Find your Home space.

➤ Show me how you make a 2-point shape other than just using your feet.

➤ 3-point shape; 4-point shape; 5-point shape.

➤ Make a long shape; a wide shape; a twisted shape; a curled shape.

➤ Find a partner. Repeat the tasks above.

➤ Groups of three: Make 3-point, 4-point, 5-point, 6-point, and 7-point shapes.

CLOSING ACTIVITIES

1. *Pink Panther.* Use the theme music, if possible. Sleepers find a Home space in the play area and get into back lying position. Fold arms across the chest, and close eyes, except for two players who are the Pink Panthers. When the music starts, the Pink Panthers keep hands behind their backs, prowl around the area, and bend down to talk to a sleeping player. Panthers, be clever and humorous as you try to get a sleeping player to wake up. If the sleeping player moves in any way, he or she is automatically awakened and becomes a Pink Panther helper to try to wake up other sleepers. The challenge is to see which sleeping player(s) can last the length of the song and become the best concentrator(s) of the day!

2. *Legend(s) of the Day!*

MOVEMENT STATIONS
Lesson 16, Level 3 Extension

MOVEMENT AREA: Body Control
MOVEMENT: Static Balance

TEACHING GOALS:

☛ Keep the knees slightly flexed.

☛ Use arms to assist in balancing.

☛ Keep head up and eyes focused straight ahead on a fixed point.

EQUIPMENT REQUIRED:

Wooden blocks or soft dome markers
Beanbags
Hoops
Individual and partner balance cards
Balance benches or beams
Large rope
Assessment Recording Sheet

MOVEMENT STATIONS

1. ***Balance Object Play.*** Explore and practice balancing tasks:

   ➤ Balance on different body parts using wooden blocks or soft dome markers.

   ➤ Balance a beanbag on different body parts.

   ➤ Use a hoop to create different balanced positions.

2. ***Balancing Challenges.*** Perform individual balancing challenges. (See page 329.) Enlarge these onto cards and have children perform.

3. ***Static Balance—Assessment.*** Observe and record performance in doing a static balance. (See Book 1, *Ready-to-Use Fundamental Motor Skills & Movement Activities for Young Children*, for a Recording Sheet.)

4. ***Balance Bench/Beam Challenges.*** Explore different ways of balancing on the bench or beam on 1, 2, 3, and 4 body parts. (Mats should be placed around the apparatus for safety.)

4.

5. ***Partner and Three's Balances.*** (See page 330.) Enlarge these onto cards and have the children work first in pairs, then in three's to perform the balancing positions.

6. ***Large Rope Balancing.*** Using a large rope, children together explore different ways of balancing cooperatively.

6.

INDIVIDUAL BALANCING CHALLENGES

BALANCES IN THREE'S

PARTNER BALANCING CHALLENGES

FOUNDATION MOVEMENT REVISION
Lesson 17, Level 3

ORGANIZATION: Identify the play area by setting up cone markers around the perimeter. As a general rule, space cone markers every 10 feet (3 meters) apart, using about 15 markers for a play area that is 60´ by 30´ (20m by 10m). Signals are reinforced. Team concept of "Islands" is revised.

EQUIPMENT REQUIRED:

15 cone markers placed in a large circle or oval
Suitable music; cassette/CD player
1 large sheet of drawing paper for each team
2 different colored marking pens per team
1 set of bibs per team, beanbags for tagging
Several hoops
4 sets of different colored flags—one color per set

WARMING-UP/FITNESS SIGNALS

Superstar Warm-up. Listen carefully for my signal as I turn you into Superstars!

➤ "Scrambled Eggs—Hockey Player!" Move in and out of each other dribbling the puck like a hockey player. "Iceberg!" "Score a goal!"

➤ "Homes—Figure Skater." In your Home space create different movements as a figure skater.

➤ "Activity Circle Clockwise—Formula I Driver!" Show me how you move in and out of each other as a racing car driver. "Iceberg!"

➤ "Black Line—Kick Boxer!" Run to a corner of the play area and perform karate kicks and boxing arm actions.

➤ "Corners—Tennis Player!" Find a corner and show me how you can move as a tennis player.

➤ "Home/Line—Tightrope Walker" Find a Home space on a line, and show me how you would walk across a suspended wire. Careful!

➤ "Blue Line—Basketball Player!" Pantomime dribbling a basketball for a lay-up, jump-stop, pivot, shoot!

HOCKEY PLAYER

FIGURE SKATER

FORMULA I DRIVER

KICK BOXER

TENNIS PLAYER

TIGHT ROPE WALKER

BASKETBALL PLAYER

MOTOR MEMORY

1. *The Eye Box.* (Refer to Lesson 8, page 304, for description.) Stand tall in a Home space. Make sure that you can all see the Eye Box. Now march in place, touching your hands lightly to your knees and listen to what I say: top middle, bottom left, top right, bottom middle, top left; bottom right. Move only your eyes to those places. Remember that your head must stay still! Observe actions and comment.

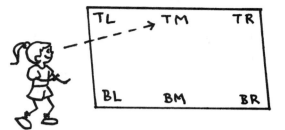

SPATIAL AWARENESS

1. *Colors Team Tag.* Give each team a set of colored pinnies to wear (red, green, blue, yellow). Select the Red team to be the tagging team and give each team member a tagging object. On signal "RED Tag," Red team members try to tag as many of the other players as they can in 30 seconds. A tagged player must jog on the spot. At the end of 30 seconds count the number of tagged players. This is the Red team's score. Each team has a turn at being the IT team and is given the tagging objects. Which team will make the most number of tags?

   ➤ *Variation:* Use 4 different sets of colored flags.

2. *Islands.* Create several "islands" using hoops scattered throughout the play area. On signal "Scrambled Eggs—Jogging" (each time vary locomotor movements used), move in and out of the islands without touching them. On signal "Islands!" quickly find an island and jump into it. You will need to share your island with others. Each time we "Scramble Eggs" I will take away one or two islands. Eventually the islands will become more and more crowded. You will have to cooperate in order to all fit into your island. Do so carefully!

BODY AWARENESS

Create a Being. Mark out several team "Islands" as shown. Assign each team to an island. Let the team choose a name for the island. Each team is given marking pens and a large sheet of drawing paper.

➤ One team member gets into back lying position on the large piece of paper. Using a marking pen, trace an outline of this member onto the paper. Then, taking turns, fill in the body parts: head, eyes, mouth, ears, nose, neck, body, arms, hands, fingers, and so on.

➤ Now take turns to write *inside* the body shape all the positives (attributes) you would like to have. *Outside* of the body write the negatives, the "emotional hurts." (You may wish to have the whole class contribute to the positive and negative attributes first, and write the words on the whiteboard.) Ask children to try to be a positive being for the whole day!

CLOSING ACTIVITIES

1. Curl up into a tight ball. On signal "Sunrise," slowly open to make yourself as wide and "bright" as possible. On signal "Sunset," slowly curl up into a ball, sinking, sinking until you disappear.

2. On signal "Puppets," I will pull certain strings, such as raising and lowering your right arm; lifting your left knee; making you bend forward and back. Become floppy all over. Shake gently all over, then flop to the ground.

3. In cross-leg sit position, take 4 counts to breathe in slowly; 4 counts to breathe out slowly. Repeat.

4. *Legend(s) of the Day!*

TEACHING SESSION
Lesson 18, Level 3 Extension

MOVEMENT AREA: Body Control
MOVEMENT: Dynamic Balance

TEACHABLE POINTS:

1. Feet are flat on the floor with toes extended.
2. Feet remain slightly bent.
3. Hips, back, and shoulders remain straight.
4. Arms are extended out to the sides for balance.
5. Head is up and upper body remains steady.
6. Eyes are focused and looking straight ahead at a fixed point.

HEEL-TOE

EQUIPMENT REQUIRED:

Firm even surface with line markings
Beanbags as tagging objects
Cone markers
Floor tape or lines on floor
Music with steady 4/4 beat; cassette/CD player

TEACHING GOALS:

☞ **Keep head up and eyes focused.**
☞ **Keep feet flat on the floor.**

TEACHING PROGRESSIONS

1. Have children walk forward, then backward along the line with arms out to the side.
2. Combine forward and backward walking with turns along the line.
3. Have children walk sideways along the line.
4. Combine these 3 types of walking.
5. Have children perform the above activities with hands on hips.
6. Have children walk heel to toe, forward then backward, with arms out to sides.
7. Have children walk heel to toe forward with hands on hips. Repeat walking backward.
8. Explore other ways of traveling along the lines.

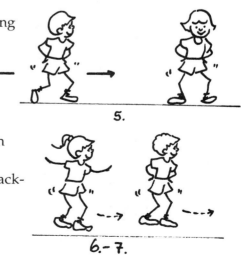

5.

6.- 7.

ACTIVITIES

1. ***Horses, Knights, and Cavaliers.*** Children move to music like prancing horses to the signal "Scrambled Eggs—Prance!" When music stops, teacher calls out one of the following signals:

    ➤ "Horses": One partner on all fours, the other gently straddling this partner.

    ➤ "Knights": New partners, one partner in kneeling position with one knee up; other partner gently sitting on knee of kneeling partner (and putting one foot in the air).

    ➤ "Cavaliers": New partners, one partner standing and supporting legs of other partner, who is standing on hands.

2. ***Hoppo Bumpo.*** Partners, about the same size, take up a position of right hand holding the left foot behind, while left hand is used to gently push the other partner off balance. After 3 attempts, challenge a new partner.

    ➤ Reverse leg–hand hold and repeat activity.

3. ***Heel–Toe Relay.*** Split the class into 4 teams. For each team, mark on the floor 4 long lines (5 yards [5 meters]) using floor tape. Have each team position in shuttle formation, with 3 members at the start of the line, facing 3 other members at the finish. Children must walk heel-toe along the line and tag the teammate on the opposite side. If a teammate comes off the line, he or she must start over again.

    ➤ *Variation:* Backward Heel–Toe Relay.

ORGANIZATION: Identify the play area by setting up cone markers around the perimeter. As a general rule, space cone markers every 10 feet (3 meters) apart, using about 15 markers for a play area that is 60′ by 30′ (20m by 10m). The shuttle formation signal is revised, practiced, and reinforced through relays.

EQUIPMENT REQUIRED:

15 cone markers	Tagging objects
Cassette/CD player	1 jump-hoop per relay team
Climbing frame	1 ball per relay team

WARMING-UP/FITNESS SIGNALS

1. **Grand Prix.** Mark out a large oval area using cone markers. Ideally have one cone marker for each child in your class.

    ➤ You are Formula I racing car drivers moving around a track. Everyone stand on the outside of a cone marker, rev up your engine, and wait for your start signal!

    ➤ When you hear the signal "Circle Up—Clockwise" (clockwise hand signal), race around the oval in a clockwise direction, like the hands of a clock.

    ➤ The rule at this race track is that you pass on the *outside* only!

    ➤ On signal "Circle Up—Counter-clockwise" (counterclockwise hand signal), travel in the opposite direction.

1.

    ➤ On signal "Pitstop," stop where you are and do the task for 5 seconds: "Bridge"; "Periscope!;" "Bucking Bronco;" "Thread-the-Needle."

2. **Crab Walk Greeting.** In crab walk position, greet everyone on your team by "shaking feet" (touching bottom of foot to partner's). Alternate feet each time you do a greeting.

2.

MOTOR MEMORY

Climbing Frame. Move between the rungs using right/left concepts. Example: move right hand, then left foot as you climb upward, across, through, in, and out; and so on.

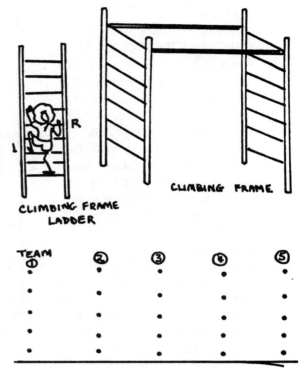

CLIMBING FRAME LADDER

CLIMBING FRAME

SPATIAL AWARENESS

1. *Team Leapfrog.* Teams position in file formation behind a listening line. Check for good spacing. (See diagram.) Leapfrog by placing hands gently on the back of the player in front who curls up on all fours and keeps head down. Straddle jump over this player.

   ➤ Co-captain Frog at the back begins the race by leap-frogging over the backs of each member in front. Once you reach the front, squat down and call out "Ribbet," which is the signal for the next Frog to go. Which team will be the first to get all its Frogs across the opposite listening line?

TEAM ① ② ③ ④ ⑤

LISTENING LINE

LEAP-FROGGING

LISTENING LINE

2. ***The Black Hole.*** Give each team a "Star Wars" name such as Han Solo; Luke Skywalker; Chewbacca, C3PO; or R2D2. Select one team to be the IT team (Darth Vader and Storm Troopers) who stand in the middle of a circular area ("the black hole"). See diagram. The other teams "fly" around the outside of this circular area, saying "Whose spaceship are you?" Darth Vader can give several answers, but when he/she says "Yours!" the chase is on. Outside spaceships must fly to the safe zones (outside boundary lines of play area). If a spaceship is captured (tagged), that spaceship must join Darth Vader and his/her team.

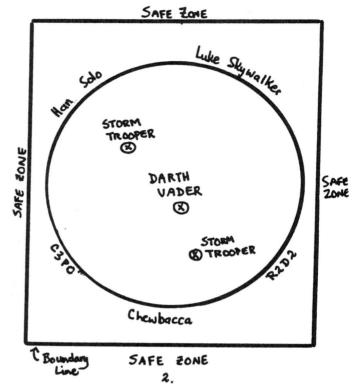

BODY AWARENESS

Human Shapes.

Partners:

➤ Make the letter A, T, L, H, C . . .

➤ Make the following numbers: 3, 6, 8, 19 . . .

➤ Make two-letter words.

Three's

➤ Make triangles, circles, squares, diamonds.

➤ Make different letters.

➤ Make different numbers—single, double, and triple digits.

➤ Make simple words.

CLOSING ACTIVITIES

1. *Shuttle Relays.* Shuttle formation. (See Formation Signals, page 9.)

   ➤ Run to opposite side giving high
     tens for the next player to go.
   ➤ Run to the opposite side bouncing
     a ball to the next player in line.
   ➤ Run to the opposite side dribbling
     a ball to the next player in line.
   ➤ Zigzag through the markers to the
     opposite line.

SHUTTLE RELAY - BALL DRIBBLING

   ➤ Do different locomotor movements: slide-step, walk backwards, skip, hop.
   ➤ Do different Animal Walks.
   ➤ Use a jump-hoop to travel to the other side.

2. *Legend(s) of the Day!*

MOVEMENT AREA: Body Control
MOVEMENT: Dynamic Balance

TEACHING GOALS:

☞ Keep head up, feet flat on the ground.

☞ Keep upper body quiet (relatively still).

EQUIPMENT REQUIRED:

Cone markers
Long ropes
Wooden blocks or dome markers
Large mats
Balance boards (Duck Walkers), foam
   stilts or bucket steppers
Low box horse, hurdles, climbing frame
Balance benches or beams
Assessment Recording Sheet

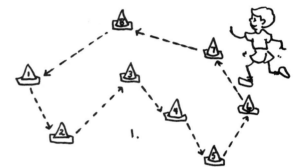

MOVEMENT STATIONS

1. **Snake Run.** Use numbered cones to mark out a "Snake Run" course as shown in the diagram. Children take turns running through the course. Each cone must be touched without knocking it over. Time each other, if possible.

2. **Balancing Challenges.** Print tasks on posterboard. Children stand on mats.

   ➤ Balance on one leg for a count of 5. Repeat balancing on the other leg.

   ➤ Balance on one leg on 2 dome markers/ blocks of wood as shown; balance on 1 dome marker/wooden block.

   ➤ Balance on one knee and one hand; balance on the other knee and hand.

   ➤ Explore balancing on other 2-point combinations.

   ➤ Explore other 3-point balances.

   ➤ Balance on one knee; balance on the other knee.

   ➤ Explore other 1-point balances.

   ➤ Repeat these tasks with eyes closed.

3. ***Dynamic Balance—Assessment.*** Observe and record performance of dynamic balance. (See Book 1, *Ready-to-Use Fundamental Motor Skills & Movement Activities for Young Children*, for a Recording Sheet.)

4. ***Balance Walk Challenges.***

   ➤ Explore using foam stilts or foam bucket steppers to travel.

   ➤ *Balance Board Challenge.* Use commercial (Duck Walker) or homemade boards and try to balance as you rock side-to-side; spin 360 degrees on a smooth surface; "walk like a duck."

5. ***Jumping Challenges.*** Explore different ways of jumping off or over different objects such as a bench, low box horse, medium box horse; from a climbing frame; over hurdles set at different heights. Practice landing onto a soft mat.

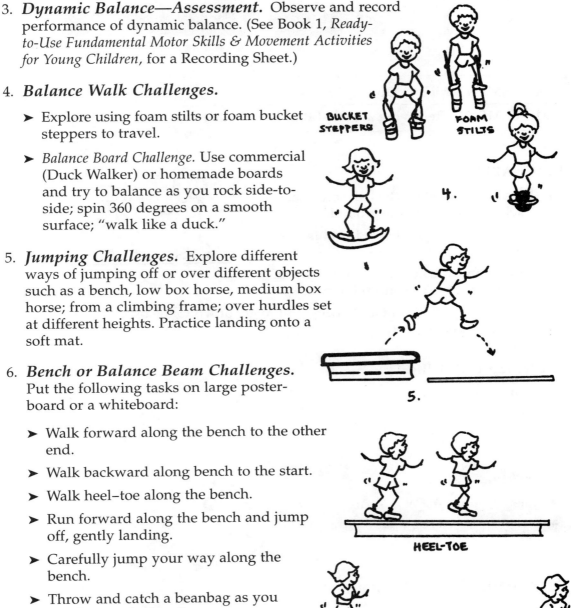

BUCKET STEPPERS

FOAM STILTS

4.

5.

6. ***Bench or Balance Beam Challenges.*** Put the following tasks on large poster-board or a whiteboard:

   ➤ Walk forward along the bench to the other end.

   ➤ Walk backward along bench to the start.

   ➤ Walk heel–toe along the bench.

   ➤ Run forward along the bench and jump off, gently landing.

   ➤ Carefully jump your way along the bench.

   ➤ Throw and catch a beanbag as you walk along the bench.

   ➤ Try moving along bench with one foot on the bench and the other foot on the floor.

   ➤ Explore other ways of traveling along the bench.

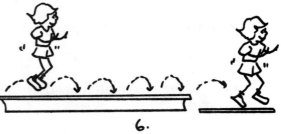

HEEL-TOE

6.

> **MOVEMENT AREA:** Object Control
>
> **MOVEMENT:** Receiving a Rolled Ball (small ball)

TEACHABLE POINTS:

1. Eyes are focused on the ball source and track the ball along the ground.
2. Child moves to get the body behind the ball.
3. Fingers are spread and face downward, ready to receive the oncoming ball.
4. Preferred leg is in front and knees bent to get down to the ball.
5. Child takes the ball cleanly in the hands.

EQUIPMENT REQUIRED:

Firm even surface
Variety of small balls
Large cone markers

> TEACHING GOALS:
> ☛ **Keep head up and eyes focused.**
> ☛ **Use correct body and hand position.**

TEACHING PROGRESSIONS

1. Revise teaching skills for rolling a ball:

   ➤ Hold the ball in both hands; feet shoulder-width apart.

   ➤ Swing arms back on your favorite side (right side for right-hander).

   ➤ Step forward with the opposite foot and swing your rolling hand forward and through.

   ➤ Release the ball downward with your favorite hand as you follow through.

   ➤ Cue Words: "Ball"—"Swing Back"—"Step Forward"—"Swing Through."

2. Revise receiving position. Have children copy you. Practice rolling the ball against the wall.

3. Have children practice moving down into the receiving position from standing still to bending at the knees. Repeat, going down on one knee. Let them decide which is more comfortable. Instruct children to roll the ball toward each other, emphasizing to keep eyes fixed on the ball. Check for hands in the correct position to receive the ball.

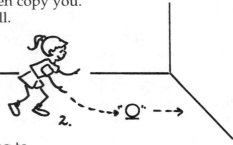

4. Repeat #3 in a standing position. At this stage, emphasize the importance of bending from the knees to reach down to the ball.

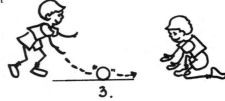

5. Repeat #4, gradually increasing the distance between you and your child.

6. ***Roller Ball Derby.*** Find a partner, collect a ball, and go to a Home space. Stand 5 giant steps away from each other on opposite lines, facing as shown. At the same time, roll the ball straight ahead to your partner's line. Partner moves to get in line of oncoming ball and receive it.

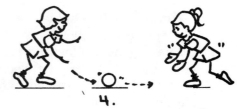

 ➤ Gradually have them increase the rolling distance.

7. ***Rolling Stunts.*** Find a Home space and stand tall holding your ball. Always roll your ball into an open space.

 ➤ Roll the ball ahead of you and try to jump back and forth over the ball.

 ➤ Roll the ball ahead of you. Run after it to get in front and field the ball.

 ➤ Keep the ball rolling. Change its direction, but don't let it touch any of the other rolling balls.

 ➤ Roll the ball along a line on the floor. Follow its path to see how long it will roll along the line.

 ➤ Roll the ball in a figure-8 between your legs.

 ➤ Create a rolling stunt of your own.

ACTIVITIES

1. *Modified Leaderball.* Field of play is a semi-circle with a radius of 5 yards (meters). Class is divided into teams of 4, with each team spaced safely apart. Members number off: 1, 2, 3, 4. #1 player stands at the center of the semi-circle line, as shown. On the "Roll" signal, #1 rolls the ball to #2, who receives the ball and rolls it back to #1. Then #1 rolls the ball to #3 and #4 in turn. #1 then goes to stand on the side of #4, and #2 takes over as the new leader. After everyone has had a turn at being leader, the group quickly sits down. The winning team is the one that completes the rotation first and sits down.

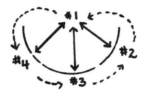

2. *Tunnel Ball.* Divide the class into files of 5–6 players and position each file at a start line, equally spaced apart from each other. Each member of the file is spaced 2 yards (meters) behind the child in front. On the "Roll" signal, players must roll the ball backward between their legs to the player behind. The ball must be stopped and controlled before passing it back. When the last player in the line receives the ball, he/she picks it up and runs to the start of the line as the rest of the team moves back one space. Every child in the team has a turn at running to the front. The first team that has the original leader back in front and in cross-leg sit position is the winner.

3. *Ball Wars.* Divide the class into 2 teams. Mark out a rectangular area with a center line as shown. At either end of each half is a goal line that must be defended. Place 6 small playground balls on each side. Have each team go into one half of the play area. On signal "Roll!" each team rolls balls into the other team's half attempting to score a goal for every ball that rolls over the opposition's endline.

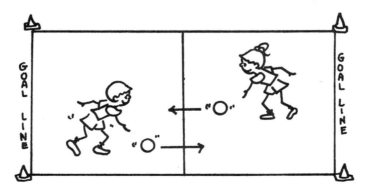

MOVEMENT STATIONS
Lesson 22, Level 3

MOVEMENT AREA: Object Control
MOVEMENT: Receiving a Rolled Ball (small ball)

EQUIPMENT REQUIRED:

Small playground balls
Bowling pins or plastic bottles
Cone markers
Ball on a long rope
Box
Garbage bin
Assessment Recording Sheet

MOVEMENT STATIONS

1. ***Guard the Pin.*** Five of the children in the group form a semi-circle. The sixth child stands in the middle of the circle to protect a bowling pin from being knocked down by the children in the circle who roll the balls at the pin. When the middle child stops the ball, he or she rolls it to the next person in the circle. Each child has a turn in the middle. Emphasize that children take turns at rolling the ball. Use 3 small playground balls.

2. ***Circle Pattern Roll.*** Members of group knee-sit in a circle. One player starts with the ball and rolls it across the circle to a player who is not on either side of them. Each player in turn does the same. When the ball returns to the first player, the pattern begins again.

> ➤ How many times can this pattern be repeated before moving to the next station?

3. ***Bowling Challenge.*** Set up 2 5-pin bowling stations as shown. (Plastic jugs or small traffic cones could also be used.) In turn, take 2 tries to knock over as many pins as possible. Organize your station so that there is a Bowler, a Setter-Up, and Ball Returner.

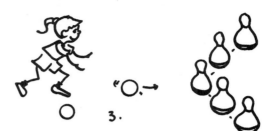

4. ***Receiving a Rolled Ball— Assessment.*** Observe and record performance of receiving a rolled ball. (See Book 1, *Ready-to-Use Fundamental Motor Skills & Movement Activities for Young Children*, for a Recording Sheet.)

5. ***Jump the Ball.*** Play each game with 3 players. Two play-ers stand facing each other, spaced 5 giant steps apart. The other player stands in the mid-

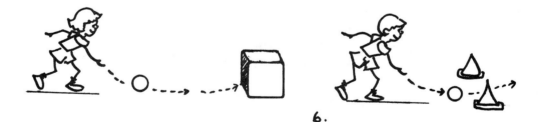

dle. The two outside players roll the ball back and forth to each other. The mid-dle player tries to jump or leap over the ball. After 5 jumps, change roles until everyone has had a turn in the middle.

6. ***Rolling Targets.*** Set up different targets: an open box on the side; 2 large cone markers; or a garbage bin laid on its side. Children take turns rolling the ball into or through the targets.

➤ Vary the distance to be rolled. Vary the size of the target opening to increase the challenge level.

MOVEMENT AREA: Object Control
MOVEMENT: Slide-Stepping

TEACHABLE POINTS:

1. Body is side on to the intended direction of travel.
2. Head is held up and still, and eyes look in the direction of travel.
3. Slide-step is on the forefoot.
4. Leading leg side-steps, followed by a sliding action of the trailing leg, back to the leading leg.
5. Width of the slide-step is not too wide or too narrow, about shoulder-width apart.
6. Knees are slightly bent throughout the movement.
7. Arms remain relaxed but may assist the movement.
8. Child can slide both ways.
9. Movement should be smooth and rhythmical.

EQUIPMENT REQUIRED:

Firm even surface
Cone markers
Hoops
Deckrings
Music with a steady 4/4 beat;
cassette/CD player

SLIDE   TOGETHER   SLIDE

TEACHING GOALS:

☛ **Be sure a step then a slide are evident.**
☛ **Be sure body is side on to direction of travel.**
☛ **Push off the trailing leg as leading leg side-steps.**

TEACHING PROGRESSIONS

1. Revise the slide-stepping action, emphasizing the teaching goals.
2. Have child slide-step to the right; slide-step to the left, on signal have them "Jump Stop." "Scrambled Eggs— Slide Step!"
3. Scatter hoops, small cones, and deckrings around the floor. Have children slide-step around the objects.

4. Have children slide-step in a big circle; slide-step in a zigzag pattern; slide-step a square pathway.

5. On signal "Foursome!" children join hands in a group of 4 and slide-step for 8 counts in one direction; then 8 counts in the opposite direction.

➤ On signal "New Foursome!" children form a new group of 4 and slide-step. Use music to which to slide-step.

ACTIVITIES

1. ***This Way and That Way.*** Have children stand facing you in "wave" formation. Point with your right hand to slide-step to the right; left hand to slide-step to the left; both hands pointing to floor to "stutter step" or quickly move feet in place; both hands in air to have children jump up high.

➤ *Variation:* Add other hand signals, such as extended hands out front with fingers pointing upward as if to gently push children backward. They respond by carefully jogging backward. Motion them with hands to move forward.

2. ***Slide-Step Chasey.*** Play simple tag using the slide-step movement. Establish a "safe" position by freezing for a 3-second count in a static balance such as a "Stork Stand." Have 3 taggers each with a tagging object. Change taggers frequently. *Variation:* Use other locomotor movements.

➤ Play as above, but pair players, who must hold hands as they slide-step around.

MOVEMENT STATIONS
Lesson 24, Level 3

MOVEMENT AREA: Object Control
MOVEMENT: Slide-Stepping

TEACHING GOALS:

- Be sure a step then a slide are evident.
- Be sure body is side on to direction of travel.
- Push off the trailing leg as leading leg side-steps.

EQUIPMENT REQUIRED:

Locomotion signs
Cone markers
Beanbags
Laundry basket or box
6 dome markers
10 numbered large cone markers
Large rolling balls
Foam stilts, foam bucket steppers, LoLo®
  Ball, or Bigfoot Striders™
Acessment Recording Sheet

MOVEMENT STATIONS

← -- CRAB-WALK
HOP →

↑ POWER-WALK / SPRINT -- ↑

← --- JOG BACKWARDS
SLIDE - STEP →

1.

← JUMP
PUPPY-DOG WALK -- →

2.

1. ***Locomotion Circuit.*** Mark out a rectangular area. At each corner set up a sign that indicates the movement to be done along this line, as shown: Power Walk a length; Hop a width; Slide-Step a length; Jump a width. After completing two circuits, children stop to stretch, then travel in the reverse direction: Sprint a length; Puppy Walk a width; Jog backward a length; Crab Walk a width.

2. ***Beanbag Circle Toss.*** Underhand toss beanbags into a laundry basket or box from markers set up in a circle formation as shown. Increase the throwing distance by moving marker with every successful 2 throws.

349

3. ***Slide-Step Shuttle Lines.*** Mark off a series of lines using cone markers as shown. Number the lines 1, 2, 3, 4, and 5, with line 1 being the start line. Children slide-step from starting line across to touch line 2 with two hands, then return to line 1 facing the opposite direction as the slide-step. Then slide-step to line 3, returning to line 1; continue to slide-step to each line, touch, and return to starting line. When they complete set of lines, take a Stretch Break and do the lines again.

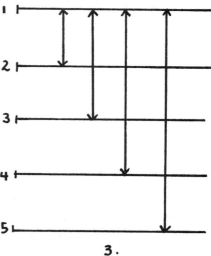

3.

4. ***Slide-Stepping—Assessment.*** Observe and record performance. (See Book 1, *Ready-to-Use Fundamental Motor Skills & Movement Activities for Young Children*, for a Recording Sheet.)

5. ***Roller Ball Derby.*** In pairs, collect a ball and go to a Home space. Stand 5 giant steps away from each other on opposite lines, facing as shown. At the same time, roll the ball straight ahead to your partner's line. Partner moves to get in line of oncoming ball and receive it.

➤ Gradually increase the rolling distance.

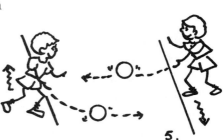

5.

6. ***Balance Walk Challenges.***

➤ Explore using foam stilts or foam bucket steppers to travel.

➤ *Balance Board Challenge:* Use commercial (Duck Walker™) or homemade boards and try to balance as you rock side-to-side; spin 360 degrees on a smooth surface; "walk like a duck."

➤ *Advanced Balancing:* LoLo® Ball, Bigfoot Striders™

6.

MOVEMENT AREA: Object Control
MOVEMENT: Underhand Throwing a Small Object (for Accuracy)

TEACHABLE POINTS:

1. Stand square on to target.
2. Keep a balanced position with the feet comfortably spread.
3. Weight transference from back to front foot during the throw by stepping forward with the foot opposite to the throwing arm.
4. Ball held in the fingers.
5. Good arm extension in the wind-up; then in the throw and follow-through.
6. Release the ball in front of the body.
7. Follow-through toward the target.
8. Eyes focused on the target.

EQUIPMENT REQUIRED:

1 beanbag per child
1 small ball (tennis ball) per pair
Cone markers
1 hoop per pair
Wall to throw at, if possible

TEACHING GOALS:
- ☛ Use good extension in wind-up and follow-through.
- ☛ Obtain accuracy through correct release and direction of follow-through.

TEACHING PROGRESSIONS

1. Revise and demonstrate the correct technique for underhand throwing, emphasizing the goals for the lesson.

DOWN-BACK   SWING-THROUGH
2.

2. Revise holding a beanbag or tennis ball with the correct grip. Then have children stand with feet shoulder-width apart, square on to a wall in front of them, holding object with both hands. Throwing arm swings down and back, then swings through. Practice.

3. Practice stepping forward with the opposite foot to throwing hand as hands swing through, releasing beanbag "up and out" toward wall. Cue words: "Down, back; step and swing through; throw up and out." Emphasize good follow-through and holding beanbag in fingers.

351

4. Repeat #2 having children use the nonpreferred hand.

5. Have children pair up, collect 2 beanbags and hoop, and find a Home space. One partner underhand throws the beanbag through a hoop held by the other partner who stands near a wall. Switch roles after every 3 throws. Gradually increase the throwing distance.

6. Partners stand back to back, walk 2 giant steps away, jump-turn, and face each other. At this distance begin under throwing a small ball back and forth to each other. After every 4 throws, take a walking step away from each other. Continue in this way. Emphasize throwing "up and out" to partner and catching with hands in the correct position.

ACTIVITIES

1. *Pass the Beanbag Tag.* Pair children. Have one partner collect a beanbag; then the pair finds a Home space to start game. On signal "Pass the Beanbag" partners jog around the play area gently passing their beanbag back and forth to each other. On signal "Beanbag Tag!" partner holding the beanbag at this time is IT and gives chase to the other partner. IT tries to hit his/her partner below the knees, using an underhand throw, before the whistle blast is heard and the next signal "Pass the Beanbag!" is called. If successful, IT earns a point. Then partners once again toss the beanbag back and forth to each other. Continue in this way.

2. ***Stuck in the Middle.*** Divide the class into teams of 6. Each team forms a circle of 3 giant steps diameter with captain of team in the middle. Circle players throw the beanbag around and across the circle, trying to keep it away from the middle player. If the middle player intercepts the beanbag, the circle player making the throw comes to the middle. If middle player cannot intercept the beanbag after a certain time, then choose another player to be "stuck" in the middle!

3. ***Throw and Deliver Relay.*** Place children into 4–5 teams. Members of each team stand in a file, spaced 3 yards (meters) apart. On either side of the leader is a hoop. (See diagram.) One hoop is empty; the other has 4 tennis balls in it. The leader must throw a ball to the first person, who turns and throws to the second, continuing until the last person in the line receives the ball. Last person then runs to the front, places the ball in the empty hoop and becomes the new leader. The original leader runs to the front of the file and the rest of the team shuffles 1 place backward. Continue in this way until all the balls have been transferred to the second hoop.

MOVEMENT STATIONS
Lesson 26, Level 3 Extension

MOVEMENT AREA: Object Control
MOVEMENT: Underhand Throwing a Small Object (for Accuracy)

TEACHING GOALS:

- ☞ Use good extension in wind-up and follow-through.
- ☞ Obtain accuracy through correct release and direction of follow-through.

EQUIPMENT REQUIRED:

Deckrings
Beanbags
Buckets (varying sizes)
Cone markers
Skittles
Plastic bottles
Bench and low box horse,
Tennis balls
Power-walk and jog signs
Deckring on a long rope
Assessment Recording Sheet

MOVEMENT STATIONS

1. ***Deck Ring/Beanbag Play.*** Pair children, each with a beanbag and a deckring between the two.

   - ➤ *Beanbag Basketball.* One partner throws beanbag through partner's deckring held horizontally with both hands. Partner with deckring tracks beanbag so that it will go through. Change roles after 3 throws. Find a new partner and repeat.

   - ➤ *Beanbag Horseshoes.* Deckring is placed on the floor or ground at a certain distance away from throwers. Partners take turns tossing their beanbag at the ring to see whose beanbag can get closer. Play best 2 out of 3 and challenge a new partner. Gradually increase the throwing distance.

2. ***Bucket Toss.*** Working in pairs, partners underhand throw beanbags into a bucket from marked distances as shown; 3 markers, each 1 yard (meter) apart with the first marker 2 yards meters) from the bucket. Each partner gets 2 tries at each marker. Score 1 point for hitting the bucket and 2 points for landing the beanbag in the bucket. Vary the size of the buckets.

3. ***Underhand Throwing— Assessment.*** Observe and record performance. (See Book 1, *Ready-to-Use Fundamental Motor Skills & Movement Activities for Young Children*, for a Recording Sheet.)

4. ***Knock-Over.*** Create 3 different targets using skittles, plastic bottles, and small cones set on a bench, box horse, or floor. Set targets at different throwing and rolling distances as shown. Children in pairs, take turns, to underhand throw or roll 2 tennis balls at the targets, knocking them over. Pairs rotate to different targets after a certain time.

5. ***Power Walk & Jog Circuit.*** Set up a power walk and jog circuit as shown. Children complete a circuit then take a Stretch Break for 30 seconds (3 different stretches—10-second count), then do the circuit again. Start in clockwise direction, then change to counterclockwise direction next time circuit is done.

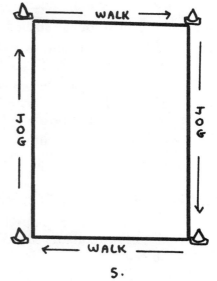

6. ***Jump the Ring.*** One child swings a deckring attached to a rope in a large circle along the ground. Children try to jump the ring each time it passes under their feet.

MOVEMENT AREA: Object Control
MOVEMENT: Catching Small Objects (Different Sizes and Shapes; Two Hands/One Hand)

TEACHABLE POINTS:

1. Keep in a balanced position.
2. Body is positioned behind the ball.
3. Arms reach for ball; fingers spread and curved, ready to receive the oncoming ball.
4. Hands adjust for the size of the ball.
5. Arms bend at the elbows and give when the ball meets the hands.
6. Fingers face upward, thumbs close together for a high ball; downward with little fingers closer together for a low ball.
7. Fingers wrap around the ball, not "clap" it.
8. Eyes focused on the ball.

EQUIPMENT REQUIRED:

Different sized and shaped balls (tennis balls, whiffle balls, small playground balls, mini-footballs, size 5 basketballs or medium-sized playground balls)
Beanbags
Deckrings
Cone markers

TEACHING GOALS:

☞ Keep eyes focused on the ball.
☞ Use correct body positioning.
☞ Use correct hand positioning.

TEACHING PROGRESSIONS

1. Revise and demonstrate the "catching" action. Emphasize having the hands the right distance apart, fingers relaxed and spread, body in alignment with the oncoming ball, and eyes watching the ball all the way into the hands.

As children perform these tasks, have them exchange objects with other class members after a certain time.

2. In Home space, children practice the following tasks:

   ➤ Throw object with preferred hand and catch ball in 2 hands.

   ➤ Throw object with preferred hand and catch ball in preferred hand.

   ➤ Throw object with other hand and catch in 2 hands.

   ➤ Throw object with other hand and catch in 1 hand.

   ➤ Throw from one hand to the other hand.

   ➤ Throw, clap, and catch; throw, clap twice, and catch; etc.

   ➤ Create a throw–catch stunt of your own!

3. Find a partner:

   ➤ Throw to partner with preferred hand; catch in 2 hands.

   ➤ Throw to partner with preferred hand, catch in preferred hand.

   ➤ Throw to partner with other hand; catch in both hands.

   ➤ Throw to partner with other hand and catch in that hand.

   ➤ Throw high, throw low, throw to one side, other side.

   ➤ Create your own throw–catch stunt with partner!

ACTIVITY

Triangle Pass and Catch. Divide class into groups of 3. Each group finds a Home space and stands in a triangle formation about 3 giant steps apart from each other as shown. Children underhand pass the beanbag in this order: player 1 passes to player 2 who passes back to player 1; then player 1 passes ball to player 3 who returns pass to player 1. Then player 2 becomes the lead passer. Continue in this way.

➤ How many catches can be made in a certain time?

➤ *Challenge:* Use 2 beanbags. As one beanbag is passed by player 1 to player 3, another beanbag is being sent to player 1 from player 2.

MOVEMENT STATIONS
Lesson 28, Level 3

MOVEMENT AREA: Object Control
MOVEMENT: Catching Small Objects (Different Sizes and Shapes; Two Hands/One Hand)

TEACHING GOALS:
- ☞ Keep eyes focused on the ball.
- ☞ Use correct body position.
- ☞ Use correct hand position.

EQUIPMENT REQUIRED:

Foxtails or balls in long socks

Variety of balls: mini-basketballs, footballs, tennis balls, whiffle balls, squellet balls, spider balls

Large square grid on plastic sheet, or floor tape, or colored chalk

3 beanbags per pair (different color for each pair)

Cone markers

Fit-Kid Circuit cards

Balance benches, balance boards

Assessment Recording Sheet

MOVEMENT STATIONS

1. *Foxtail™ Catch.* Children pair off and underhand throw or "windmill throw" a foxtail (or ball in a long sock) to each other. A "windmill throw" is performed by grabbing the tail midway and swinging the tail outwards (clockwise) in a large circle, then letting go. Catch is made by grabbing the tail.

2. *Make the Catch.* Children pair off and explore throwing and catching a variety of small objects such as: mini-footballs, tennis balls, whiffle balls (plastic balls with holes in them), Squellet Balls™ (soft balls filled with beads), Spider Balls™, etc.

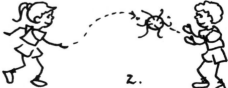

3. *Catching a Small Ball—Assessment.* Observe and record performance. (See Book 1, *Ready-to-Use Fundamental Motor Skills & Movement Activities for Young Children*, for a Recording Sheet.)

4. *Shuffle Grid.* Mark out a large square divided into 9 areas using floor tape, or large sheet of plastic, or colored chalk on tarmac. Each square is marked with a 1, 2, or 3 as shown. Have children stand with a partner two giant steps away (cone markers) on either side of square. Each partner takes 3 throws of the beanbag into the grid and keeps score. Each pair should have a different colored set of beanbags to toss.

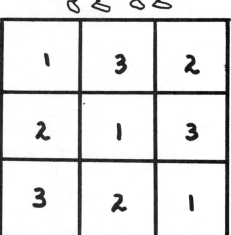

4.

5. *Fit-Kid Circuit.* Children complete a fitness circuit of stretches, runs, and strength activities. (See Fitness Strategies on page 15.) Place these on cards.

6. *Toss and Balancing Tasks.*

   ➤ Walk in general space tossing and catching a beanbag.

   ➤ Walk along a bench tossing and catching a beanbag.

   ➤ One partner tosses beanbag back and forth to a partner who is standing on the bench.

   ➤ Balance on a Duck Walker while tossing and catching a beanbag.

   ➤ Create your own toss-and-balance stunt!

5.

6.

MOVEMENT AREA: Object Control
MOVEMENT: Overhand Throwing

TEACHABLE POINTS:

1. Stand side on to target, head and eyes facing target.
2. Keep in a balanced position with the feet comfortably apart.
3. Ball held in the fingers, wrist cocked, nonthrowing arm points at the target.
4. Throwing arm moves in a downward and backward arc.
5. Weight transferred onto back foot.
6. Elbow bends as throwing hand moves behind head.
7. Front foot steps forward as weight transfers from back foot.
8. Hips, then shoulders rotate forward.
9. Forearm and hand lag behind upper arm.
10. Follow-through down and across the body.

EQUIPMENT REQUIRED:

Cone markers
1 beanbag per child
1 small ball per child
2 sets of 4 bases

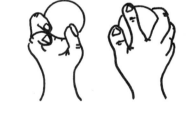

TEACHING GOALS:
- ☞ Use side-on stance while throwing.
- ☞ Use good extension in the wind-up.
- ☞ Use correct follow-through.

TEACHING PROGRESSIONS

1. Demonstrate the overhand throw emphasizing the focus points.
2. Now have children hold a beanbag with the correct grip (with their fingers) and stand side on to the target Nonthrowing arm points at the target. Use the cues: "Swing down and back, bend elbow, step and throw."
   - ➤ Practice the action first without a beanbag in the hand.
   - ➤ Then practice overhand throwing the beanbag at the wall.

3. Now have children focus on the wrist snap by holding the beanbag in their fingers, cocking wrist back, and then snapping it forward. Let hand follow in the line of direction. Now complete the whole action, as in activity 2.

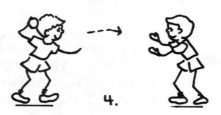

4. In pairs have the children overhand throw back and forth. Start close and gradually move further away as the children begin to master the task. Be aware of catching ability.

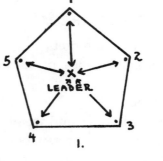

5. Repeat #2, #3, then #4 using a small ball, such as a tennis ball or whiffle ball.

ACTIVITIES

1. *Corner Spry.* Children are placed into 4 teams. For each team, players stand on a corner of a polygonal shape, with a leader from each team standing in the middle as shown. Team members number off 1, 2, 3, . . . On signal "Spry!" the leader overhand throws the beanbag to each team member in turn. When the last player returns the beanbag, that player goes in the middle to replace the leader who then becomes the first player.

2. *Beat the Ball.* Divide the class into 4 teams. Mark out two fields of play as shown in the diagram, opposite each other so that the teacher can control both games. Game consists of a running team and throwing team. The first runner must overhand throw the ball as far as possible into the field of play. The throwing team must collect the ball and throw it around the bases. In this time the runner earns a point for every circuit of the running area he/she completes before the ball has been thrown around all the bases.

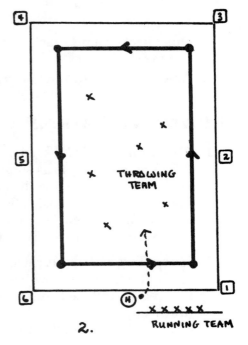

MOVEMENT STATIONS
Lesson 30, Level 3

MOVEMENT AREA: Object Control
MOVEMENT: Overhand Throwing

TEACHING GOALS:
- ☛ Use side-on stance while throwing.
- ☛ Use good extension in the wind-up.
- ☛ Use correct follow-through.
- ☛ Be accurate.

EQUIPMENT REQUIRED:

3 different wall targets
Skittles, small cones, plastic bottles
Beanbags
Floor tape
Hoops with ropes and weights
Mini-footballs or vortex footballs
Large numbered cone markers
Small playground balls
Large mats
Quiet background music; cassette/CD player
Assessment Recording Sheet

MOVEMENT STATIONS

1. *Overhand Target Throw.* Set up 3 different wall targets as shown and mark off 3 different throwing distances using floor tape. Children pair off with each pair facing a target. Taking turns, partners overhand throw beanbags at targets. Each partner has 3 turns. Keep score.

2. *Hoop Target Throw.* Suspend a hoop from a basketball framework or other suitable fixture. Secure it with a rope and weight to the floor as shown. Children work in three's and take turns to overhand throw a football or Junior Vortex Howler™ (throwing football) into the hoop. If possible, set up two identical hoop targets. Use cone markers to set distances.

   ➤ *Variation:* Suspend a hoop between two chairs or in a grooved cone marker.

3. ***Overhand Throwing—Assessment.*** Observe and record performance. (See Book 1, *Ready-to-Use Fundamental Motor Skills & Movement Activities for Young Children*, for a Recording Sheet.)

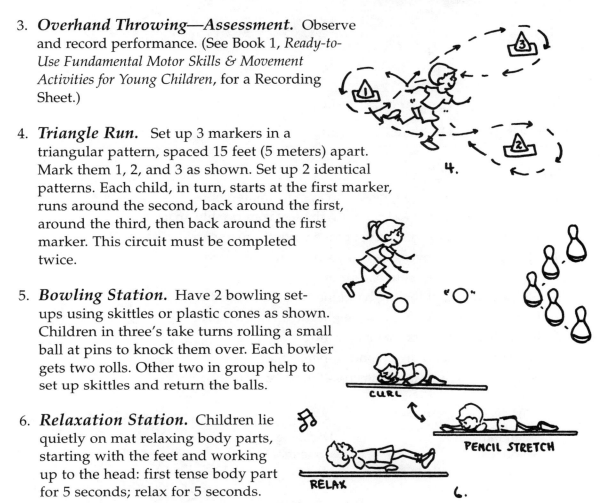

4. ***Triangle Run.*** Set up 3 markers in a triangular pattern, spaced 15 feet (5 meters) apart. Mark them 1, 2, and 3 as shown. Set up 2 identical patterns. Each child, in turn, starts at the first marker, runs around the second, back around the first, around the third, then back around the first marker. This circuit must be completed twice.

5. ***Bowling Station.*** Have 2 bowling set-ups using skittles or plastic cones as shown. Children in three's take turns rolling a small ball at pins to knock them over. Each bowler gets two rolls. Other two in group help to set up skittles and return the balls.

6. ***Relaxation Station.*** Children lie quietly on mat relaxing body parts, starting with the feet and working up to the head: first tense body part for 5 seconds; relax for 5 seconds.

➤ Finally do an overall body stretch. Pencil Stretch—curl up into a ball—Pencil Stretch.

MOVEMENT AREA: Object Control
MOVEMENT: Overhand Throwing

TEACHABLE POINTS:

1. Stand side on to target, head and eyes facing target.
2. Keep in a balanced position with the feet comfortably apart.
3. Ball held in the fingers, wrist cocked, nonthrowing arm points at the target.
4. Throwing arm moves in a downward and backward arc.
5. Weight transferred onto back foot.
6. Elbow bends as throwing hand moves behind head.
7. Front foot steps forward as weight transfers from back foot.
8. Hips, then shoulders rotate forward.
9. Forearm and hand lag behind upper arm.
10. Follow-through down and across the body.

EQUIPMENT REQUIRED:

Small balls	Deckrings
Beanbags	Cone markers
Foxtails™ or balls in sock	Hoops

> **TEACHING GOALS:**
> ☛ **Use good weight transference.**
> ☛ **Extend in wind-up and follow-through.**
> ☛ **Throw for distance.**

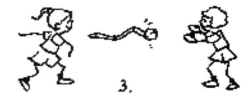

TEACHING PROGRESSIONS

1. Revise and demonstrate the overhand throw emphasizing the goals.

2. In pairs, children overhand throw to each other. Explore using different objects to overhand throw, such as tennis balls, beanbags, small playground balls. Emphasize receiver setting a target with hands. Gradually increase the throwing distance. Observe throwing and catching ability.

3. Use Foxtails™ or balls in socks to overhand throw. Emphasize follow-through which can be seen in the "tail" of the foxtail as it is thrown.

   ➤ Throw high, throw low; throw to right side, left side.

   ➤ *Pepper Throw and Catch:* Which pair can complete 20 throws and catches the quickest and then knee sit?

4. Use the "Listening Line" signal to have children stand on one of the sidelines of the play area, with one partner in front and the other partner behind. Check for ample spacing between each pair. First partner runs forward with a deckring, which will be used to mark second partner's throw. Second partner has two attempts to over-hand throw beanbag as far as possible. Change roles and continue.

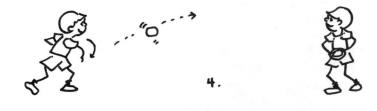

4.

ACTIVITIES

1. *Stinger Tag.* Children pair off, one partner with a beanbag or small soft ball, both in a Home space standing back-to-back to start game. On signal "Sting!" the partner with the beanbag counts to 5, then gives chase to the free partner trying to hit  him/her below the knees with the beanbag, using an overhand throw. If success-ful, the "stung" partner becomes IT and gives chase. Emphasize that everyone look where they are going to avoid collisions.

2. *Catch and Capture.* Divide the class into 4 teams and set up two playing areas. Playing area is a large rectangle with a neutral area in the middle about 5 yards (meters) wide. On the outside of the court at either end is a hoop. The game is start-ed by a member of the throwing team calling the name of a child on the opposite team. The ball is then thrown over to any team member on this team, who must catch the ball. If not caught, the child whose name was called must stand in the hoop at the opposition team's end. A team may free a prisoner by calling out his/her name. If the ball is dropped by the opposition, prisoner is freed.

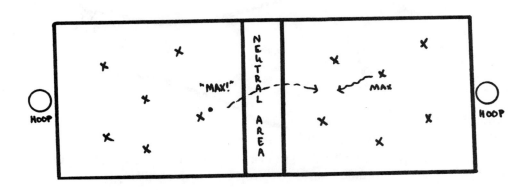

MOVEMENT STATIONS
Lesson 32, Level 3

MOVEMENT AREA: Object Control
MOVEMENT: Overhand Throwing

EQUIPMENT REQUIRED:

Music; cassette/CD player Foxtails™ or balls in socks
Hoops Long rope
Cone markers Posts
Beanbags Fling-It™ Nets or small sheet
Wall space Small balls
Tennis balls Assessment Recording
Sheet

MOVEMENT STATIONS

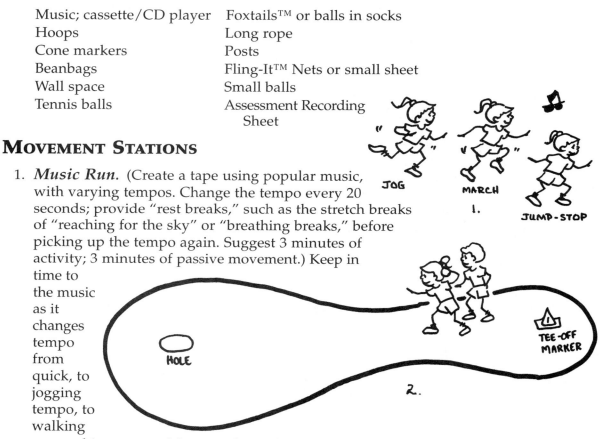

1. *Music Run.* (Create a tape using popular music, with varying tempos. Change the tempo every 20 seconds; provide "rest breaks," such as the stretch breaks of "reaching for the sky" or "breathing breaks," before picking up the tempo again. Suggest 3 minutes of activity; 3 minutes of passive movement.) Keep in time to the music as it changes tempo from quick, to jogging tempo, to walking or marching tempo. Move on the spot or in general space, watching where you are going. When the music stops, you stop by jump-stopping!

2. *Mini Golf.* Set up a number of "fairways" using hoops as holes and marker cones as tees as shown. Children pair off and take turns overhand throwing beanbags around the course. Each pair keeps track of its score. *Variation:* Use spider balls.

3. ***Wall Throw and Catch.*** Children pair off, and find a free wall space to throw and catch a small playground ball. Use the overhand throw and catch ball on one bounce, then no bounces, if possible.

4. ***Continue Overhand Throwing—Assessment.*** Observe and record performance. (See Book 1, *Ready-to-Use Fundamental Motor Skills & Movement Activities for Young Children*, for a Recording Sheet.)

5. ***Foxtail™ Throw.*** Group in three's, on opposite sides of a roped area as shown. Throw 2 foxtails (or balls in socks) back and forth A side scores a point for each time the foxtail lands in the opposition's court. Emphasize receiver tracking ball all the way into the hands.

6. ***Fling-It™ Play.*** Children pair off and, using Fling-It™ Nets or lightweight sheets (about the size of a towel), send a ball up into the air and catch it in the net.

MOVEMENT AREA: Object Control

MOVEMENT: Catching on the Move; Throwing at Moving Targets

TEACHABLE POINTS:

1. Eyes focused on the target.

2. When catching on the move, move toward oncoming ball, hands in correct positioning. Reach for ball and give with impact.

3. When throwing at moving targets, hand follows through, releasing the ball in the line of direction.

EQUIPMENT REQUIRED:

1 small ball or beanbag per pair
Cone markers

TEACHING GOALS:

☞ Have eyes stay focused on the ball.
☞ Use correct hand positioning.
☞ Use correct body positioning.

TEACHING PROGRESSIONS

1. Demonstrate catching a ball on the move, emphasizing the teaching goals.

2. Children pair up and start in a Home space. One partner has a beanbag or small ball. On signal "Run and Pass," partners move about in general space passing the ball back and forth with an underhand pass.

3. Children travel further apart and overhand pass to each other. Remind them to look for free spaces to move into.

ACTIVITIES

1. ***Simple Keep-Away.*** One pair versus another pair in a marked off 5-yard (-meter) square. As skills improve, play game 3-on-3.

1.

2. ***Line Passing.*** Form groups of 3 players. Have each group get a medium-sized ball and stand side-by-side as shown in the diagram. One of the outside players has the ball. All 3 players start running in step with each other. Use the underhand throw to pass the ball down the line and back again. How many times can they pass the ball in two minutes?

2.

3. Play ***Stinger Tag.*** (Refer to Lesson 31.)

4. ***Spaceship Attack.*** Divide the class into 3 teams. Two teams are the "Asteroids." Each Asteroids team stands on a sideline, spaced arm's length apart. The sidelines are 8 yards (meters) apart as shown in the diagram. The third team is the "Spaceships" which fly through the field. Each Asteroid team is given 3 foam balls. These balls can be rolled, or thrown underhand or overhand at the spaceships as they fly through the field from one end to the other. A Spaceship can only be hit below the knees. A hit spaceship is "captured" and must join the Asteroid team until all Spaceships have been caught. Then an Asteroid team and Spaceship team change roles and a new game begins. Spaceships must wait for the signal "Fly Away!" to move from one endline to the other each time.

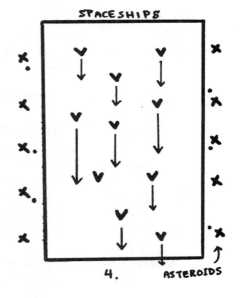

4.

➤ *Variation:* Player making the "hit" exchanges places with the Spaceship.

MOVEMENT AREA: Object Control
MOVEMENT: Catching on the Move; Throwing at a Moving Target

TEACHING GOALS:

☛ Have eyes stay focused on the ball.
☛ Use correct hand positioning.
☛ Use correct body positioning.

EQUIPMENT REQUIRED:

Cone markers
Small playground balls
Medium-sized playground ball
Deckrings
Stretching/Strengthening chart
Assessment Recording Sheet

MOVEMENT STATIONS

1. ***Monkey in the Middle.*** Play game in 3's, with two throwers and one player in the middle trying to intercept the ball. If middle player is successful, he/she changes places with the thrower. Emphasize playing game in designated space (identified with cone markers).

2. ***Pattern Pass.*** Group forms a circle, facing inward. One player has a medium-sized ball and starts the pattern. Use the overhand pass to send ball across the circle to another player who is not on either side of throwing player.

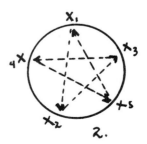

3. ***Catching a Ball on the Move—Assessment.*** Observe and record performance. (See Book 1, *Ready-to-Use Fundamental Motor Skills & Movement Activities for Young Children*, for a Recording Sheet.)

4. ***Deckring Play.*** Explore the following tasks which are put on posterboard:

➤ Toss with one hand, catch with one hand.

➤ Repeat with the other hand.

➤ Toss, clap, catch; toss, two claps, catch; etc.

➤ Toss ring from one hand to the other.

➤ Flip ring in the air, try to "ring it" on your arm.

➤ Toss and catch with a partner.

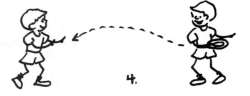

➤ Throw ring like a Frisbee back and forth to partner.

➤ Foot-pass ring to partner.

➤ Roll ring like a tire back and forth to partner.

➤ Create a ring stunt with your partner.

4.

5. ***Tugs and Pulls.***

➤ *Hoppo Bumpo.* Partners, about the same size, take up a position of right hand holding the left foot behind, while left hand is used to gently push the other partner off balance. After 3 attempts challenge a new partner. Reverse leg-hand hold and repeat activity.

➤ *Palm Wrestles.* With palms of hands against partner's palms, try to push each other over a Line behind each.

➤ *Wrist Tugs.* Using a wrist hold, try to pull partner over a line. Use either hand.   **5.**

6. ***Stretching/Strengthening Station.*** Do the following stretches, holding them for a 10-second count:

Stretching

➤ Foot Artist

➤ Periscope Stretch

➤ Side Stretcher

Strengtheners

➤ Hand Walkers

➤ Ankle Taps

➤ Thigh Lifters

Display stretches and strengtheners on a wall chart.

FOOT ARTIST   SIDE STRETCHER

PERISCOPE   ANKLE TAPS

HAND WALKERS   THIGH LIFTERS

6.

> **MOVEMENT AREA:** Object Control
>
> **MOVEMENT:** Two-Handed Passing

TEACHABLE POINTS:

1. Ball is held on the sides; thumbs up, fingers spread, elbows in.
2. Contact with the ball is on the fingers, not the whole hand.
3. Stance is square on to the target, feet shoulder-width apart.
4. Ball is brought toward the belly button–chest area, then arms straighten, and fingers push the ball away.

5. At the same time that arms extend, a step forward is taken.
6. Arms follow-through in line of direction, with fingers extended and back of hands facing.

EQUIPMENT REQUIRED:

Cone markers
1 large playground ball per child
15–18 bibs

TEACHING GOALS:

- Hold ball in fingers, thumb up, elbows in to start.
- Step forward, releasing ball with a push off fingers.
- Extend arms in follow-through.

2.

TEACHING PROGRESSIONS

1. Demonstrate passing the ball through the air using two hands, emphasizing the goals (chest pass).
2. Children stand facing a wall, about 2 giant steps away, and practice sending ball to the wall. Observe and offer feedback.

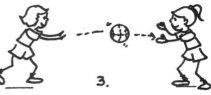

3.

3. Children, in pairs, 3 giant steps away, send the ball back and forth to each other with two-handed passing.

4. Demonstrate the same technique, but now send the ball to the floor (bounce pass). Discuss where the ball should hit the floor so that it bounces into the receiver's hands at about waist height.

5. Let children explore bouncing the ball closer to passer; about half-way; two-thirds of the way. Which is best? Emphasize that the ball should bounce about two-thirds of the way to the receiver.

6. Children practice the bounce pass at a wall, if possible, as for #2 . Emphasize that the bounce pass starts the same way as the chest pass. Some children may have a tendency to start the bounce pass by holding the ball overhead.

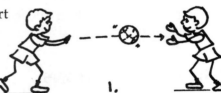

ACTIVITIES

1. *Twenty Passes.* Children pair off, collect a ball, and stand facing about 3 giant steps apart in a Home space. On signal "Chest Pass!" they pass back and forth to see which pair can complete 20 passes the quickest! Knee-sit when finished.

   ➤ Play game again using signal "Bounce Pass!"

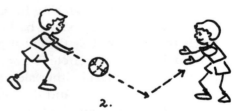

2. *Shuttle Chest Pass.* Form teams of 6, with each team in shuttle formation. Chest pass to opposite teammate, then run across and join end of opposite line. Which team can complete twenty passes the quickest?

   ➤ *Shuttle Bounce Pass.* As for above, but emphasize passing first, then moving.

SHUTTLE BOUNCE

3. *Two-on-Two Keep Away.* Designate an area for each 2-on-2 play. Players can bounce pass or chest pass to try to keep the ball away from the opposition. Emphasize that each player must have an opposition player to "guard" and not just run after the ball. Have one pair wear bibs.

MOVEMENT AREA: Object Control
MOVEMENT: Two-Handed Passing

TEACHING GOALS:

☞ Hold ball in fingers, thumb up, elbows in to start.

☞ Step forward, releasing ball with a push off fingers.

☞ Extend arms in follow-through.

EQUIPMENT REQUIRED:

Medium-sized balls
Lummi stick (12-inch [30-cm] doweling, 1-inch [2.5 cm] in diameter) per child
Deckrings
Blindfolds
Obstacles such as mats, chairs, hoops, cones, ropes, low hurdles
Assessment Recording Sheet

MOVEMENT STATIONS

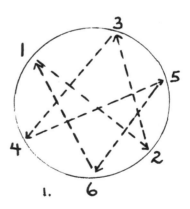

1. ***Circle Pattern Pass and Follow.***
   Group forms a circle, facing inward. One
   player has a medium-sized ball and
   starts the pattern. Use the chest pass to
   send ball across the circle to another
   player who is not on either side of
   throwing player. Pass and then run to
   the place (person) you have just passed
   to, taking his/her spot. Meanwhile, this
   person will have received the ball,
   passed to a circle player, and run to that
   place. Continue in this way.

2. ***Twenty Mixer Passes.*** One partner
   chest passes, while the other partner
   bounce passes. After completing 10 of
   these, switch roles and repeat.

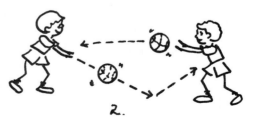

374

3. ***Slide-Step and Pass.*** Group stands in a line, arm's length apart as shown. First player with ball comes to the front of line and slide-steps down the line and back up again, chest-passing ball back and forth to each player in turn. First player then joins the end of the line; second player comes out and becomes new passer; everyone else shuffles one place to the left. Continue in this way.

4. ***Two-Handed Passing—Assessment.*** Observe and record performance. (See Book 1, *Ready-to-Use Fundamental Motor Skills & Movement Activities for Young Children*, for a Recording Sheet.)

5. ***Lummi Stick/Deckring Play.*** (Enlarge drawings and put on posterboard for this station.)

   ➤ Eyes closed, pass the stick from hand to hand, around your body, through the legs.

   ➤ Holding one end, flip the stick over once and catch it on the same end. Try this with the other hand. Flip it from one hand to other hand.

   ➤ Twirl stick like a baton.

   ➤ Balance stick in the palm of your hand; on your pointer finger.

   ➤ One partner tosses a deckring, while the other partner tries to ring it with the stick.

   ➤ Send ring along the floor back and forth to each other by using lummi sticks.

6. ***Trust Walks.*** For each pair, blindfold one partner and take him/her through an obstacle course using mats, ropes, chairs, hoops, small cones, low hurdles, etc., scattered across the floor. Then switch roles. *Emphasize safety!*

MOVEMENT AREA: Object Control
MOVEMENT: Single-Handed Striking—Forehand

TEACHABLE POINTS:

1. Hold racquet in the "shake hands" grip.
2. Start in ready position, keeping balance with feet comfortably apart.
3. Keep the knees bent through the movement.
4. Side-on body position is achieved when hitting.
5. Transfer the weight forward by stepping into the swing.
6. Take a big backswing
7. Keep the head of the racquet slightly above the wrist; keep the wrist firm.
8. Follow-through in the intended direction.
9. Eyes are focused and head is kept steady throughout the movement.

EQUIPMENT REQUIRED:

Small paddle racquets
Medium-sized plastic balls
Cone markers
Tall witch's hats or T-ball stands
2 chairs, long rope per pair

TEACHING GOALS:
- Use big backswing.
- Use correct weight transference.
- Use correct follow-through.
- Keep wrist firm.

TEACHING PROGRESSIONS

1. Demonstrate the forehand strike, emphasizing the teaching goals.

2. Ask children to stand side-on to a wall or side-line in a Home space. On signal "Back" or "Front," they move their weight from the front foot to the back foot and back again.

3. Now add the arm swing, making the action rhythmical and counting "one and two." "One" is the backswing; "and" is the pause at the top; and "two" is the downswing and follow-through.

"ONE" "AND" "TWO"

4. Children now stand in a ready position or square stance, facing you, then step to the side-on position. (For a right-hander, the left foot will step forward.) Use signal "Ready Position, lift and step." Practice.

5. Now add the arm swing as for rhythmical count in #3. Check that wrists are firm, not "floppy."

SQUARE   SIDE-ON

4.

6. In pairs, one partner is the Striker; the other, the Tosser. Striker lets the ball bounce once, then hits it with the open hand. Use a medium-sized ball. Remind striker to step to the side-on position, keep eyes on ball, swing, and follow through! After 5 attempts to strike the ball, switch roles.

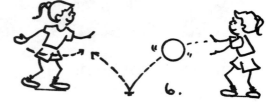

6.

7. Now have children collect a racquet and go to a Home space. Put racquet down and *shake hands* with partner. Then "shake hands" with the racquet. This is the grip for holding the racquet.

– Bounce a plastic ball on your racquet, holding it with the (*forehand*) grip. How many times in a row can you do this before losing control?

7.

8. Practice the swinging action with the racquet as for activities 3, 4, and 5. Cues: "Ready Position." "Side-on Position," Swing Back, Pause, Swing Through, Finishing High."

9. Hit the ball to a wall from the forehand position. Check for firm wrists.

ACTIVITIES

1. *T-Ball Play.* Children, in three's, take turns striking a medium-sized ball off a large cone or T-ball stand. Remind striker to be side on to ball, and keep eyes on ball as hand swings through; then follow through. Have one striker and two fielders. Each striker takes 3 hits.

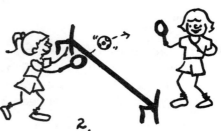

1.

2. *Racquet Ball Play.* With a partner, use racquets to hit a light plastic ball to a wall. *Variation:* Hit ball back and forth over a low rope strung across two chairs, as shown.

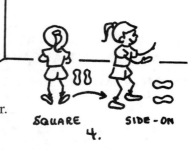

2.

MOVEMENT STATIONS
Lesson 38, Level 3

MOVEMENT AREA: Object Control
MOVEMENT: Single-Handed Striking—Forehand

TEACHING GOALS:
- ☞ Use big backswing.
- ☞ Use correct weight transference.
- ☞ Use correct follow-through.
- ☞ Use firm wrist.

EQUIPMENT REQUIRED:

Balloon balls
Paddle racquets
Totem tennis set-ups
Light plastic balls
Wall or 2 chairs/long rope per pair
Shuffle grid
Different colored beanbags
Cone markers
Fit-Kid Circuit cards
Assessment Recording Sheet

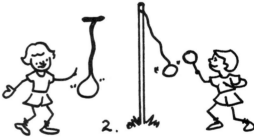

MOVEMENT STATIONS

1. **Balloon Ball Play.** Children, in pairs, keep the balloon afloat using hand, then paddle racquets. (Balloon balls are cloth spherical covers with a large inflated balloon inside.)

2. **Totem Tennis.** Children take turns striking a suspended ball in a stocking with an open hand. If possible, set up two totem tennis areas.

3. **Racquet Ball Play.** With a partner, use racquets to hit a light plastic ball to a wall. *Variation:* Hit ball back and forth over a low rope suspended between 2 chairs.

4. ***Single-Handed Striking—Assessment.*** Observe and record performance. (See Book 1, *Ready-to-Use Fundamental Motor Skills & Movement Activities for Young Children*, for a Recording Sheet.)

5. ***Shuffle Grid.*** Mark out a large square divided into 9 areas using floor tape, or large sheet of plastic, or colored chalk on tarmac. Each square is marked with a 1, 2, or 3 as shown. Have children stand with a partner two giant steps away (cone markers) on either side of square. Each partner takes 3 throws of the beanbag into the grid and keeps score. Each pair should have a different colored set of beanbags to toss.

6. ***Fit-Kid Circuit.*** Children complete a fitness circuit of stretches, runs, and strength activities. (See Fitness Strategies on page 373.) Place these on cards.

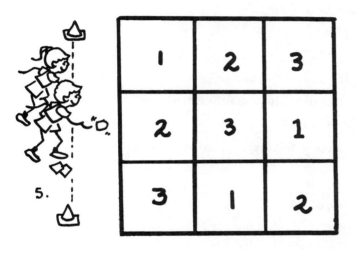

6.

MOVEMENT AREA: Object Control
MOVEMENT: Single-Handed Striking—Backhand

TEACHABLE POINTS:

1. Hold racquet in the "shake hands" grip.
2. Start in ready position, keeping balance with feet comfortably apart.
3. Step forward on foot that is on the same side as striking arm.
4. Side-on body position is achieved when hitting.
5. Shoulder of striking arm is turned toward target.
6. Take a big backswing.
7. Keep the head of the racquet slightly above the wrist; keep the wrist firm.
8. Pull arm across body, following through in the intended direction.
9. Keep the knees bent through the movement.
10. Eyes are focused and head is kept steady throughout the movement.

EQUIPMENT REQUIRED:

Small rackets	T-ball stands
Tall witch's hats	Cone markers
Various sized balls	Floor tape or colored paint or chalk

TEACHING GOALS:
- ☞ Use correct body positioning.
- ☞ Use big backswing, firm wrist.
- ☞ Follow-through in the direction of the target.

TEACHING PROGRESSIONS

1. Structure free play with small bats and different sized balls.
2. Children use a small racket to see how many times they can bounce the ball with their racquet; hit the ball up and down on the racquet. Revise the "shake-hand" grip.

3. Revise the forehand striking motion. Have children stand in ready position, move to forehand position, and swing racquet through. Use cue words: "Ready Position," step to forehand-swing.

4. Demonstrate the backhand striking motion, emphasizing the goals. Show children how to move from ready position into stance to do a backhand swing. Have class face a wall and practice footwork and swinging action. Use cue words: "Ready Position," step to back-hand-swing.

5. Have children practice footwork moving from forehand to backhand positions on the cue words: "Ready Position," step to forehand-swing, "Ready Position," step to backhand-swing.

6. Have children practice sending a ball to a wall off the paddle by gently bouncing the ball, letting it bounce once. As it comes upward, hit it against the wall with a forehand strike. This is called the "bounce serve."

7. Same as for #6, but continue to hit the ball back and forth off the wall using forehand and backhand strikes.

8. *Partner Serve.* Stand facing a partner 4–5 giant steps away. Serve the ball to your partner using the bounce serve, then strike the ball using forehand or backhand hits. (If possible, partners could hit across a bench or a low rope secured between two chairs as shown.)

ACTIVITIES

1. ***Rounders.*** Place children in teams on a large rectangle field. Hitting team strikes a medium-sized soft ball from a tee. When struck, the hitter must run to the far end of the marked court. The fielding team must attempt to throw the ball and hit the runner. The runner must return on the next player's hit. Up and back scores 1 run. It is simple to run 2 games simultaneously once the children have the concept of the game.

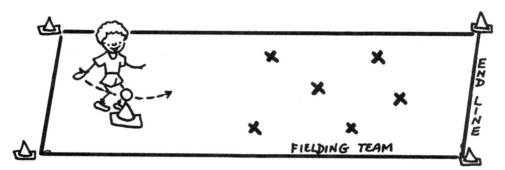

2. ***Two Square.*** Use floor tape or colored paint or chalk to mark out as many 1 yard (meter) by 2 yard (meter) courts and center line as needed. Have children pair off. Each pair gets a whiffle ball, then stands facing each other in one side of the two-square court. One partner starts the game by bounce-serving the ball with the open hand into the other player's square. Continue hitting back and forth until one player misses. Play to 5 points, then challenge a new partner. "On the line" is considered "in"; on the bounce serve and on each hit, the ball must clear the center line and bounce in the other partner's side. Encourage players to use either hand and emphasize fair play at all times.

Variations:

➤ Use paddle racquets.

➤ *Four Square.* Mark out several 8-foot square courts as you have groups of four players. Divide the court into four smaller squares. Name each A, B, C, and D. A player stands in each of the squares. Player in Square A starts the game by bounce-serving the ball to a player in any of the other 3 squares. The receiving player must let the ball bounce once, then strike it into any of the other 3 squares. A point is scored by the striker if the receiver fails to return the ball properly into another court.

MOVEMENT STATIONS
Lesson 40, Level 3

MOVEMENT AREA: Object Control
MOVEMENT: Single-Handed Striking—Backhand

TEACHING GOALS:
- ☛ Use correct body positioning.
- ☛ Use big backswing, firm wrist.
- ☛ Follow-through in the direction of the target.

EQUIPMENT REQUIRED:

Paddle racquets
Whiffle balls
Low nets or ropes
Chairs
Long ropes
Hoops
Rope and weights
Framework

Mini-footballs
Cone markers
Basketballs
Blindfolds
Obstacle course of mats, ropes, chairs, hoops, cones, low hurdles
Assessment Recording Sheet

MOVEMENT STATIONS

1. *Paddle Play.* In pairs, face each other on opposite sides of a low net (rope/two chairs) as shown. Cone markers can mark out each paddle court. Use forehand and backhand hits to send a whiffle ball back and forth over the net. Let ball bounce once before hitting it over.

2. *Long Rope Jumping.* Children split up into threes. Each group has two turners and one jumper. Jumpers perform the following tasks:

   ➤ Start in the center and try to jump the turning rope as long as you can.

   ➤ Run in front door (at the top of the rope turn as the rope turns toward you); jump 5 times; run out.

   ➤ Run in front door and straight out.

   ➤ Run in front door and do jump-turns.

   ➤ Create your own jumping stunt!

3. *Overhand Target Throw.* Suspend 2 hoops at different levels from a framework as shown. Children take turns overhand throwing mini-footballs or small playground balls through the hoops. Use cones to mark off throwing lines.

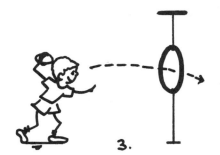

4. *Single Striking Backhand— Assessment.* Observe and record performance. (See Book 1, *Ready-to-Use Fundamental Motor Skills & Movement Activities for Young Children*, for a Recording Sheet.)

5. *Double Passes.* In pairs, each partner has a ball and stands about 3 giant steps apart. One partner bounce passes, while at the same time, the other partner chest passes ball. After a while switch roles.

6. *Trust Walks.* For each pair, blindfold one partner and take partner through an obstacle course using mats, ropes, chairs, hoops, small cones, low hurdles, etc., scattered across the floor. Then switch roles. *Emphasize safety!*

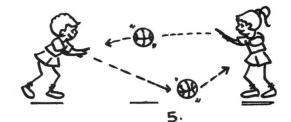

MOVEMENT AREA: Object Control
MOVEMENT: Single-Handed Striking (moving ball)

TEACHABLE POINTS:

1. Eyes are focused on the ball, head steady throughout movement.
2. Knees are bent through the movement.
3. Body is moved to the side-on position.
4. Weight is transferred forward by stepping into the swing.
5. Good shoulder turn occurs in backswing.
6. Nonpreferred arm remains relatively straight in backswing.
7. Hit starts with the hips rotating toward the target.
8. Good extension in the follow-through is evident.

EQUIPMENT REQUIRED:

Firm even surface
4 bases, 1 bat, 1 whiffle or tennis ball per group of 4
T-ball stands
Cone markers
1 small bat per group of 4

TEACHING GOALS:
- Keep head up and eyes focused.
- Use side-on stance.
- Transfer weight.

TEACHING PROGRESSIONS

A two-handed strike is used in a number of sports. This lesson will focus on a strike with a T-ball bat.

1. Revise and demonstrate the stance, hand positioning, and swinging action of a two-handed strike emphasizing the goals.

2. Have children stand side- on to a wall or sideline and shift weight back and forth from front foot to back foot on your call.

3. As #2, but have children practice swinging their arms in time with the weight trans ference. Arm swing starts with a small action backward, then slowly increases as the arms swing through and around the body. Make the action rhythmical by calling out a "one and two" count: "one" is the backswing; "and" is the pause at the top; and "two" is the swing through.

4. Children are in groups of 4: a Hitter, a Catcher, and two Fielders, with 2 balls per group. The Hitter strikes the ball with a small bat from a tall witch's hat or T-ball stand. The Fielders return the ball to the Catcher who places the ball on the stand. Rotate positions after 3 hits each.

ACTIVITY

T-Ball. Introduce the basics of T-ball. You will need to modify the rules; for example, the runner is out if the ball is thrown and caught by any baseman. No tagging is required; no base sneaking. Keep it simple. This introduction to the popular game will allow you to view many aspects of a child's motor development, such as throwing, catching, hitting, and running, as well as social skills, enthusiasm, etc. When the children are playing the game, keep up the feedback on their movement skills and promote enthusiasm.

MOVEMENT STATIONS
Lesson 42, Level 3

MOVEMENT AREA: Object Control
MOVEMENT: Two-Handed Strike—Moving Ball

TEACHING GOALS:

- ☛ Keep head up and eyes focused.
- ☛ Use side-on stance.
- ☛ Transfer weight.

EQUIPMENT REQUIRED:

Home base	Cone markers
Medium-sized balls	Paddle racquets
Cricket bats	Light plastic balls
Hoops	Large mats
Foam ball	Assessment Recording Sheet
1 small bat	

MOVEMENT STATIONS

1. ***Smack the Ball.*** Batter uses a small bat to try to hit a pitched ball as far as possible. After every 3 attempts, a new batter takes a turn, with every one rotating one position.

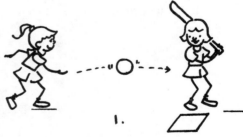

2. ***Cricket Ball Play.*** Children in three's find a Home space. Each threesome has a medium-sized ball, a modified cricket bat (smaller, lighter), and hoop. One player is the striker; second player, the roller; and a third, the fielder. (See diagram.) Players change roles after striker has hit a rolled ball 3 times.

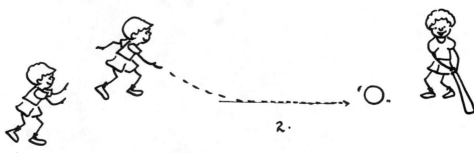

3. ***Stuck in the Middle.*** Group forms a circle with one player "stuck" in the middle. Group underhand throws or rolls ball toward middle player trying to hit him/her below the waist. Middle player tries to last for 5 attempts; then another player comes in the middle.

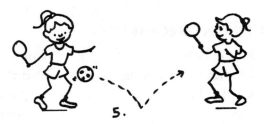

4. ***Two-Handed Striking— Assessment.*** Observe and record performance in doing a two-handed strike. (See Book 1, *Ready-to-Use Fundamental Motor Skills & Movement Activities for Young Children,* for a Recording Sheet.)

5. ***Racquet Ball Play.*** In pairs, using small racquets, children practice hitting a light plastic ball back and forth to each other.

6. ***Partner-Stretch Like Me.*** In pairs, partners stretch together, mirroring each other's actions. Emphasize slow, gentle stretching, holding each stretch for 10 seconds.

MOVEMENT AREA: Object Control
MOVEMENT: Two-Handed Striking—Moving Ball

TEACHABLE POINTS:

1. Eyes are focused on the ball, head steady throughout movement.
2. Knees are bent through the movement.
3. Body is moved to the side-on position.
4. Weight is transferred forward by stepping into the swing.
5. Good shoulder turn occurs in backswing.
6. Nonpreferred arm remains relatively straight in backswing.
7. Hit starts with the hips rotating toward the target.
8. Good extension in the follow-through is evident.

EQUIPMENT REQUIRED:

Firm even surface
1 soft medium-sized ball per pair
1 small ball per pair
1 plastic bat, 1 cricket bat per pair
1 T-ball stand or large cone per pair
Cone markers
2 sets of baseball bases

TEACHING GOALS:
☞ Use side-on stance.
☞ Use large backswing.
☞ Transfer weight.

TEACHING PROGRESSIONS

1. Revise the two-handed strike emphasizing the goals.
2. Children stand back to back with their partner. Without moving their feet, they turn and pass a ball to each other. Arms must be relatively straight when passing the ball. Stress to the children this is the shoulder turn they should try to feel in their backswing.

2.

3. In pairs have children further practice this by hitting a large light ball positioned on a tee or high cone.

4. Repeat #3 using a smaller ball.

5. Children are in four's: 1 Batter, 1 Pitcher (thrower), 1 Fielder, and 1 Catcher. Pitcher underhand tosses a whiffle ball toward Batter who stands side on to a base. Pitcher aims between the Batter's knees and chest area, sending ball across the base. Rotate one position after every 3 pitches. Ensure that each group is well spaced apart.

> *Variation:* Use a medium-sized bouncing ball and allow one bounce before striking the ball.

6. In partners, one partner rolls a large ball to other partner who strikes it with a cricket bat. Change roles after 3 hits.

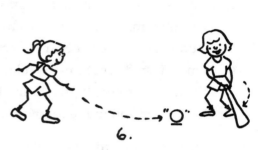

7. Repeat #6 using a smaller ball like a tennis ball.

8. Repeat #6 with thrower tossing ball so that it bounces before batter can strike it with the cricket bat.

ACTIVITIES

1. *Mini Softball Game.* Played in groups of 6: 2 Batters, 1 Catcher, 1 Pitcher, and 2 Fielders. Batter makes the hit, then runs to tag the base. Batter can decide to stay there and wait for teammate to hit, then return to home base. Fielding team tries to put Batter out by catching an air ball, tagging him/her at the base before he/she can get there, or tagging him/her at home base.

2. *Mini Cricket Ball Game.* Played as above except the Batter uses a cricket bat and carries bat with him/her to tag the base (or hoop).

MOVEMENT AREA: Object Control	
MOVEMENT: Two-Handed Strike—Moving Ball	

TEACHING GOALS:
- ☛ **Use side-on stance.**
- ☛ **Use large backswing.**
- ☛ **Transfer weight.**

EQUIPMENT REQUIRED:

Cone markers
T-ball stand or large cone
Marker
Medium-sized balls
Medium lightweight balls
Bats
Soccer-type balls
Plastic whiffle balls per pair
Scoops™
Relaxation music; cassette player/CD
Large mats
Assessment Recording Sheet

MOVEMENT STATIONS

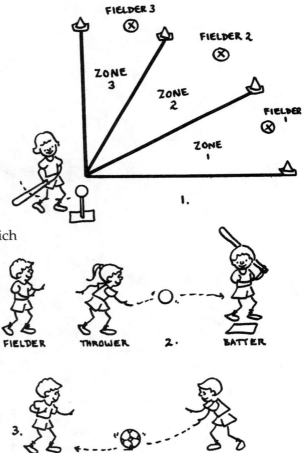

1. *Batter's Box.* Mark out a right angle and use 4 cone markers to divide this angle equally into 3 zones as shown. The batter hits off the batting tee or high cone, but now must select into which zone he or she will hit the ball. Batter must try to hit beyond the markers. Fielders position beyond the markers. Have players rotate one position after every 3 hits.

2. *Strike the Moving Ball.* Children are in 3's: one Batter, one Thrower, one Fielder. Practice striking an underhand tossed ball. Rotate one position after every 3 attempts.

3. *Kick the Moving Ball.* As for station #2, but ball is rolled and kicker attempts to kick the ball.

4. *Two-Handed Striking—Assessment.* Observe and record performance in doing a two-handed strike. (See Book 1, *Ready-to-Use Fundamental Motor Skills & Movement Activities for Young Children*, for a Recording Sheet.)

5. *Scoop Ball™ Play.* Children are in pairs, with a scoop each and a plastic whiffle ball between the two. Explore sending and receiving the ball using the scoops. "Flick" the ball from the scoop, track it, and gently reach and give with the ball as it comes into the scoop.

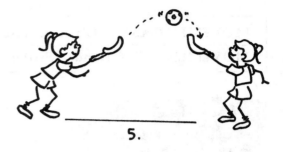

5.

6. *Relaxation Tape.* Lie quietly on mat. Listen to the music. Relax. Close your eyes. Think of something very pleasant. Now gently tense and stretch your body parts, starting with your feet and working your way up to the head.

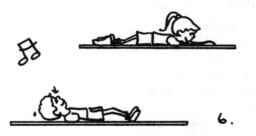

6.

TEACHING SESSION
Lesson 45, Level 3 Extension

MOVEMENT AREA: Locomotion
MOVEMENT: Hopping, Leaping, and Skipping

TEACHABLE POINTS:

Hopping

1. Hop starts on one foot and lands on the same foot (both on the forefoot).
2. Swinging leg remains bent and moves back and forth during the hop, in opposition to the support leg, assisting in the forward movement.
3. Hopping leg bends to absorb the landing force.
4. Arms move in opposition and nonsupport leg assists in the forward movement.
5. Head remains stable with the eyes looking forward.
6. Keep it smooth and in balance.

Leaping

1. Leaping action is on the balls of the feet during take-off and landing, springing from one foot to the other.
2. Knees flex at landing to absorb the force of the landing.
3. Arms assist in the propulsion by extending forward and upward vigorously as the legs extend forcefully.
4. Head remains up with eyes focused forward during the action.
5. Movement is continuous and rhythmical.

Skipping

1. Skipping action is done on the balls of the feet.
2. Use the command "Step, hop."
3. Arms and legs move in opposite direction to each other.
4. Head remains up with eyes focused forward during the action.
5. Keep in balance.

TEACHING GOALS:

Hopping

☛ Promote knee drive from nonsupporting leg.
☛ Promote correct arm action.
☛ Promote correct landing.

Leaping

☛ Promote correct take-off.
☛ Promote correct landing.

Skipping

☛ Be sure action is on the balls of the feet.
☛ Use correct arm swing.
☛ Use rhythmical action.

EQUIPMENT REQUIRED:

Firm flat surface
Cone markers
3 beanbags
20 hoops
Music; cassette/CD player

TEACHING PROGRESSIONS

HOPPING

Hopping is an extremely fatiguing movement and should be used in conjunction with other movements. When hopping, the duration should be short with adequate rest between efforts. Encourage hopping on both legs.

1. Revise and demonstrate the correct hopping action to the children, emphasizing the teaching goals.

2. Have the children complete one hop and then balance in place without and then with the hands on the hips. Emphasize using their arms to drive.

3. How many hops does it take to reach a certain spot? Emphasize knee drive.

4. Hopping to music, change hopping foot every 4 beats.

5. Pantomime rope jumping while hopping on one foot for 4 counts, then on the other foot for 4 counts; then 3-count hops; then 2-count hops.

6. Hop in and out of a hoop. Try this with the preferred foot first, rest, then try with the other foot.

7. Form teams of 4 and have a Hopping Relay in shuttle formation. Keep the hopping distance to about 8 yards (meters).

8. Play **Hoppo Bumpo** with a partner. Hop on one foot while holding other foot with the opposite hand. Use the free hand to gently push partner to lose balance.

LEAPING

1. Revise and demonstrate the correct leaping action, emphasizing the goals.

2. Have children run forward, leap off one foot into the air, and land softly on 2 feet. Repeat, leaping off the other foot. Try to convey the feeling of "flying" through the air.

2. "FLYING!"

3. Now explore leaping off one foot, landing on the other, and leaping off it. Leap across the play area in this way. How can your arms help you to leap?

4. Children leap over lines on the floor or over stretched rope.

5. Leap over low hurdles.

4.

5.

6. Run forward, spring off one foot at a marker, and land on 2 feet on a mat as shown.

7. Leapfrog with a partner across the play area.

8. Leap upward to touch the bottom of the basketball net, or a ball in a sock suspended from a framework.

7.

8.

SKIPPING

1. Revise and demonstrate the correct technique, emphasizing the goals.

2. Have children start in a Home space. Step and hop, using the cues: "Step right, hop; step left, hop."

3. Now do this skipping action, moving forward in general space. Make slight changes of direction.

4. Ask children to skip in a happy way, swinging arms and lifting knees high.

2. STEP — HOP

5. Have children skip to music, then with a partner.

6. Skip in different pathways and patterns: circle, rectangle, zigzag, backward, etc.

5.

6.

ACTIVITIES

1. *Artful Dodger.* (Refer to Lesson 6, page 298.) Use a variety of locomotor movements: power walking; jogging; skipping; hopping; jumping; leaping; slide-stepping. Try backward, forward.

2. *Shark Attack!* Scatter several hoops throughout a marked play area. Choose 3 players to be the "Sharks" who each hold a beanbag. All players ("Fish") move ("Swim") around the play area by skipping (or designate other ways of moving, such as slide-stepping, hopping, power-walking, etc.). Sharks try to tag free players with their beanbags. Fish that are caught must step-hop in place. Fish can jump into any hoop to be safe from a Shark; only one Fish per hoop, and after a 3-second count ("one shark– two sharks–three sharks") must swim away. After a certain time, count all the Fish that the Sharks caught. Choose new Sharks and play again using a different way of traveling.

SAFE AREA

SHARK

TAGGED

2.

3. *Dance.* Have each team create a dance that involves hopping, skipping, walking, clapping, and balancing. Use suitable music with a steady beat.

3.

MOVEMENT AREA: Locomotion
MOVEMENT: Hopping, Leaping, and Skipping

TEACHING GOALS:

Hopping

☛ Promote knee drive from nonsupporting leg.
☛ Promote balance.
☛ Promote correct landing.

Leaping

☛ Promote correct take-off.
☛ Promote correct landing.

Skipping

☛ Be sure action is on the balls of the feet.
☛ Use correct arm swing.
☛ Use rhythmical action.

EQUIPMENT REQUIRED:

Long ropes
Cone markers
Long rope with ball attached
Variety and different types of medium and large balls
Short skipping ropes
Assessment Recording Sheet

MOVEMENT STATIONS

Suggest that children *skip* as the way of traveling on rotation from one station to the next.

1. ***Alligator Leap.*** Place 2 long ropes at an angle to each other as shown, about 1 yard (meter) at the narrow end and about 3 yards (meters) at the wide end. Children, in turn, attempt to leap across the "river" which is full of alligators. With each successful leap, child attempts to leap across a wider part.

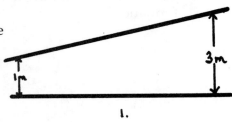

397

2. ***Hopping Sprint.*** Use markers to set out a certain traveling distance and have children in turn hop through this distance. Emphasize using arms to assist in hopping action.

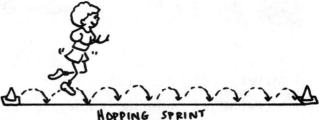

HOPPING SPRINT
2.

➤ Use preferred foot to hop; then hop using the other foot.

➤ *Variation:* Leap through a certain distance, counting the number of leaps taken.

3. ***Jump the Ball.*** One child in group swings a ball attached to a rope in a circle along the ground. Other children try to hop, leap, or jump over the ball each time it passes under their feet. Switch rope swinger after every 5 complete swings. If rope catches someone's feet, that player must run around the circle, then back in place to continue.

3.

4. ***Hopping, Leaping, Skipping— Assessment.*** Observe and record performance. (See Book 1, *Ready-to-Use Fundamental Motor Skills & Movement Activities for Young Children,* for a Recording Sheet.)

5. ***Ball Throw and Catch.*** Children in pairs practice overhand throwing and catching. Use a variety of different types of balls at this station.

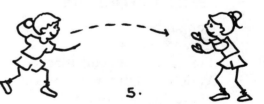

5.

6. ***Short Rope Jumping.*** Children practice jumping a short rope.

➤ *Variation:* Use skipping hoops in shuttle formation.

6.

TEACHING SESSION
Lesson 47, Level 3

MOVEMENT AREA: Object Control
MOVEMENT: Dribbling with a (Floor Hockey) Stick

TEACHABLE POINTS:

1. Stick is held in both hands with one hand on top and the other 6–8 inches (15–20 cm) below it.
2. For a right-hander, the right hand should be down the stick.
3. Edge of the blade of the stick rests on the floor.
4. Knees are bent slightly.
5. Ball or puck is moved in front rather than to side with short taps from one side of blade to other.
6. Keep head up and "feel" the puck on the stick.

EQUIPMENT REQUIRED:

Firm even surface
1 floor hockey stick per child
1 ball or puck per child
Cone markers

TEACHING GOALS:
- ☞ Use correct hand positioning on stick.
- ☞ Control puck (ball) with short taps.

TEACHING PROGRESSIONS

1. Each child collects a stick and finds a Home space. Stick is placed on the floor in front to do the following:

   ➤ Jump from side-to-side over stick.
   ➤ Walk along stick like a tightrope walker.
   ➤ Run and leap over stick.
   ➤ "Thread the Needle" with the stick.
   ➤ Stretch with your stick.
   ➤ Build a bridge over your stick.
   ➤ Play stick tug-o-war with a partner.
   ➤ Jump over the stick held by partner.

2. (Demonstrate the proper hand positioning on the stick.) Have children experiment with letting right hand be the lower hand down the stick, then left hand. Which feels better?

3. On signal "Run and Carry!" children hold stick in both hands, with the blade as low to the floor as possible, and run straight ahead. On signal "Change!" do sudden changes of direction. Emphasize heads up, looking for open spaces.

4. (Demonstrate how to use the stick to move the ball (dribbling). Emphasize the teaching goals.) Have children collect a ball or puck. Move it along the floor so that it always stays in contact with the blade, one side only. This is called "carrying" the ball.

5. In Home space have children move the puck from side-to-side with short taps. This is called "stick-handling." Keeping the puck in front rather than to the side, travel in general space. This is called " dribbling." Practice dribbling.

6. Form groups of 4–6 and have each group stand in files behind a starting line, facing a row of 4 cone markers, spaced 2 yards (meters) apart. Children in turn dribble a puck in and out of markers. When the end marker is reached, they dribble straight back to group. As soon as one dribbler has reached marker 3, the next dribbler can go. Continue in this way. Emphasize keeping the puck under control!

ACTIVITIES

1. ***Shuttle-Stick Relay.*** Form teams of 6 players. Each team sets up in shuttle formation facing the other half about 10 yards (meters) apart. First player of one side has a puck. On signal "Stick-Handle!" this player stick-handles the puck across to the first player of the opposite file and leaves the puck for this player, who then repeats the action. Continue in this way.

   ➤ *Variation:* Place 3 cone markers between sides and have dribblers stick-handle puck in and out of cone markers.

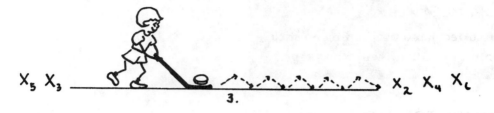

2. ***Stick Pirates.*** Select one-third of the class to be the "Stick Pirates," who each have a stick and stand in the center of the play area to start. Have the rest of the class collect a hockey stick and puck (or ball), scatter, and find a Home space to start. Pirates try to stick-handle the puck away from a free player; if successful, this free player then becomes a Pirate. Emphasize that no body contact is allowed; sticks must stay low to the ground at all times; watch where they are moving; and play fair!

3. ***Square-Box Dribble.*** Teams position around a large square and number off as shown. A circle in the center contains 4 pucks. On signal "3's," for example, the number 3 players run to the middle, collect a puck, dribble it back out through their spot, and dribble around the square in a clockwise direction back to place. First player back scores 4 points for his/her team; second player scores 3; third player scores 2; and fourth player scores 1.

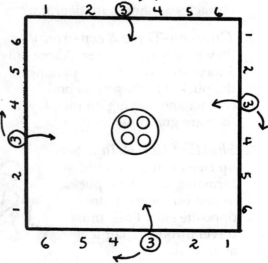

MOVEMENT STATIONS
Lesson 48, Level 3

MOVEMENT AREA: Object Control
MOVEMENT: Dribbling with a (Floor Hockey) Stick

TEACHING GOALS:

☛ **Use correct hand positioning on stick.**

☛ **Control puck (ball) with short taps.**

EQUIPMENT REQUIRED:

Obstacles such as mats, hoops, cones, chairs
Hockey sticks
Pucks
Chairs
Paddle racquets
Light whiffle ball or small Balloon
    Ball™
Low nets/posts
Assessment Recording Sheet

MOVEMENT STATIONS

1. ***Stick-Handle Obstacle Course.***
   Dribblers in turn dribble puck through the
   obstacle course. Emphasize control. Use
   obstacles as shown in diagram.

2. ***Three-on-Three Keep-Away.***
   Play in designated area. Allow only
   3 traveling steps before passing
   the puck. Emphasize no body
   contact and staying on the player
   they are guarding!

3. ***Shuttle Stick Relay.*** Set
   up two identical shuttle
   formations. Dribble puck
   in and out of chairs to
   opposite side. Puck must
   travel through chair legs
   as shown.

4. ***Dribbling with a Stick—Assessment.*** Observe and record performance. (See Book 1, *Ready-to-Use Fundamental Motor Skills & Movement Activities for Young Children*, for a Recording Sheet.)

5. ***Racquet Ball Play.*** Set up as shown with 3 players on one side of a low net (badminton net) and 3 on the other side. Use a large whiffle ball or small Balloon Ball™. Allow one bounce before hitting ball back to other side.

6. ***Stick Stretches.*** Children explore stretching with a stick in different ways as shown in the diagram. Enlarge drawings and place on posterboard.

MOVEMENT AREA: Object Control

MOVEMENT: Passing, Trapping, and Shooting with a (Floor Hockey) Stick

---

TEACHABLE POINTS:

Passing

1. Position hands slightly further apart on stick as for dribbling position.
2. Keep stick blade upright and use a smooth, sweeping motion.
3. Stick blade stays in contact with floor with forward swing.
4. Ball stays in contact with blade until pushed away.
5. Lower hand guides the stick down to push through the puck.
6. Elbows bend slightly and wrist of lower hand snaps through.
7. Follow-through is in the line of direction toward target, keeping stick low.
8. Check the puck/ball first, then concentrate on the target.

Trapping

1. Keep eyes on the ball or puck as it travels along.
2. Slight forward tilt of stick blade over the ball or puck to trap it.
3. Cushion the pass by allowing stick blade to "give" at moment of impact.
4. Control the ball or puck first before sending.

EQUIPMENT REQUIRED:

Firm even surface
1 floor hockey stick per child
1 ball/puck per child or pair
Cone markers

TEACHING GOALS:

Passing

☛ Use smooth sweeping motion.
☛ Snap through wrist of lower hand.
☛ Follow-through toward target; keep stick low.

Trapping

☛ Tilt blade slightly forward over ball to make trap.
☛ "Give" or cushion to absorb impact.

TEACHING PROGRESSIONS

1. Demonstrate how to pass and trap the ball/puck, emphasizing the goals.

2. Find a partner and stand about 5 giant steps away from each other. Practice passing the ball or puck to each other. Emphasize trapping the ball/puck first, gently absorbing the impact; then pass it to partner. Gradually increase the distance.

3. While one partner stays still, pass the puck to the moving partner who stops the puck and then passes it back to first partner who is now moving. Pass slightly ahead of moving partner. This is called a "lead pass."

4. Now have partners pass the puck back and forth while on the move.

5. Demonstrate how to execute a "wrist shot," emphasizing the goals." Have children practice at a wall. Gradually they should move farther away to take wrist shots. Emphasize keeping stick blade along the floor and snapping wrist to send the puck/ball to the wall. Trap the rebound and shoot again. Caution children that the stick is not to be raised above the waist on the follow-through.

6. Practice wrist shot and trapping puck with a partner. Start about 8 giant steps away and gradually increase distance.

7. Have partners set up two cone markers halfway between them with markers spaced 2 giant steps apart to start. Practice accuracy in shooting. Gradually they can increase their distance apart from each other and decrease the space between the markers.

ACTIVITIES

1. **Shuttle Pass Relays.** Teams of 6 set up in shuttle formation with sides spaced about 8 yards (meters) apart. Puck is passed to opposite player; then passer runs to join the end of opposite side. Receiving player must first trap ball/puck before passing across. Continue in this way.

   ➤ *Challenge:* Which team can complete the most number of passes in a certain time?

2. **Clear-Away Hockey.** For each game, mark out a large rectangular area with a center line as shown. On signal "Clear-away!" each team has 3 pucks and tries to shoot the pucks into the opposition's half. On signal "Stop!" each team counts the number of pucks in its half. The team with the fewest number of pucks wins this game. Play best of 3; then have teams rotate to play another match with new opposition.

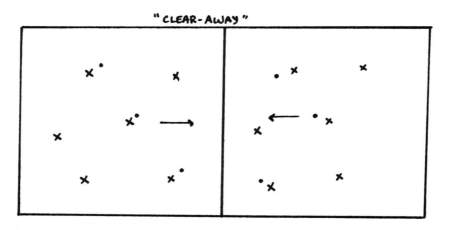

MOVEMENT STATIONS
Lesson 50, Level 3

MOVEMENT AREA: Object Control
MOVEMENT: Passing, Trapping, and Shooting with a (Floor Hockey) Stick

TEACHING GOALS:

Passing
- ☛ Use smooth sweeping motion.
- ☛ Snap through wrist of lower hand.
- ☛ Follow-through toward target; keep stick low.

Trapping
- ☛ Tilt blade slightly forward over ball to make trap.
- ☛ "Give" or cushion to absorb impact.

EQUIPMENT REQUIRED:

12 skittles
18–20 hockey sticks
Cone markers
10–12 pucks
Dome markers
6–7 scoops per child
3 whiffle balls per pair
6–7 jump ropes per child
Music; CD/cassette player
Assessment Recording Sheet

MOVEMENT STATIONS

1. *Skittle Shoot.* Set up 6 skittles as shown in 2 stations. Players are in groups of 3 with one shooter, one puck retriever, and one player who counts skittles knocked over and then resets them. Rotate positions after every 2 shots. Players all keep their own score. Gradually increase shooting distance each round.

2. *Goal Hockey.* In pairs, near a wall, one partner is the goalie; other partner, the shooter. Each shooter takes 3 shots at goalie, trying to score, then they switch roles. Emphasize that the follow-through is low and puck must travel along the ground.

3. ***Shuttle Pass Relay.*** Mark off 2 lines, A and B, that are 15 yards (meters) apart. In pairs, pass puck back and forth from line A to B. After each pair has had a turn, pair up with a different partner and repeat task from lines B to A. As soon as one pair is halfway, then the next pair can go. Continue in this way.

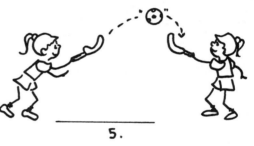

4. ***Passing, Trapping, and Shooting with a Stick—Assessment.*** Observe and record performance. (See Book 1, *Ready-to-Use Fundamental Motor Skills & Movement Activities for Young Children*, for a Recording Sheet.)

5. ***Scoop™ Ball Play.*** Each pair has a scoop and a plastic whiffle ball. Explore sending and receiving the ball using the scoops. "Flick" the ball from the scoop, track it, and gently reach and give with the ball as it comes into the scoop.

6. ***Short Rope Jumping.*** Use music and have children explore jumping a short rope in time to the music. Use the rope to take stretch breaks when tired, then continue jump roping.

TEACHING SESSION
Lesson 51, Level 3

MOVEMENT AREA: Object Control
MOVEMENT: Dribbling and Trapping with Foot

TEACHABLE POINTS:

Dribbling

1. Ball is kept close to the body.
2. Ball is controlled with the inside and outside of the foot.
3. Control is attained before speed.
4. Arms are used for balance.
5. Head is up and eyes focused.

Trapping

1. Keep in balance.
2. Nontrapping foot placed near and to side of the ball.
3. Knee is bent on contact.
4. Trap with the inside of the foot.
5. Arm opposite the kicking leg is away from the body assisting balance.
6. Give with the ball to cushion on contact.
7. Eyes focused on the ball.

EQUIPMENT REQUIRED:

Firm even surface
4 cone markers per group
1 large playground ball or soccer ball per child
2 hoops per team

TEACHING GOALS:

Dribbling
☞ **Control ball movements before speed.**
☞ **Use insides and outsides of either foot.**
☞ **Keep the ball close.**

Trapping
☞ **Keep in balance.**
☞ **Place nontrapping foot near and to side of the ball.**
☞ **Trap with the inside of the foot.**

TEACHING PROGRESSIONS

1. Demonstrate using the insides or outsides of the foot to move the ball, emphasizing the teaching goals.

   ➤ Have children start in a free space, then dribble the ball with the inside of either foot in general space.

   ➤ Dribble the ball with the outside of the feet.

   ➤ Dribble the ball with inside or outside of either foot.

2. Revise and demonstrate trapping the ball with the inside of the foot and the sole of the foot.

   ➤ In pairs, 1 child rolls a ball slowly to his/her partner, who stops the ball with the sole of the foot. As the ball comes toward trapper, lift foot to make a "wedge" with the ground so that the heel of foot is closer to the ground than the toes. Trap with either foot. Gradually increase the rolling speed.

   ➤ In pairs, 1 child rolls the ball slowly toward and slightly to the side of the partner. Children move toward the ball and trap it with the inside of the foot, then kick it back to the partner.

   ➤ In pairs, have 1 child kick a stationary ball toward a wall. Contact with ball is made on the inside of the foot by turning the kicking foot out to the side. As the ball rebounds off the wall, have partner stop (trap) the ball by using the inside of the foot. Gradually increase the distance away from the wall.

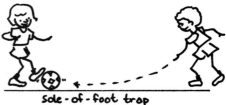

Sole-of-foot trap

inside-of-foot trap

2.

3. On signal "Scrambled Eggs—Dribble!" children dribble the ball in and out of each other. On signal "Iceberg!" ball is immediately stopped with a sole-of-the-foot trap or inside-of-the-foot trap.

ICEBERG!
3.

4. *Bubbles.* Children dribble their balls ("bubbles") around the play area. They must not let their bubble touch anyone else's; otherwise, the bubble will "burst." If that happens, then they must trap the ball and jog in place for a 10-second count.

5. *Pirates.* Every third player returns soccer ball. These are the "Pirates" who try to steal the balls from the dribblers. A player without a ball becomes a new Pirate. Emphasize heads up and no body contact!

5. "PIRATES"

"BUBBLES!"
4.

ACTIVITIES

1. ***Zigzag Dribble Relay.*** Divide class into groups of 4. Each group stands in a file behind a starting line facing a row of cone markers, spaced 3 giant steps apart as shown. Children, in turn, dribble soccer ball in and out of cone markers and then back to starting line. Each group has 2 soccer balls. As soon as dribbler reaches the end cone, the next dribbler can go. Continue in this way.

2. ***Shuttle Dribble Relay.*** Have each team of 6 set up in shuttle formation with sides spaced 10 yards (meters) apart. Equally space two hoops between the two sides as shown. Dribbler travels across to the opposite side in and out of hoops. Opposite player traps ball with sole-of-foot trap or inside-of-foot trap, and dribbles across. Continue to shuttle dribble in this way. Which group can complete the most number of crossings in 3 minutes?

MOVEMENT AREA: Object Control
MOVEMENT: Dribbling and Trapping

TEACHING GOALS:

Dribbling

- ☞ Control ball movements before speed.
- ☞ Use insides and outsides of either foot.
- ☞ Keep the ball close.

Trapping

- ☞ Keep in balance.
- ☞ Place nontrapping foot near and to side of the ball.
- ☞ Trap with the inside of the foot.

EQUIPMENT REQUIRED:

Cone markers
Chairs
Hoops
Soccer balls
2–3 junior soccer goals or wall tape
3–4 Fling-It™ Nets
3–4 frisbees or whoosh rings
Beanbags, small balls, other objects
Assessment Recording Sheet

MOVEMENT STATIONS

1. *Zigzag Dribble.* Set up 2 different courses using cones, chairs, and hoops as shown. Children take turns dribbling in and out of markers. Once they reach the end marker, dribble straight back.

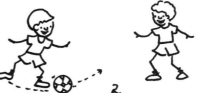

2. *Free Kicking.* Children explore kicking the ball and trapping it with the sole-of-the-foot or the inside-of-the-foot trap. Emphasize safety, kicking into open space.

3. ***Dribble, Kick, 'n Score.*** Use 2 junior soccer goals or wall goals with a dribble line and a kicking line marked off as shown. Children, in 3's, take turns to dribble up to a kicking line and kick the ball into the goal.

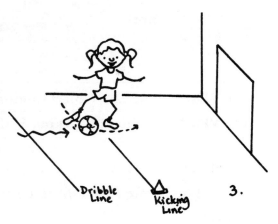

4. ***Dribbling and Trapping—Assessment.*** Observe and record performance in dribbling and trapping the ball. (See Book 1, *Ready-to-Use Fundamental Motor Skills & Movement Activities for Young Children*, for a Recording Sheet.)

5. ***Fling-It™ Play.*** Children pair off and use Fling-It™ Nets to send and receive different objects. One pair can then try to send object into another pair's net, or both pairs can send their object at the same time. (Light sheets can also be used.)

6. ***Frisbee (or Whoosh Ring) Play.*** Children pair off and explore throwing a frisbee back and forth to each other. Emphasize being side on to partner, holding Frisbee with thumb on top, pointer finger along the edge, and rest of fingers underneath. Flick the Frisbee with a side-arm action. Catch the Frisbee in two hands: thumbs up for a low catch; thumbs down for a high catch.

TEACHING SESSION
Lesson 53, Level 3

MOVEMENT AREA: Object Control
MOVEMENT: Ground Kicking Skills

TEACHABLE POINTS:

Kicking with the Instep for Distance

1. Keep in balance.
2. Nonkicking foot placed near and to side of the ball.
3. Knee is bent on backswing (at least 90 degrees).
4. Kick with the instep (shoelaces) and contact at bottom of ball.
5. Arm opposite the kicking leg is away from the body assisting balance.
6. Follow-through toward the target.
7. Eyes focused on the ball.

Accuracy Kicking with the Inside of the Foot

INSIDE OF FOOT

1. Keep in a balanced position.
2. Nonkicking foot is placed beside the ball.
3. Kicking foot is turned so that the inside of the foot faces the ball.
4. Opposite arm swings forward as the kicking leg moves back and assists in balance.
5. Ball is contacted on the inside of the kicking foot.
6. Arm on same side as kicking leg swings away from the body assisting balance, as the kicking leg swings through.
7. Follow-through toward the target.
8. Head is down with eyes focused on the ball throughout the movement.

EQUIPMENT REQUIRED:

Firm even surface
Cone markers
Wall targets, wall tape

1 kicking ball per child or per pair
Carpet squares or flat markers

TEACHING GOALS:
- ☞ Keep head up and eyes focused.
- ☞ Use correct placement of kicking foot
- ☞ Use correct contact with foot.
- ☞ Control the ball by trapping.

TEACHING PROGRESSIONS

1. Revise and demonstrate the instep kicking action, emphasizing the teaching goals.

   ➤ Children demonstrate the kicking action in slow motion to you. Note the children who fall off balance while doing this. These children may find the kick difficult.

   ➤ In pairs have the children stand 10 yards (meters) apart. Children send ball to each other using the instep kick and trap with the sole-of-the-foot trap. Emphasize stopping the ball first, then kicking it to partner. Gradually increase the distance.

   ➤ Children, in pairs, have 1 ball between each pair and 2 markers. From a kicking line and on the signal "Kick," one of the pair kicks the ball as far as he/she can. The partner marks the ball where it stops. Children take alternate turns to kick for distance. Ensure that you keep emphasizing the main points and provide feedback to individual children.

2. Revise and demonstrate the inside-of-the-foot kick. Children do the action in slow motion. Emphasize the teaching goals.

   ➤ Children, in pairs, kick back and forth to each other using the inside of either foot. Use the inside-of-the-foot trap. Control the ball first, then kick. Gradually increase the kicking distance.

   ➤ Partners place two cone markers between them and try to kick between the markers. Start at two giant steps apart, then gradually decrease the distance apart of the markers. Use either foot to kick.

3. Repeat #2, with child approaching ball from a 3-step run as shown. Kick the ball to a wall; into a wall target; to a partner. Use the instep kick or inside-of-the-foot kicks.

ACTIVITIES

1. *Goal Kicking.* Divide the class into groups of 6. Each group has 3 soccer balls, 3 flat markers or carpet squares, and 2 cone markers. The group sets up goals with markers 2 giant steps apart, then randomly place the squares at least 5 yards (meters) from the goals. One child is the goal keeper, another 2 back up the goal keeper, and the other 3 take turns at kicking from the markers. Have kickers and goal keepers switch roles after a certain time.

2. *Kicking Croquet.* Divide the class into groups of 4. Explain how to set up course as shown in the diagram. Ensure good spacing to allow for successful accuracy when kicking. Establish a start and a finish to the course. Each kick must go through the markers before going on to the next set of markers. As skill level improves, increase the distance and reduce the space between the 2 markers.

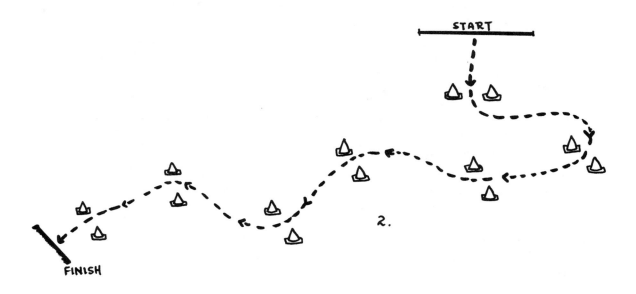

MOVEMENT STATIONS
Lesson 54, Level 3

MOVEMENT AREA: Object Control
MOVEMENT: Ground Kicking Skills

TEACHING GOALS:
- ☞ Keep head up and eyes focused.
- ☞ Use correct placement of kicking foot.
- ☞ Use correct contact with foot.
- ☞ Control the ball by trapping.

EQUIPMENT REQUIRED:

Large playground balls or soccer balls
Wall targets
Cone markers
Bases
Catchballs™
3 juggling scarves per child
3 small goal nets
Assessment Recording Sheet

MOVEMENT STATIONS

1. *Wall Target Kick and Trap.* Children pair off and face a wall target as shown. One partner kicks a playground ball into wall target. Other partner tries to trap the ball with the sole-of-the-foot or inside-of-the-foot trap as the ball rebounds off the wall. Then partner kicks ball to wall. Gradually increase the distance of the kick. *Variation:* Kick into junior soccer goals in groups of 3.

2. *Kick-Ball.* Have two kickers, one catcher, one roller, and two fielders for a group of 6. Kickers take turns to kick a rolling ball. Fielders must field the ball and return it to catcher before kicker can run to touch a base and return to touch a home base. After each kicker has had two kicks, everyone rotates one position.

CATCHER   KICKER

2.

ROLLER

FIELDER

417

3. ***Kicking Golf.*** Set up 3 fairways with a "tee-off" and a "green" for each as shown. Have children pair off, with each partner kicking in turn and counting the number of kicks taken to kick the ball through the hole.

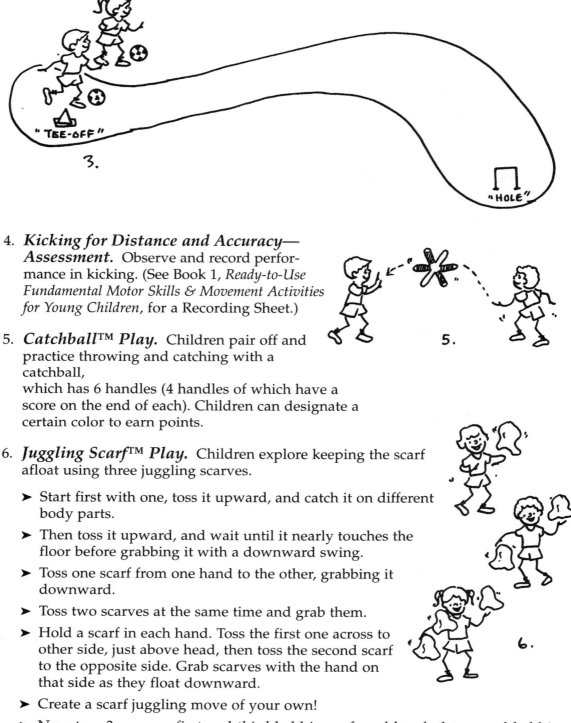

4. ***Kicking for Distance and Accuracy—Assessment.*** Observe and record performance in kicking. (See Book 1, *Ready-to-Use Fundamental Motor Skills & Movement Activities for Young Children*, for a Recording Sheet.)

5. ***Catchball™ Play.*** Children pair off and practice throwing and catching with a catchball, which has 6 handles (4 handles of which have a score on the end of each). Children can designate a certain color to earn points.

6. ***Juggling Scarf™ Play.*** Children explore keeping the scarf afloat using three juggling scarves.

   ➤ Start first with one, toss it upward, and catch it on different body parts.

   ➤ Then toss it upward, and wait until it nearly touches the floor before grabbing it with a downward swing.

   ➤ Toss one scarf from one hand to the other, grabbing it downward.

   ➤ Toss two scarves at the same time and grab them.

   ➤ Hold a scarf in each hand. Toss the first one across to other side, just above head, then toss the second scarf to the opposite side. Grab scarves with the hand on that side as they float downward.

   ➤ Create a scarf juggling move of your own!

   ➤ Now toss 3 scarves; first and third held in preferred hand; the second held in other hand. Toss in order, 1-2-3; remember that each hand takes a turn, and the toss is across the body to above and in front of the opposite shoulder.

TEACHING SESSION
Lesson 55, Level 3

MOVEMENT AREA: Object Control
MOVEMENT: Punt Kicking

TEACHABLE POINTS:

1. Ball is held in front of body at hip height with both hands.
2. Head is down with eyes focused on the ball.
3. Step is forward onto nonkicking foot.
4. Knee of kicking leg is bent on the backswing.
5. Ball is guided down (not dropped) with the hand on the same side as kicking leg.
6. Ball is contacted on the instep of the kicking foot.
7. Arm opposite kicking leg moves forward during the kick.
8. High follow-through occurs in the direction of the target.
9. Body leans backward on contact and into follow-through.

EQUIPMENT REQUIRED:

Firm even surface
Cone markers
1 beanbag per pair
1 balloon, beachball, or large round ball per child
1 foam or soft ball per pair
1 oval-shaped ball per pair

| STEP | SWING | THROUGH |

2.

3.

TEACHING GOALS:

☛ **Keep head down, eyes focused on ball.**
☛ **Guide ball down; do not drop it.**
☛ **Follow-through in direction of target.**

TEACHING PROGRESSIONS

1. Demonstrate the punt kick, emphasizing the goals.
2. Have children go through the kicking action slowly on cues: "Step, swing, kick through."
3. Now have children practice punt kicking action using a balloon or beachball. Observe that contact is on the instep (shoelace) of the kicking foot. Emphasize keeping head down and guiding the ball down with the hands, not letting it drop.

419

4. Kick a foam or soft ball to a wall. Remember to keep your eyes on the ball and follow-through high in the direction of target.

5. Punt kick a round ball back and forth to partner. Gradually increase the kicking distance

6. Repeat #5 using an oval-shaped ball.

7. *Kick and Mark.* One partner is the kicker; the other partner is the marker. Kicker takes 3 punt kicks. Marker places a beanbag where the best kick lands. Then switch roles.

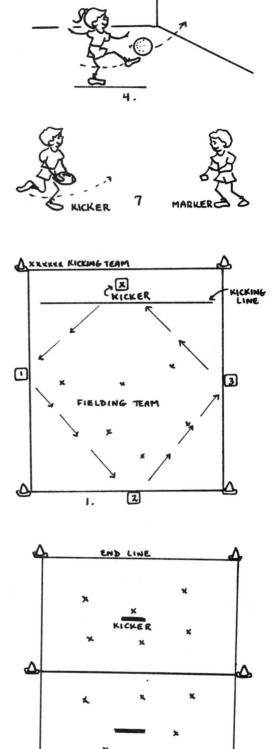

ACTIVITIES

1. *Soccer T-Ball.* For each game have 2 teams of 6–8 players. One team is the kicking team; the other, the fielding team. Everyone on the kicking team has a turn at punt kicking the ball into the field, then running around the bases, tagging each base in turn, before the fielding team, using only feet, can get the ball across the line to the catcher who traps the ball. Fielding team cannot use hands. Kicking team must punt kick the ball across a designated line as shown in the diagram. Kicking team keeps score of each successful run, then fielding team has a turn.

2. *Forcing Back.* For each game form 2 teams of 6–8 players. Each team scatters on opposite sides of a large play area, divided in half by a middle line and marked out with cone markers as shown. One team starts the game with a player punt kicking into the opposition's half from a marked spot halfway in that player's half side. The ball must be kicked from wherever it is caught or stopped. A point is scored by kicking the ball over the opposition's endline. This ball is again kicked from the starting mark.

MOVEMENT STATIONS
Lesson 56, Level 3

MOVEMENT AREA: Object Control
MOVEMENT: Punt Kicking

TEACHING GOALS:
- ☛ Keep head down, eyes focused on ball.
- ☛ Guide ball down, do not drop it.
- ☛ Follow-through in direction of target.

EQUIPMENT REQUIRED:

Goal posts
Hoops or ropes
Soccer balls
Beanbags
Plastic bottles, skittles or small cones
Cone markers
Bases
Small playground balls
Balloons
Balloon Balls™
Light foam balls
Assessment Recording Sheet

MOVEMENT STATIONS

1. *Spot Kicking.* Use hoops or rope circles to designate 6 kicking spots around a goal area as shown. Each spot is worth so many points according to difficulty (as indicated on cone marker). Children pair off with one partner being the kicker; the other, the retriever. Kicker punt kicks from each spot to send the ball through goal area; then the two change roles.

2. *Partner Punt and Receive Play.* Group pairs off; each pair has a soccer ball and each kicker has a beanbag. Kickers start 5 yards (meters) apart using the beanbags to mark the spot, and punt kick to each other from this spot. If both players successfully catch the kicked ball, then players can take a step backward. Beanbags are moved to mark the spot for the next kick. Continue in this way.

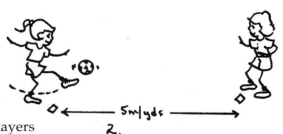

421

3. ***Five-Pin Kick.*** For each group of 3, set up 5
plastic bottles, skittles or cones near a wall in
a triangular pattern as shown. Vary the
kicking distance using cone markers.
Children take turns using the inside-of-
the-foot kick to try to knock over the
pins. Each player gets two attempts.
Keep score.

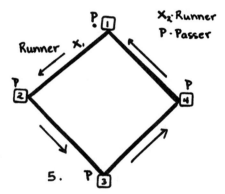

4. ***Punt Kicking—Assessment.*** Observe
and record performance. (See Book 1, *Ready-to-Use
Fundamental Motor Skills & Movement Activities for
Young Children*, for a Recording Sheet.)

5. ***Baseball Diamond Run.*** Set up 4 bases in
the shape of a diamond, with bases spaced 5
yards (meters) apart as shown. Two runners
take turns running the bases with a foot tag at
each base. The other players tag up on each
base as shown. Base players underhand or overhand pass a small playground ball around the
bases, from home base back to home base, trying
to beat the runner. Home base player gives the
"Go!" signal.

6. ***Soccer Juggling.*** Children explore keeping
the ball in the air using knees and feet. Use
balloons, balloon balls, light foam balls, or
other types of soft balls to foot juggle.

MOVEMENT AREA: Object Control
MOVEMENT: One-Handed Bouncing

TEACHABLE POINTS:

1. Keep in a balanced position with the feet comfortably spread.
2. Eyes are focused just in front of the ball.
3. Ball is pushed down with hand by extending arm downward.
4. Fingers are relaxed and spread.
5. Be in ready position to receive the bouncing ball, with elbow slightly bent.
6. Let arms give or move slightly upward as ball contacts the hands.
7. Bounce ball in front of and to side of the body.

EQUIPMENT REQUIRED:

Firm even surface
Cone markers
Variety of large bouncing balls,
   1 per child
1 hoop or carpet square per child

TEACHING GOALS:

☛ **Keep head up and eyes focused.**
☛ **Use pumping action, not slapping at ball.**

TEACHING PROGRESSIONS

1. Get the feel of the ball by holding it in both hands, and moving hands around the ball. Try this with your eyes closed.

   – Toss the ball from hand to hand by gently pushing it off the fingers. Try this with your eyes closed.

1.

2. Revise the stance for the Pocket Bounce: Stand so that your knees are bent and feet are shoulder-width apart. Put your foot opposite the bouncing hand slightly ahead. Now bounce the ball in your preferred hand in the "pocket" formed by your body and feet.

➤ Reverse body stance and bounce ball with your other hand.

➤ Do 4 bounces; crossover; 4 more bounces. Continue this pattern while bouncing ball in place.

3. Travel from one sideline to the opposite sideline by bouncing your ball in the following pattern: forward bounce – 2 – 3 – 4.

4. *Shake Hands—Bounce.* On "Scrambled Eggs—Bounce," bounce your ball with one hand as you move in and out of each other. Listen for my "Shake Hands" signal. Use your free hand to shake hands. On "Scramble Eggs—Bounce," bounce your ball with the other hand while moving in and out of each other.

5. *Ball Stunts.*

➤ Roll the ball through your legs in a figure-8 pattern.

➤ Pass the ball around your waist. Go the opposite direction.

➤ Bounce the ball from standing position to kneeling position to sitting position, and back up again. Repeat.

➤ Bounce the ball in place while you walk around it.

➤ Bounce the ball around you while you stand in place.

➤ Try to get the ball bouncing from its stationary place on the floor.

➤ Spin the ball on your finger.

➤ Roll the ball down your back and bounce it between legs to catch in front.

➤ Hold ball between your legs, one hand in front; other, behind. Let ball bounce once while you quickly reverse hand hold.

➤ Think up a stunt of your own!

ACTIVITIES

1. ***Mirror Bouncing.*** Children mirror your movements and ball-bouncing positions.

   ➤ Pass the ball in a figure-8 between your legs.

   ➤ Bounce the ball in a figure-8 between the legs.

   ➤ Bounce ball while marching in place, jogging in place, jumping in place.

   ➤ "Pocket bounce—crossover—pocket bounce" pattern.

   ➤ On signal "Freeze," children jump-stop and hold the ball in both hands near hip (opposite to leading foot).

   ➤ Hold ball and "Pivot" by keeping the toe of one foot in touch with the floor as the other foot is used to push off and turn you in different directions.

2. ***Knock Away.*** Play this game in a circular marked-out area. Everyone has a ball and starts with 2 "lives." Try to knock away each other's ball with the free hand while using the other hand to keep the ball bouncing. If ball is knocked away you lose "one life" and must bounce your ball to touch a boundary line; then you can come back into the game. Once both "lives" are lost, you must stand outside of the circular area and cross-over bounce the ball until the game is finished.

   ➤ *Rules:* You cannot touch the ball with both hands; cannot carry the ball at any time; cannot stop and hold the ball, then bounce it again.

FOUNDATION MOVEMENT
Lesson 58, Level 3

MOVEMENT AREA: Object Control
MOVEMENT: One-Handed Brouncing (large ball)

TEACHING GOALS:
- ☛ Keep eyes on ball.
- ☛ Use arms in pumping action, as fingers push ball downward; do not slap ball.

EQUIPMENT REQUIRED:

Hoops, ropes, mats, chairs, cones, low box, large balls
Cone markers
Balance feathers
Tennis tins and tennis balls
Balance bench, foam stilts, bucket steppers, balance boards, Lolo® Ball,
Bigfoot Striders™
Assessment Recording Sheet

ACTIVITY STATIONS

1. *Obstacle Course.* Scatter several objects—such as chairs, mats, hoops, ropes, cones, low box, bench—around the station area. Children bounce their ball in and out of objects; across or along; on and off; over and under. Every time they come to a hoop they must cross-over bounce their ball 5 times inside the hoop before traveling onward.

2. *Zigzag Bounce.* Set up 2 identical zigzag courses using cone markers as shown. Children take turns bouncing ball in and out of cone markers. When the last marker is reached, they return directly to the starting line, bouncing the ball all the way back.

426

3. ***Balance Feathers.*** Explore balancing a feather on different parts of your hand: palm of hand; back of hand; fingers; wrist; right hand; left hand.

   ➤ Balance feathers on other body parts: elbow, knee, shoulder, forehead.

   ➤ Balance your feather from one body part to another; for example, palm of hand to back of hand.

   ➤ Create a feather balance of your own.

4. ***Bouncing Ball with One Hand— Assessment.*** Observe and record performance. (See Book 1, *Ready-to-Use Fundamental Motor Skills & Movement Activities for Young Children*, for a Recording Sheet.)

5. ***Target Bounce.*** Each person has an empty tennis tin and a tennis ball. Perform the following tasks:

   ➤ Bounce tennis ball and catch it in the tennis tin.

   ➤ Bounce tennis ball off a wall and catch in tennis tin.

   ➤ Bounce ball to a partner who tries to receive ball in tennis tin.

   ➤ Create a stunt of your own!

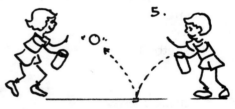

6. ***Balance & Travel Challenges.*** Explore using:

   ➤ bench or balance beam
   ➤ foam stilts or foam bucket steppers
   ➤ homemade balance boards, such as commercial Duck Walkers™
   ➤ LoLo® Balls
   ➤ Bigfoot Striders™

MOVEMENT AREA: Object Control

MOVEMENT: One-Handed Bouncing (changing directions)

TEACHABLE POINTS:

1. Keep in a balanced position with the feet comfortably spread.
2. Eyes are focused on the ball. When skill increases, eyes can look away from the ball.
3. Ball is pushed down with hand by extending arm downward. Fingers are relaxed and spread.
4. Be in ready position to receive the bouncing ball, with elbow slightly bent.
5. Let arms give or move slightly upward as ball contacts the hands.
6. Bounce ball in front of and to side of the body.

EQUIPMENT REQUIRED:

Firm even surface
Cone markers
Variety of large bouncing balls, 1 per child
Chairs
Hoops
Basketballs

TEACHING GOALS:
- ☛ Use footwork.
- ☛ Have ball control.
- ☛ Use pumping action on cross-over.

TEACHING PROGRESSIONS

1. ***"V" Bounce or Cross-over Bounces.*** Stand square on; bend your knees. Bounce the ball from one hand to the other. The ball travels in a "V" pathway on the cross-over. Remember to stay low, with knees bent!

1.

2. ***Pattern Bouncing.*** Pocket bounce with preferred hand. Cross-over bounce and switch to other hand. Pocket bounce with other hand. Cross-over bounce, and switch back to preferred hand. Continue this pattern.

> ➤ Pocket bounce (preferred hand) for 3 counts; cross-over bounce on fourth count; pocket bounce (other hand) for 3 counts; cross-over bounce on fourth count. Continue this pattern: "bounce–bounce–bounce, cross-over."

3. Travel and bounce ball in this pattern from sideline to sideline.

4. Divide class into teams of 6. For each team set up a zigzag course with cone markers spaced 2 yards (meters) apart. Children zigzag dribble the ball through course in a follow-the-leader fashion. Observe dribblers and offer feedback.

ACTIVITIES

1. ***Circle Bounce Relay.*** Divide the class into 2 equal teams that stand in a circle, facing the center. Have players of each team number off consecutively, as shown in diagram. On signal "Circle Bounce," each player in return bounces the ball while traveling clockwise around the circle, back to place. Hand the ball to the next player in line who repeats the task. Who will be the first team to finish in cross-leg sitting position?

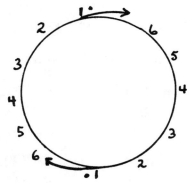

2. ***Figure-8 Scramble.*** For each game, have two teams stand facing each other on opposite sides of the play area. Teams number off as shown. Place a hoop in the center between the two teams and two balls inside the hoop. Set up two chairs as shown. Call out a number, for example, "3's!" The number 3 players run to the center to each grab a ball from the hoop, dribble around one chair and then around the other in a figure-8 fashion, return ball to hoop, and join their respective lines. First one back in place scores a point for the team. Continue in this way.

MOVEMENT STATIONS
Lesson 60, Level 3

MOVEMENT AREA: Object Control
MOVEMENT: One-Handed Bouncing (changing directions)

TEACHING GOALS:

☞ **Keep eyes on ball.**

☞ **Pump arms as fingers push ball downward (do not slap ball).**

EQUIPMENT REQUIRED:

Hoops	Poles and low net
Chairs	Paddle racquets
Cone markers	Large plastic whiffle ball
Ropes	Wall targets
Large balls	Beanbags
Basketballs	Assessment Recording Sheet

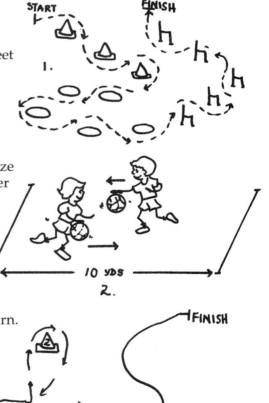

MOVEMENT STATIONS

1. *Zigzag Obstacle Course.* Set up an obstacle course as shown, and have children bounce ball in and out of obstacles. Emphasize keeping control. Encourage them to use either hand.

2. *Line Shuttle Speed Dribble.* Mark out two lines that are 10 yards (meters) apart as shown. Three dribblers bounce their balls at a time from one line to the other. Use the preferred hand to travel across to the opposite line, then the other hand to return.

3. *Speed Dribble.* Set up 2 different speed dribble courses as shown. Team members take turns going through the courses. Children could record each other's times.

4. ***One-Handed Bouncing—Assessment.*** Observe and record performance. (See Book 1, *Ready-to-Use Fundamental Motor Skills & Movement Activities for Young Children*, for a Recording Sheet.)

5. ***Paddle Ball Play.*** Set up a mini-court as shown in the diagram. Children play 3-on-3 paddle ball. Ball can bounce before being struck.

6. ***Hit the Target.*** Use wall targets as shown. Have 2–3 different targets set up. Children take turns overhand throwing bean-bags at targets from varying distances. Emphasize good follow-through.

TEACHING SESSION
Lesson _____, Level _____

MOVEMENT AREA:	
MOVEMENT:	

TEACHABLE POINTS:

EQUIPMENT REQUIRED:

TEACHING GOALS:

TEACHING PROGRESSIONS

ACTIVITIES